The Art of Kubernēsis (1 Corinthians 12:28)

The Art of Kubernēsis
(1 Corinthians 12:28)

Leading as the Church Board Chairperson

Larry J. Perkins

WIPF & STOCK · Eugene, Oregon

THE ART OF KUBERNĒSIS (1 CORINTHIANS 12:28)
Leading as the Church Board Chairperson

Copyright © 2019 Larry J. Perkins. All rights reserved. Except for brief quotations in critical publications or reviews, no part of this book may be reproduced in any manner without prior written permission from the publisher. Write: Permissions, Wipf and Stock Publishers, 199 W. 8th Ave., Suite 3, Eugene, OR 97401.

Wipf & Stock
An Imprint of Wipf and Stock Publishers
199 W. 8th Ave., Suite 3
Eugene, OR 97401

www.wipfandstock.com

PAPERBACK ISBN: 978-1-5326-6798-5
HARDCOVER ISBN: 978-1-5326-6799-2
EBOOK ISBN: 978-1-5326-6800-5

Manufactured in the U.S.A.

With thanks to Larry Nelson and Lyle Schrag
for the wonderful collaboration.

Contents

Preface | ix
Introduction | xi

Chapter 1: Foundational Paradigms and Principles: The Nature of Governance Leadership within a Local Church | 1

Chapter 2: Roles and Responsibilities of Church Boards: "Examples to the Flock" (1 Pet 5:3) | 22

Chapter 3: Models of Church Board Governance | 38

Chapter 4: Discerning and Building Your Leadership Character as Church Board Chairperson | 60

Chapter 5: Church Board Chairperson and Lead Pastor Relations | 73

Chapter 6: Leading the Church Board as a Ministry Team | 89

Chapter 7: Developing and Sustaining Church Board Effectiveness | 102

Chapter 8: Chairing an Ethnically Diverse Church Board | 123

Chapter 9: The Church Board Chairperson and Key Board Operational Issues: Internal Matters | 134

Chapter 10: The Church Board Chairperson and Key Board Operational Issues: External Relations | 155

Chapter 11: Church Board Chairpersons, Legal Issues, and Finances | 173

Chapter 12: Chairing in the Midst of "Black Swan" Events | 186

Chapter 13: Keeping it Fresh | 200

Chapter 14: Finishing Well | 209

Appendices:
A. Sample Church Board Chairperson Role Description | 215
B. Sample Church Board Role Description | 219
C. Sample Church Board Chair Evaluation Instrument | 221

D. Sample Church Board Covenant | 223
E. Sample Church Board Code of Ethical Conduct | 224
F. Sample Discussion Brief and Decision Profile Templates | 226
G. Samples of Church Board Assessment Instruments | 229

Bibliography | 237

Preface

Yes, it's time! For too long, church board chairs have labored without much help or many resources. You struggle valiantly, work diligently, but often feel overwhelmed by complexity, adversarial relationships, uncertain expectations, and the lack of any road map. Yet, you do this work because you believe in the mission of Christ's church. Recent developments in nonprofit governance continue to influence how church boards understand their role, particularly within larger church settings. Whether it is the Carver "Policy Governance®" model or another paradigm, the chairperson's role is being reconceived and repositioned within church leadership structures. In this book I provide a biblically-based framework within which you, a church board chair, can find your bearings in all of these matters and provide effective leadership for your congregation's board.

I am grateful for years of collaboration with Larry Nelson and Lyle Schrag regarding these issues. As seminary president, I worked with Larry Nelson, the seminary board chairperson. I learned a tremendous amount from his wise and dedicated leadership. Together we benefited from the resources provided through InTrust. When Lyle Schrag served as a faculty member at Northwest Baptist Seminary, we collaborated in the development of a workshop entitled "Best Practices for Church Boards." Approximately sixty church boards in western Canada participated and his insights enrich this material. I am indebted to Dianne Gleave, administrative assistant at Northwest Baptist Seminary, for formatting the document.

My involvement with the board of Northwest Baptist Seminary and the opportunity to serve as part of various church boards has enriched my understanding of board operations and the role of a chairperson. I have served in that capacity for many years and know from experience the challenges that this role generates.

I am thankful to Judy, my wife of forty-five years, who patiently supported the development of this material, constantly encouraging me.

Larry J. Perkins, PhD.

Introduction

THE ROLE OF A board chairperson in a local, congregationally-led church generally has little definition among the board members, remains undervalued among the staff, and is somewhat opaque within the congregation. Few appreciate the spiritual resources this role requires for success. Many factors influence how a chairperson's role functions within the board and the congregation, including a) the church's size and culture, b) the amount of definition it receives in official documents (e.g., bylaws, board policy), c) the governance model that the board members follow, d) the role of the board within the congregation's leadership, e) the relationship between the chairperson and the lead pastor, f) the individual's sense of calling to this responsibility, and g) this individual's awareness of the responsibilities and potential inherent in this role. However, in every case, the chairperson primarily facilitates the collective strategic leadership of the board as they pursue the mission and vision of the congregation relentlessly and effectively. As John Carver indicates, the role of the chairperson is not to lead the congregation, but to lead the board to exercise its appropriate leadership, leading "individuals to become a leadership group."[1] The degree to which the board and the church can fulfill their responsibility and vision depends considerably upon the personal leadership provided by the chairperson. This becomes particularly acute when a congregation is without a lead pastor, is experiencing serious difficulties, or is embracing significant opportunities.

The purpose of this publication is very simple—to assist a church board chairperson in discerning how issues of personal *character*, church *culture*, leadership *capacity*, biblical *comprehension*, and governance *competence* contribute to successful chairperson leadership within a local congregation, and through this leadership to significantly advance the mission God has given to this local faith community. When a chairperson understands each of these elements and acts to lead accordingly, then the board, as a ministry team under that chairperson's leadership, has potential to exercise the collective spiritual leadership God intended.

1. Carver, *Carver Guide No. 4.*, 11–12.

I assume that a church board, in the context of congregational polity, represents the primary spiritual leadership of the congregation because the faith community entrusts it with the strategic ministry leadership of that congregation, i.e., to ensure that the mission adopted by the congregation is fulfilled. This center of spiritual ministry leadership, responsible for nurturing the congregation's life and service, forms the essential context for a board chairperson's work.

A pathway for training effective church board chairpersons rarely exists within local churches. Whether this neglect is due to appointment processes, failure to discern the critical importance of the role, a perception that the role is merely one of chairing a committee, lack of long-term strategic planning, or spiritual morbidity, can be debated. Regardless, it is past time that this oversight be addressed and board chairpersons receive the help they deserve in order to lead well and thus fulfill this calling with spiritual wisdom and excellence. God's church deserves no less, and the burden of leadership imposed on board chairpersons warrants our strongest encouragement and support.

Can we identify any person named in the New Testament as the chairperson of a church board? Not really, because "boards" were not invented until the development of modern commercial enterprises. It seems that the house churches operated with two or three "older males" (*presbuteroi*)[2] who filled various pastoral and other supervisory and serving roles and took care of that faith community. This care included preaching, teaching, general organizational oversight, and care ministry. Whether the role of manager/supervisor/steward (*episkopos*, or *oikonomos* [1 Tim 3:1–2; 1 Pet 5:1–4]) or assisting agent (*diakonos* [1 Tim 3:10–12]) might be compared to the role of a modern church board chairperson is unclear, but individuals (quite possibly all those fulfilling these functions were "older males"[3]) in these roles certainly had responsibilities similar to those that church board members have today. Perhaps these various leadership terms enable us to discern the diverse set of caregiving responsibilities that a church board manages effectively under a chairperson's leadership. The *presbuteros* role combines

---

2. This term probably does not define a specific "office" as we understand it today, but a function that certain individuals engaged because they filled other social roles, such as the head of a household. This domestic role would naturally lead to their involvement in some leadership capacity within a house church meeting in their household. The term *presbuteros* literally means "older male" and is a comparative adjective usually used in the New Testament as a noun (cf. 1 Tim 5:1–2).

3. We do not find any place in the New Testament where the terms "elder" and "deacon" are contrasted. I suspect that *presbuteroi* functioned both as managers (*oikonomoi, episkopoi*) and as serving assistants (*diakonoi*).

elements of caring oversight, team facilitation, strategic planning, management and serving, and requires mature spiritual discernment.

In the Canadian context,[4] most local churches are organized legally as nonprofit societies. And so a church board chairperson needs to understand the dimensions of what it means to chair the board of a nonprofit society. But we all recognize that congregations are first and foremost communities of faith, and so the chairperson should also understand the spiritual contours of the church board's role and how the chairperson must guide the board in discerning and fulfilling its primary spiritual responsibilities. This twofold nature of a local church board creates much of the leadership complexity with which a chairperson wrestles. As one of the church's spiritual leaders, a chairperson is "entrusted with God's work" (Titus 1:7). I hope that this publication will be a significant, practical resource any church board chairperson can use to accomplish that work well.

Despite the many horror stories that past and current chairpersons might tell about their experiences, the ministry of a church board chairperson has the potential to be one of the most rewarding roles that a person can experience in serving God. One of the secrets to experiencing significant satisfaction is being educated about the role. When chairpersons build their personal character, capacity, and competence, church boards have greater opportunity to lead with significant spiritual impact.

I write primarily from within the perspective of Evangelical Protestant churches and the Fellowship of Evangelical Baptist Churches (Canada) in particular. The dominant church polity in this fellowship is congregational. However, in developing these materials I have sought to present them as generically as possible so that they will have a wide application. I am also aware that some of the principles and guidelines proposed rest upon theological assumptions that I have not taken time in every case to argue or defend. To do so would mean a document that would be much lengthier. If you desire to explore some of those issues, then I would encourage you to interact with me through the www.churchboardchair.ca website which I maintain. You will find helpful resources there to assist you in your role as church board chairperson.

Many useful resources already exist whose purpose is to assist chairpersons of nonprofit boards to lead effectively. I have sought to incorporate their insights, but always with an eye to a framework of biblical values. This integrative perspective gives this book a somewhat unique perspective on

---

4. This material is written particularly with reference to the Canadian church context. However, many of the principles will apply wherever congregations are being led by church boards throughout the world.

the role of a chairperson who leads the board of a church, a faith-based nonprofit entity that has a specific mission, vision, and set of values.

I should also add that I do not presume that the chairperson in every case will be a male or that board members will be only males. I have used inclusive language in referring to the chairperson's role.

Larry J. Perkins, PhD

Professor Emeritus of Biblical Studies,
Northwest Baptist Seminary, Langley, British Columbia, Canada.

Chapter 1

Foundational Paradigms and Principles: The Nature of Governance Leadership within a Local Church

OCCASIONALLY PEOPLE IN MY workshops ask whether there are biblical/theological principles that justify the existence of church boards and the role of the chairperson. This is an important question. Usually it arises because someone is concerned lest we base our discussion about church boards upon ideas brought into the church from outside of it. In other words, the very existence of church boards smacks of business or other cultural influences, i.e., something alien to the essence of a New Testament church. To suggest that a church board chairperson has a significant role to play in the health and leadership of a local church similarly may be disturbing because the New Testament does not specifically mention this church leadership function. Further, different models of board governance are now proposed in the "nonprofit society" world and churches have to think carefully about which model will cohere most adequately with their theological and other values.

Scripture articulates principles we use today to define the nature of the church, its mission, leadership, and functions. Today we discover faith communities contextualizing these biblical principles in many diverse cultures around the world. However, it is important for church board leaders to think very deeply about the theological principles and contextual realities that have led some kinds of churches (primarily evangelical churches in North America) to adopt a governance structure that includes a board and board chairperson. Understanding this rationale generates greater leadership confidence.

In responding to these kinds of questions, we have to admit that the New Testament has very little to say about the way a local church organizes itself to accomplish its mission. The diverse faith communities that developed through the work of the apostles required some kind of leadership. In the narratives of Acts and the New Testament letters, early leaders such as Paul, Peter, James, Peter, John, and Jude give attention to issues of leadership in these emerging messianic communities. Even the Gospels from time to time reflect ways in which elements of Jesus' teaching influenced the practice of such leadership. About thirty years after the resurrection, the beginnings of recognized leadership groups become apparent. They are comprised of people termed "managers/supervisors/stewards" (*episkopoi/oikonomoi*) and "assisting agents" (*diakonoi*). The word "older male" (*presbuteros*) also seems to describe some or all of the key leaders in a local church. Within this group, some will function more specifically as pastors. This spiritual leadership cares for, teaches, protects, and encourages the congregation. Contexts such as 1 Thessalonians 5:12–15, 1 Timothy 3, Titus 1, 1 Peter 5:1–7, and selected portions in Acts (e.g., chapters 13–14, 20) provide us with this data. Occasionally Paul will talk generally about the nature of the church and its collaborative, interdependent activities (e.g., Eph 4;[1] Rom 12; 1 Cor 11–14).[2]

Some of the house churches in the early days of Christianity seem to have a plurality among their leadership (e.g., the church at Antioch in Acts 13:1–3).What decisions this leadership group made and on what basis the congregation was brought into decision-making remains disputed. Paul urges the Corinthian church collectively to exercise discipline (1 Cor 5–6). The Jerusalem church collectively—together with its elders, the apostles, and representatives from the Antioch church—discuss and come to a decision about the matter of gentile Christians (Acts 15). Similarly, in Acts 6, the apostles, together with the Jerusalem church congregation, discern a solution to the dispute about fair care for all widows in the church. Galatians 2:1–10 may also suggest that in some cases specific leadership groups met to discuss and discern God's direction. In 2 Corinthians 8:19, Paul says

---

1. Hirsch and Frost, *Shaping of Things to Come* urges churches today to constitute the primary leadership of the local church around the functional categories of apostle, prophet, evangelist, pastor, and teacher that Paul mentions in Ephesians 4:11–16. However, it is highly questionable whether Paul intended these categories to be characteristic of every local church, rather than descriptive of the various kinds of leadership competence that God has given to his entire church through history to accomplish his purposes.

2. Bible scholars have debated whether some tension existed in the earliest churches between charismatic leaders (e.g., prophets) and appointed leaders (e.g., elders). Which kind of leader truly spoke for God? Whom should the believers follow? It is theorized that, over time, appointed leadership gained control. However, the evidence for such a scenario is very limited. You can pursue this discussion by referencing Campbell, *The Elders*, 1–19.

that Titus "was chosen by the churches to accompany us as we carry the offering." Presumably the churches in some fashion (whether this means the leadership in those churches or the churches as groups of believers is not discernible) indicated to Paul their approval of Titus so that he could fulfill this leadership role.

When you study these texts and examples of church leadership, you will discern key values and principles that should guide the expression of leadership and its structures, but also realize that considerable flexibility existed with respect to such structures. Qualifications for people to participate as spiritual leaders in the church are provided (1 Tim 3; Titus 1; 1 Pet 5:1–7). As we have reviewed, some stories (e.g., Acts 6, 15; 1 Cor 5) suggest that the leadership group took care to include the congregation in the final decision when major issues were under consideration. Beyond these elements, the Holy spirit seems to have let the good sense and wisdom of the initial leadership develop effective leadership and organizational means to advance the church's mission, with some attention paid to the cultural patterns in their diverse contexts. Care was taken to preserve the values Christ expected his people to exhibit and to enable the people individually and collectively to present the gospel clearly. The terms *episkopos* ("manager/supervisor") and *oikonomos* ("steward"), for instance, were common secular terms used to describe administrators and managers, particularly of large agricultural estates. Often these individuals would be slaves. Similarly, the word *presbuteros* (older male) described the head of a household unit, someone whom others discerned to be wise and responsible because of age and social position.

It is probable, for example, that in some cases Jewish Christians adapted some aspects of synagogue life and leadership to guide the development of the emerging messianic assemblies. In the Greco-Roman world, societies were common, regulated by specific laws, but organized for many different reasons, some of which were religious in nature. People in the early church felt free to borrow leadership ideas from their Jewish and/or Greco-Roman cultural surroundings, so long as the theological principles defining the nature of the Messiah's new people and its leadership were sustained. Different organizational arrangements were possible and early leaders were creative in developing house churches in centers such as Jerusalem, Antioch, and Ephesus.

I would suggest that the situation is similar today. In Canada, most evangelical churches have a senior spiritual leadership group defined as pastor/elders, or deacons, or a mixture of people filling these ministry roles. In recent decades as well, most of these churches have been defined as nonprofit charitable agencies, organized in accordance with government regulations for such entities.[3] Maintaining the theological principles expressed in the New Testament concerning the nature of the church, church leadership, and congregational relations, while operating within legal boundaries of these government regulations, does pose some challenges. For example, there is some tension between the church as faith community and the church as organization. However, this form of contextualized church governance (i.e., organized as a nonprofit charity) does enable the church to appoint and enjoy the benefit of spiritual leadership described in the New Testament, while at the same time taking full advantage of the benefits offered by being a nonprofit charitable ministry agency. So long as the leadership understands the essence of the church and is aware of the primacy of the spiritual values, care, and mission essential to the church, then the kind of governance pattern required for a nonprofit charity can integrate well with the communal life of a local church and its mission.

Now, there is no necessity for a church to organize itself as a nonprofit charitable society in Canada. However, it has advantages related to taxation, legal liability, and other matters. Provided a local church is able to accomplish its spiritual work by adopting and using such a structure, it will be appropriate theologically. Should a local church decide to constitute itself differently, it still has to sort out issues of leadership, authority, accountability, and governance, and exercise appropriate care to prevent untoward abuses. As a church grows in size, the governance patterns will have to change to keep pace. The local church's history, denominational traditions, age, size, and culture will all influence how governance actually functions. Another factor in all of this will be the theological perspective of the lead pastor, and how he views the church board's role within the congregation.

If a local church does decide to function as a nonprofit charitable society, then the governance leadership role of the board and its chairperson needs to be acknowledged. Personally, I do not believe that this kind of governance structure detracts from congregational authority, the ability of pastoral leadership to fulfill its appropriate spiritual ministry, or the opportunity for the church board to consider all of its work as spiritual work necessary for sustaining and deepening the spiritual health of a local church. Again, I would emphasize, the spiritual leaders, i.e., the church board members, have to ensure in all of this that the nature of the church as the body of Christ is not compromised, but rather enabled to flourish.

---

3. Several reasons explain this choice of legal structure in Canada, but a primary one would be the opportunity for members of such societies to receive tax deductions for gifts to these agencies.

Perhaps a comment of clarification would be helpful here. John Carver noted "a flagrant irony in management literature where opportunity for leadership is greatest, job design for leadership is poorest."[4]

I think this remains a significant issue for local church boards, board chairpersons, and lead pastors. This is not to say that individuals are incompetent, lack giftedness, or have deficient passion. The opposite is the case in most instances. However, the lack of clarity about the role of the board and the role of its chairperson in many congregations prevents board members from exercising the effective governance leadership they desperately desire to offer and should be offering.

Confusion about who leads within the local church creates needless tension between pastoral staff and church boards and creates congregational uncertainty. Much of the literature[5] that pastors study in order to define their professional and vocational activity urges them to be the leader God has called them to be. Such publications argue that a lead pastor has the prerogative to define the vision for the congregation among whom they serve, and thus provide the strategic leadership within a congregation. The church board collectively serves to advise and assist, but not to exercise any meaningful form of strategic leadership. However, these ideas are, in my opinion, a distortion of what the New Testament teaches about the plurality of leaders within local churches, which includes both paid and volunteer leaders.[6] The strategic leadership God provides for a local church is a collective, formed from the mature spiritual leaders that the congregation appoints to be the governance leadership team. They accomplish a significant part of their service by constituting the church board (or forming a major part of it). The chairperson of such a church board leads in ways that facilitate its collective, strategic leadership on behalf of the congregation. This collective, strategic, and spiritual leadership team will include the lead pastor and the church board members (whatever title a local congregation chooses to use to describe such individuals in these roles). Together they provide the missional governance a local church needs.

Given that a local church board (usually composed of elders, including primary pastoral personnel and/or deacons who exemplify the spiritual and

---

4. Carver, *Boards that Make a Difference*, 8.

5. See for example Hybels, *Courageous Leadership*; Roxburgh and Romanuk, *Missional Leader*; Nanus, *Visionary Leadership*.

6. In many churches, the elders/pastors are complemented in their leadership by a cadre of deacons. Not everyone will agree that the terms "elder" and "pastor" are used synonymously in the New Testament. However, texts such as Acts 20:17, 20:28, and 1 Peter 5:1–4 encourage us to consider "pastors" as a subgroup within or synonymous with the "older men" selected to guide a congregation.

personal traits Paul defines in 1 Timothy 3 and Titus 1) forms the essential strategic, spiritual leadership body in a local church, then the role of the chairperson in guiding such a body takes on critical significance. The board usually chooses the chairperson from among its members appointed by the congregation as board members. The chairperson, in facilitating this group of spiritual leaders in a local church, has a responsibility to serve board members individually and collectively in an exemplary way. The relationship of the chairperson to the lead pastor will be the most significant relationship in the church. Further, a board chairperson must demonstrate certain kinds of giftedness, if the board is to do its spiritual work well. Lastly, because this person chairs the strategic leadership team in the church which is entrusted with the responsibility to advance the church's mission, the chairperson exercises considerable spiritual influence in the life of the church. All of a church board's work is spiritual work because it focuses on advancing the church's mission, exercising missional governance.

If you serve in the leadership of a church in a region of the world other than Canada, then you will need to contextualize the principles of church leadership and governance in ways which are appropriate to your cultural and legal context. However, what we have learned about these matters in some segments of the Canadian Evangelical church may be helpful for you to consider.

The role of a church board or a nonprofit charity's board frequently is associated with the term "governance." It seems that much of what a church board does today concerns good governance. However, what does governance mean when the word is applied to a church board? What constitutes bad governance and why is this so detrimental to church health? Does this word cover everything a church board does or just one part of its work? What does a church board chairperson need to know about governance in order to fulfill his or her responsibility? Is governance a biblical concept that nestles snugly within the principles of congregational polity?

To answer the last question first, one can argue that the spiritual gift defined by Paul in 1 Corinthians 12:28 as *kubernēsis*, often translated as "administration" (as in the NIV), is related to governance, at least etymologically. The term describes the skill and experience that a pilot requires to navigate a ship safely to its intended harbor. Within the context of a church board, a chairperson facilitates the board's collective ability to provide such navigation so that the congregation reaches its destination, i.e., its mission. While the concept of governance does not occur explicitly with much frequency in the New Testament, Paul acknowledges in 1 Corinthians 12:28 that the Holy Spirit provides this ability as one of his gifts to enable the body of Christ to flourish. Sometimes when we hear the word "governance," we immediately think of authority asserted in a dictatorial manner. However, within the context of the New Testament, governance (*kubērnesis*) expresses a stewardship of the congregation's mission entrusted by that same congregation to selected mature spiritual leaders. Governance is the spiritually appropriate wisdom and action required to enable the congregation to achieve its discerned goals in accordance with kingdom values.

To paraphrase a definition offered by G. Douglass Lewis, governance within a local church involves

> the processes by which the leadership group, entrusted by a congregation with specific authority and spiritual care, discerns, plans and makes decisions that enable that congregation to fulfill its mission, with due regard for its values, bylaws, resources, reputation and stakeholders.[7]

Good governance will provide stability for the congregation, but also allow, encourage, and perhaps mandate movement and change, so that over time the faith community achieves its biblical vocation and desired vision in relevant ways. Good governance, including strategic leadership, occupies the mind of a church board, while worship guides its soul.

The concept of governance includes three critical elements: *purpose, process, and care*.[8] Everything that a church board does, i.e., its primary *purpose*, must advance the congregation's mission. This requires a future orientation for church board discussions and a concentrated focus on "value creation"[9] through its work. If over time this does not occur, then the board is failing to live up to the trust the congregation has given to it. To achieve this requires deep commitment and consistent discipline on the part of individual board members and the collective group.

The board only makes progress in achieving the mission if it develops and pays attention to beneficial and effective *processes*. Sometimes the bylaws define processes (e.g., certain items need to have congregational approval); sometimes external authorities define them (e.g., certain annual taxation reports, regional labor laws); and sometimes the board itself creates operational policies that define how it will work cooperatively and in a principled manner to achieve good decisions (e.g., decisions by consensus or by motion, code of conduct, etc.).

---

7. Lewis, "Governance," 26

8. Cf. Lewis, "Governance."

9 The phrase "value creation" describes the contribution that the work of a governance board makes to the life of the congregation. All of its work should add value to the congregation's efforts to achieve its God-given mission.

A church board employs various means to provide the spiritual care necessary for congregational health. These means include prayer, teaching, provision of spiritual care, policy development, decision-making, strategic planning, hiring and caring for key leaders, stewarding resources, assessing staff and programs, managing risk, and public relations/communication. All of these various elements involved in governance enable the congregation to flourish. A congregation gives a church board the authority necessary to exercise such care on its behalf and for its healthy development. A church board is accountable to the congregation for its stewardship of this trust.

A church board chairperson must understand the essence of good governance as it finds expression in and through the board's work. Several aspects are particularly critical for the chairperson to manage well:

1. *Assisting the board to keep its focus on mission.* This includes defining clear ends to guide the board, sustaining the spiritual ethos in the board, agenda preparation, meeting evaluation, facilitating effective decision-making, ensuring assessment of outcomes/goals, and encouraging consistent accountability.

2. *Assisting the board to understand process.* This includes board assessment, education, board orientation, mapping decision pathways, alerting the board to inappropriate behavior or risk, communicating on behalf of the board to the congregation or the public, knowing the rules (i.e., bylaws, legalities, and policies), strategic planning, and managing employee reviews well.

3. *Assisting the board to exercise spiritual care for the congregation in all it does.* This includes not abusing the congregation's trust, conducting all board work with deliberate attention to worship, and enabling the board to exercise its authority in ways that contribute to church health. Church board members will be modeling exemplary spiritual wisdom and ethical behavior because they are spiritually mature leaders within the congregation.

The better a chairperson understands governance, the more ably he or she can facilitate a church board's functions and help it continually improve its work. Much of this board leadership depends upon Spirit-guided common sense and wisdom. This is particularly the case when a board is engaged in intense discussion about an issue. The chairperson has the responsibility, more than any other board member, to keep everything that happens within the bounds of Christian values[10] and good governance. When things get dis-

---

10. Within a faith community, one document that defines these values will be the Statement of Faith, which defines the congregation's theological framework. Board

ordered, the chairperson must help the board members recover and reestablish good order. When a church board is not following proper process, the chairperson must call the board to account. When a church board requires spiritual wisdom, the chairperson must call the board members to prayer. When relationships between two or more board members become strained, the chairperson must work to generate reconciliation. In all of these various challenges, the chairperson is the board's servant and coach.

Good governance in essence is a form of shepherding. When the congregation appoints the church board, it is the sheep appointing other sheep to guide the flock. These sheep take on some shepherdlike qualities to protect, nourish, organize, and lead the flock (1 Pet 5:1–4). A lead pastor is not the only one responsible for shepherding the congregation. The entire church board in its collective work is responsible for the total care of the congregation, ensuring effective organizational leadership and providing wise governance.

Decisions in a local church are often tricky things to manage, yet governance cannot occur in the absence of decision-making. In fact, the primary work of a church board is decision-making. For instance, a group in the church may be urging the pastoral leadership to initiate a ministry to seniors. Who decides whether this should happen? How is that decision to be processed? The answers to such questions and acting to achieve decisions that are in the best interests of the congregation's mission form the central responsibility defined by good governance. These questions include:

- Which groups in the congregation should speak into this decision and who decides?
- Does such a ministry advance the mission of the congregation and specifically enable it to fulfill its vision?[11]
- Is it a substantive change to the previously approved strategic plan?
- If the decision is positive, who decides which person or group will be responsible to implement? How will this person or group be accountable and within what timeframe?

---

members have a fiduciary responsibility to govern within the boundaries of that theological framework.

11. In this publication, the term "mission" refers to the essential, unchanging purpose of a congregation as defined in Scripture. This mission will be shared with all Christian congregations. The term "vision" describes how a particular congregation determines the appropriate shape that this mission will take in its particular context, and employs the particular gifts and other resources the Holy Spirit has placed within it.

- Is this a governance matter and so the responsibility of the board, or a management issue, which should be delegated to the administration for implementation?
- Who determines what resources should be devoted to this initiative? What is their source?
- If there is risk involved, who is responsible to manage this risk so that the congregation does not become liable or suffer harm in other ways?
- How will success be defined and over what timeframe?

Good governance enables a congregation to sort through these matters, reach an appropriate decision, and implement that decision well. Church board chairpersons often find that that they work at the very center of these processes. Like an umpire, the chairperson ensures that the rules of the game, i.e., the bylaws, policies, and legal boundaries of the congregation and the board, are sustained and respected as the decision-making proceeds.

The fact is that various internal (and sometimes external) entities share authority for major decisions within congregational polity. The congregation retains ultimate governance authority within a local church that operates within the terms of congregational polity. The congregation entrusts the board with specified authority to make sure that the mission, values and processes, as stated in its constitution, bylaws, and statement of faith, are followed fairly, transparently, completely, and in a timely manner, limiting any risk to the welfare of the congregation. If the board believes that changes need to be made to the congregation's foundational documents, it works these through in full accord with stated process. A church board cannot arbitrarily ignore or change such documents. The congregation will require the board to refer some matters to it for decision (e.g., major facility development, borrowing money, annual budget approval, appointment of the board members, appointment of the lead pastor, etc.). The board in turn delegates to the ministry staff appropriate responsibility and authority to achieve the ends mandated by the board and to implement other assorted decisions. So governance becomes a shared commodity among the congregation, the board, and the ministry staff, and the chairperson helps the board manage this sharing of governance so that the best decisions are achieved.

One understanding of shared governance is that various groups within the agency, by virtue of role, assigned responsibility, and competence, have a legitimate voice in respective decisions. Sometimes bylaws or policies mandate this voice and sometimes it occurs because a particular group has special competence that can inform a good decision, or because the proposed change will affect a group significantly. Theologically, this concept of shared governance honors the concept of the church as body, respects the priesthood of believers, empowers those who exercise ministry oversight, and enables the board members to hear the wisdom of the Holy Spirit through various people within the body.

Good governance will understand, appreciate, and respect these various roles and ensure that the board has all the necessary input to make a good decision. Taking time to get this right will usually result in good decisions and sustained unity.

1. *The congregation's bylaws will define the decisions that the congregation must discern.* In the example previously used, the introduction of a seniors' ministry will probably require additional financial resources, i.e., an adjustment to the annual budget. Often the congregation must approve such budgetary changes. The new ministry may require the hiring of a new ministry staff person. Depending upon the status of this role (e.g., it may be a pastor, a coordinator, or something else), the bylaws may require the congregation to appoint the candidate by direct vote.

    The rationale for giving the congregation voice in the decision would include the fact that:

    a. they are primary stakeholders;

    b. they must have confidence in the spiritual competency of their ministry leaders;

    c. as members in the charity, they must ensure that financial decisions are being handled properly;

    d. many in the congregation will probably be affected by this ministry initiative;

    e. the congregation's by-laws require it.

2. *The ministry staff will have some voice in this decision because they possess a certain competence that will help the congregation and board make a good decision.* Also, they will have to work closely with the proposed, new staff person and so enabling their input expresses how the congregation and board value them as leaders. Further, probably more than anyone else in the congregation and board, the ministry staff will appreciate the change in dynamics that this new ministry will generate, particularly with respect to adjustments to current ministries, and the kind of person necessary to lead it successfully. Usually the staff will develop and submit proposals to the board for their consideration.

3. *The board will play a pivotal role.* First, they will have to discern whether this proposed initiative will advance the mission of the church. Second, they will have to consider whether this initiative, among others, has priority and why this is the case. Third, they will have to ask what the risks are and ensure, if it is implemented, that the congregation is adequately protected. They will have to ask whether the plan for resourcing this ministry is prudent and sustainable. Fourth, they will have to ask if the plan states who is responsible and accountable for this project. Finally, they will have to consider whether plans for implementation and ongoing evaluation are rigorous enough.

The church board chairperson, in collaboration with the lead pastor, has the responsibility to ensure that the appropriate groups have opportunities to give input and even make decisions about certain aspects of this initiative. When the proposal comes to the board, a key question in the board's deliberation will be what is the decision-making pathway and timeline that this initiative must follow, and is the board managing this appropriately? Outlining this pathway formally brings clarity for the board and removes what otherwise might be a contentious issue. When the congregation sees the board paying respectful attention to these elements of shared governance and ensuring they are implemented well, it gives them confidence in the board and its leadership.

Some board members might think that shared governance diminishes the capacity of the board to exercise its proper role. However, in shared governance the board always retains the authority entrusted to it by the congregation. What the board does is distribute the decision-making according to established principles because distributed ownership of the mission belongs to various groups within the congregation.

On the churchboardchair.ca website, you can access the article entitled "The Delicate Dance of Congregational Government," which provides more extensive biblical evidence regarding this perspective about shared governance.[12]

Governance can function in a compliant or an innovative mode. By compliance I mean that a church board does the expected business of monitoring key indicators of institutional stability (e.g., finances, reports from the lead pastor, policy reviews, etc.) and asks questions. However, it rarely involves itself in visioning the future, discerning ways and means to advance the mission, or educating itself about developments in its community, culture, or religious context. Passivity marks its mode of operation. Missional growth is not perceived by this kind of church board to

---

12. Perkins, "Delicate Dance of Congregational Government."

be an expectation emerging from the Great Commission. This board's greatest concern may be checking and poking, but even then it may not be sure what questions it should be asking. After all, the reports it receives are produced by the very people responsible for the operations the board members are seeking to check and monitor!

Monitoring for compliance to stated objectives and values and to manage risk remains a necessary and significant board member responsibility, but unduly limits the board's role to detect and protect functions. It also focuses board energy on the past, not the future. A board should expect the lead pastor or executive pastor to be providing reports regularly on the key items the board considers important, i.e., progress toward stated, annual strategic ends (goals), preservation of financial assets, operational budget risk, facility care, employee care, member care, etc. It is the board that should determine what it needs to know to assure itself that all key risks are being managed responsibly and that the congregation is healthy. *The principle is—trust, but check.* If the board is not sure about the information it is receiving, it should ask for external assistance to provide an objective view, but only after it has given the ministry leadership full opportunity to provide any clarification. Rarely should board members themselves seek to do this kind of checking on their own. It creates too many awkward issues and has the potential to damage relationships significantly.

What potential dangers occur when a church governs in a compliant mode? Compliance usually generates complicity. While board members may think they are asking good questions and receiving complete information, that may not be the case. Asking questions in response to reports is a reactive mode of governance. The circularity inherent in this process is not always appreciated. The board uses a report drafted by the person accountable as the basis for their questions, but usually has no independent source of information from which to evaluate the accuracy of the report itself.

Another danger of the compliant mode is movement into micromanagement. If the board thinks the ministry staff is not able to do the job, having evaluated their reports, then it might be tempted to take over the responsibility itself. While this might be required in an emergency, it cannot be a long-term solution. Boards have to measure, but have to measure the right things to know whether the congregational purpose is being advanced effectively. It is the board that determines what needs to be measured, by whom, and in what ways. It cannot delegate this responsibility. So the guideline is "trust but check; trust but question."

If a board thinks its work is done after it has measured compliance, then it has failed in some of its primary responsibilities, such as advancing the mission, anticipating risk, and providing strategic leadership which looks toward the future.

A church board operating with an innovative mindset, or seeking to govern forward, handles the monitoring process carefully but expeditiously because it knows that its primary job is to ensure mission fulfillment. Maintaining the status quo violates that mandate. Strategic leadership requires board members to give the majority of their time to the big questions, ensuring that their meeting agendas are not filled with busy work, but in fact keep their attention on the important issues.

What might some of these big questions be?

a. Where do we believe God wants this church to be in five years? What will it take to get there and are we attending to those matters seriously?

b. What are the biggest threats to the fulfillment of our mission and how should we respond preemptively to these threats in order to advance the mission?

c. Given the many possible things we might do, what are the two or three key things we must do (ends) in the next twelve months in order to advance our mission? These will form the core of the annual strategic plan.

d. How do we know that our ministry projects are effective? How do we measure effectiveness? Is there appropriate accountability?

e. Is our congregation healthy? How do we know? If it is not, what do we have to do in order to restore it to health?

f. Do we know what our risks are and have we done what we can to cover those risks as fully as possible?

g. Do we have the right policies in place and are these policies being used?

You can discern the question(s) which would be most stimulating and helpful for your board to consider. Discussions around such questions can be some of the most spiritually motivating conversations board members will ever experience and energize them significantly with respect to the church's vision.

Another strategy to keep the board leading and governing strategically relates to its education. Is there ever a time in the annual schedule of the board when someone with specific expertise is invited to help the board expand its understanding about a critical segment of congregational life, the external community, or theological issues? Perhaps your board is struggling to understand the issue of financial stewardship in the life of the church. Consider inviting someone (always consult others on the board about your idea before moving ahead to make sure an appropriate person is invited) who has expertise and experience in helping congregations learn how to invest financially in God's work with generosity and joy. It may be the catalyst to reach a whole new level of vision and ministry. Or perhaps your board is struggling to understand how to lead the congregation to engage in global missions in a responsible and effective way. Here again there are probably people with knowledge about this issue who could come and in forty to sixty minutes give your board new perspective, new ideas, and perhaps even discernment about the best way forward. One way to ensure such education is happening in a consistent way is to build time for it into the board's annual agenda.

Because governance is all about mission advancement, strategic leadership is an essential quality to nurture within the board so that its governance is innovative and consistent in the best sense. A chairperson has to champion this perspective and keep the board on mission in this respect. No one else in the board has the capacity or responsibility to do this. Good governance, the kind of governance Paul considers to be the Spirit's gift to his church, requires it. The phrase "missional governance" describes this kind of good governance, with the term "missional" reflecting both the congregation's mission as well as God's purposes within this world.

Debate continues as to whether the church is best defined as an organism or an organization. The tendency is to see the term organism as more adequate, because it seems to emphasize the dynamic, relational, social realities that mark a local church in its best expression. Conversely, the word organization conjures up images of a corporation or institutionalization and communicates a sense of top-down, authority-laden, static structure that seems inimical to the messianic assembly Jesus initiated to carry forward his mission.

The primary metaphors that Jesus and Paul used to capture their sense of the church were the family/household, the human body, and/or the temple. The realities behind these metaphors, i.e., household, body, flock, and temple, all represent some kind of system. The family or household is a social system, incorporating relational, structural, and practical components that work concurrently and with some degree of integration to enable the family/household unit to sustain and organize itself. Similarly, the human body, incorporating many subsystems, presents a complex network of living, highly structured, dynamic elements that collaborate to nurture, protect, and energize that body. Owners of flocks had to organize their care and protection. In antiquity, temples were tightly regulated religious entities, hierarchical in structure, and carefully organized with a view to sustaining the worship rituals appropriate to the deity associated with that precinct.

Perhaps then the whole debate about whether the church is an organism or an organization is misdirected. The New Testament presents the local church as a social system, a community with structure, designed to nurture and advance the kingdom vision that Jesus Christ initiated. As with any system, a local church will have some elements of organization. However, any organizational components will be in the service of the community and its mission. Because the church is constituted from individuals committed to Jesus Christ, it has organic character, i.e., it is a relational, dynamic, Spirit-led system. With incredible synergy, this system, the local church, organizes itself in order to care for believers[13], and they in turn, through their participation and giftedness, sustain and develop the system, i.e., the community of faith, so that Jesus Christ, their Lord, will accomplish his mission. Of course the language of the kingdom that Jesus used to define much of his message also incorporates system features.

Jesus and Paul, who employ the term *ekklesia* ("church/assembly") to define this new, kingdom community, were quite aware that this term in their day also characterized diverse assemblies of people organized in all sorts of different ways to run cities, societies, and guilds, as well as Israel in the Old Testament (cf. Acts 7:38).

Because local churches are human systems (aided by the Holy Spirit) and require some structure to flourish (as the New Testament metaphors imply), church leaders should not hesitate to incorporate insights, ideas, and processes that other organizations have discovered to be useful. Some of these ideas will come from diverse organizations whose purposes are quite different. However, if the ideas are compatible with kingdom values and are helpful in sustaining the community and mission of the local church, then they deserve consideration. If, as Evangelicals are frequently heard to say, "all truth is God's truth," then organizational truth may be helpful, so long as it remains the servant and does not become the boss.

For example, there is much written about leadership today, and within the church we are concerned similarly that we have good, competent, godly leadership. But we also know that much of the current leadership literature assumes values quite incompatible with our kingdom commitments—ideas about power, profit, ambition, ruthlessness, ego, and self-fulfillment. The leadership style and philosophy of Attila the Hun undoubtedly should not be replicated within the local church.[14] However, we might discern that good governance principles expressed in a policy-based

---

13. Congregations also provide services to people who formally are not members of that congregation.

14. Roberts, *Leadership Secrets*.

model of board governance are very compatible with kingdom values, enhance excellence in church governance, and enable the local church to sustain its community more effectively. Always we must remember that such processes or governance methodologies are tools, means to an end, never an end in themselves. Good organization, implemented humbly, honestly, and wisely, can serve powerfully to support and enhance the church community and its kingdom mission.

Case Study: Daring to Change —"Can These Bones Live?"[15]

Old habits die hard, they say. The chairperson of the board of First Baptist Church was discovering the truth of this maxim. For the past eight years the church had experienced multiple changes in pastoral leadership. Some of these changes were very hurtful, resulting in a decline in the spiritual, numerical, and fiscal health of the congregation. The periods between permanent pastoral leadership were becoming more drawn out. Discouragement was setting in among the congregation, as well as among the church board members.

The current chairperson, Ralph, who had a number of years of experience in this role, knew that the congregation probably had enough spiritual energy for one more attempt for viability. However, he wondered about the reasons for this repeated series of harmful leadership changes. Although each of the presenting reasons were different, he wondered whether a more fundamental cause was at work. Was the church board in some way responsible for this situation, or at least allowing it to continue? Was it a change in pastoral leadership that was needed or a drastic change in the way the church board provided strategic ministry leadership for the congregation?

Historically the board of First Baptist tended to be concerned with receiving reports, dealing with minor issues related to facilities or finance, advising the pastoral leadership on various matters, and overseeing the annual general meeting. Performance evaluations of lead pastors were not required, little strategic planning was done with the board members, risk management questions rarely surfaced, and only on rare occasions did the board discuss the advancement of the congregation's mission. When it came to hiring a lead pastor, the board oversaw the process, but provided little direction to the Search Committee other than to define the perfunctory

---

15. Although the story in this case study may seem to resemble a real situation, the names, places, and actual circumstances do not describe any actual church, church board, pastor, or chairperson.

position description and proposed salary and benefits package. The chairperson could not recall the last time the church board had educated itself about the function of a nonprofit board. In short, the First Baptist Church board seemed to be in a holding pattern, keeping the machinery in motion, but not addressing the critical leadership and ministry needs of the congregation. If the congregation's future was to change, then the church board had to change—a daunting prospect, but nevertheless a growing conviction for the chairperson. And if the church board was going to change, then the chairperson would have to step up and lead the charge.

Before he took any action, Ralph decided to devote two weeks to prayer and personal reflection to discern his own heart in this matter. Did he have the courage, the spiritual stamina it would take over the next two to three years to be the catalyst for change within the board? Was he willing to show the way by giving personal time to educate himself about ways that church boards can develop the capacity to provide strategic ministry leadership? If not, was he willing to let the congregation drift into greater decline and dysfunction?

During these two weeks, Ralph asked God to move in the life of another church board member and in some way bring that board person into conversation with Ralph about these matters. Ralph reasoned that if God was concerned for the health of this congregation then the Holy Spirit would be seeking to stimulate a desire for change in other church leaders. It was Friday night toward the end of the second week when Ralph received a phone call from Ken, asking whether he could have coffee on Saturday morning. He wanted to talk about the congregation and what could be done to turn this situation around. As Ralph prayed that evening, he thanked God for his direction. He felt a growing sense of confidence that God was in this desire to change the board in order to change the congregation.

When he met with Ken the next morning over coffee, Ralph asked him two questions. First, did Ken believe in his heart that God had a future for First Baptist? Second, did Ken believe that if the board changed its habits, the congregation would change too? Ken readily agreed to the first question. He told Ralph that he had been praying for several months about this situation and wondered what he could do about it. Ralph asked Ken what had prompted him to phone the night before? Ken shared that in his devotions that morning he had read Ezekiel's prophecy about the provision of a man to stand in the gap. Ken knew that God was telling him he needed to do something and so his initial step was this conversation. Beyond that he did not know what further steps might be taken.

Ken was not so sure about the relationship between effective spiritual and strategic leadership by the board and congregational health. He had never put those two things together in a cause-effect relationship. In response, Ralph suggested that the principle expressed in Proverbs—"where there is no vision, the people perish" (Prov 29:18)—applied in this instance. If the board of First Baptist Church was not able to discern, pursue, and implement a God-honoring vision, then who in the congregation would? Even if they managed to hire another lead pastor, past experience showed clearly that he could not turn things around by his own individual efforts. As Ken reflected on Ralph's comments, he found himself agreeing.

So the question then confronted them: In what ways did their church board have to change in order to provide strategic ministry leadership into a better future? And then came a collateral question: Did they have the capacity to create and generate these changes? They gave themselves over to discussing what needed to change in the board. Three ideas were generated in that discussion.

1. *They would have to reshape the culture of their church board.* Ralph and Ken knew that this would be the most difficult aspect of the necessary changes. Shifting the mindset of the board members from a compliance perspective to a strategic, innovative, missional governance model would require all of the wisdom they possessed, but as a team they believed the Holy Spirit would provide what was needed. They decided to start by evaluating the board agendas and discerning what changes they might introduce in the way meetings were planned. One of the things they discovered was that too often less important matters were given prime time. So they decided to make sure that the first two items in every board meeting after dealing with the consent agenda would always be the most strategic decisions or discussions that the board would be having at that meeting. They also decided to develop an annual agenda to make sure that in the coming twelve months the board was discussing all of the important matters necessary for congregational renewal. Finally, they decided to devote the first half hour of every meeting to prayer and Bible study, with specific focus on examples from Scripture where God enabled faithful men and women to make a difference.

2. *They would have to sharpen the focus of their church board's work on issues that advanced the congregation's mission.* When Ralph and Ken examined the board agendas from the last twelve meetings, it was difficult for them to discern items of board discussion and decision that were critical to the advancement of the congregation's mission. They knew this had to change. So they made a list of what they regarded as the key things that had to change if the congregation was

to be reinvigorated. Some of these included reviewing the vision and ensuring that all board members were passionately committed to its accomplishment; ensuring that the lead pastor position description focused on the key attributes and competencies that this individual had to bring into their context in order to support the strategic ministry leadership of the congregation and encourage the board members to own this responsibility; defining current areas of risk to the congregation and beginning to address these concerns by direct action or policy development; and improving communication with the congregation so that their confidence in the church board would improve.

3. *The board would have to become much more engaged in working with the new lead pastor.* The board of First Baptist was rather passive when it came to engagement with the lead pastor. Their default mode was to let the lead pastor make the key decisions, which they tended to rubber-stamp, after all he was the professionally trained pastoral leader. Ralph and Ken knew the board needed to respect and support whomever the congregation chose as lead pastor. However, they also knew that the board had to step up aspects of accountability, performance reviews, evaluation of ministries in light of the vision, and strategic development for the congregation. If the board accepted these responsibilities, it would dramatically alter the relationship between the board and the lead pastor.

After a short time of prayer, Ralph and Ken decided to go for it. Now the question became: How should they communicate these ideas to other board members and encourage their support?

How would you advise Ralph and Ken to proceed?

Questions for Reflection

a. Are the terms "governance" and "ministry" incompatible? Why? Why not?

b. If the most spiritually mature people, according to 1 Timothy 3, Titus 1, and 1 Peter 5, form the governance leadership team in a congregation, why then do congregants assume that it is the paid pastoral staff that have the capacity and mandate to provide the strategic ministry leadership for the congregation? Are these spiritually mature people some of the pastors/teachers, evangelists, and "prophets" whom God has gifted to the congregation (Eph 4:11–14)?

Suggested Resources

a. T. J. Addington, *High Impact Church Boards*.
b. Dan Hotchkiss, *Governance and Ministry: Rethinking Board Leadership*.
c. Aubrey Malphurs, *Leading Leaders: Empowering Church Boards for Ministry Excellence*.
d. Larry Perkins, "The Delicate Dance of Congregational Governance."

Chapter 2

Roles and Responsibilities of Church Boards

"Examples to the Flock" (1 Pet 5:3)

BOARD GOVERNANCE WITHIN THE context of a local church requires courageous faith, prudent wisdom, faith-filled endurance, and *agape* service, all concentrated toward the advancement of the Messiah's mission by sustaining the faith community. "Governance" expresses the stewardship of authority entrusted by the congregation to those who are regarded as spiritually mature, competent leaders, and vested in them for the nurture and protection of the faith community. The strategic leadership of the governing board will provide clear discernment of purpose and vision, spiritual care and health, economic vitality, careful process, good planning, and respectful communication. Board members accept such responsibility because of their desire to serve the Lord Jesus Christ and his people. In carrying it forward, they commit to being "examples to the flock" (cf. Heb 13:7) in their collective work and their commitment to biblical wisdom.

In the course of their deliberations, church boards consider the views expressed by various entities and groups that shape the life of the faith community. The board in various ways shares governance with them, including:

1. *The congregation.* The spiritual formation of the people within the congregation forms a primary responsibility for the board. Linked with this will be the development and care for the various means (facilities, finances, organizational structures, personnel, etc.) that support such nurturing. People in the congregation are both owners and beneficiaries of the agency.

2. *The staff—paid and volunteer.* Overseeing the hiring, care, and evaluation of the senior pastor forms one of the board's most critical responsibilities, but the board also ensures that they care for all staff through clear, up to date policy and attention to their concerns.

3. *Various groups of people served by the congregation's mission.* The board ensures that they offer services necessary to care for the clients/people groups defined in the congregation's mission and vision, and do so effectively, with quality, and in line with the resources that the congregation possesses.
4. *Denominational family connections.* The board nurtures the relationships with the denominational head office, churches, and agencies. The board oversees these relationships so that the congregation's mission is advanced.
5. *Civic and other entities.* The development of the congregation's relationship as a ministry agency to local civic bodies and officials, as well as other legal entities (e.g., banks, corporations, parachurch agencies, etc.), comes under the purview of the board. This would include partnerships with other ministry agencies.

These relationships and interactions are constantly changing and developing.

Church boards intent on exercising good governance and attending to the claims of these various previously identified entities and groups will give attention to three broad areas: redemptive ministry, strategic leadership, and fiduciary stewardship.

1. *Redemptive ministry* describes the board's internal spiritual dynamics and operations that enable good church boardmanship, sustain grace-filled relationships, and ensure effective alignment among church leadership (paid and volunteer). It is ministry (*diakonia*, assisting) because ultimately it requires a servant's heart and attitude, a commitment to making decisions in the best interest of the congregation's mission, and intentional collaboration to enable others to fulfill their calling in Christ. As the board members give attention to this competency, it spreads a redemptive dynamic throughout the congregation, restoring and enhancing Christian life and relationships. In this way the board exemplifies spiritual community, and encourages and advances true spirituality within the congregation.
2. *Strategic leadership* refers to aspects of governance that are oriented to the future and the accomplishment of the vision, yet are rooted in the agency's story. The board must discern the strategic dynamics required to sustain the health of the church and advance its mission. It requires a church board to develop effective conflict management and decision-making skills so that the board members sustain the priorities

necessary to advance the mission. In some respects this kind of leadership is more concerned with future stakeholders and beneficiaries, rather than current ones, because it focuses upon the congregation and local community as they will be present in the next three, five, or ten years, as God permits. With the leadership of the chairperson, a church board integrates these major priorities (ends) in some kind of planning document with which the board and staff agree, providing alignment of efforts and resources toward the mission. It will define goals or ends that all agree are crucial, thereby enabling the board members to make coherent and united decisions because they have reached a consensus about the overall direction of the congregation's life.

3. *Fiduciary stewardship* expresses a church board's responsibility to ensure that all resources within the congregation are being valued, preserved, and employed for the advancement of the mission and the achievement of the discerned ends. It is a matter of faithful accounting. Usually we think in terms of financial and facility resources, but in reality the most important resources are the people—the paid staff, volunteer leaders, and other members within the congregation. One of the key elements then for the board to oversee will be the processes by which people in the congregation, including staff, are discipled to understand their calling in Christ, their gifting, and their training in order to discern their involvement as kingdom agents in their families, the marketplace, the community, and the congregation.

Also, the church board must give attention to regular pastoral evaluation so that they can assist the lead pastor and other staff to become all they can be by God's grace and power in ministry. This will also apply to the evaluation of specific ministry programs on a regular basis (perhaps a three-year cycle) to ensure that they are accomplishing their intended goals and that there is agreement about future direction and development. In other words, quality control and improvement, as well as risk management, are part of fiduciary stewardship. Board members tend the agency's story, articulating and celebrating it as the trusted stewards of the mission.

Seven core principles and practices will enable a church board to tend well and consistently to these three key responsibilities:

1. *Future orientation that respects and honors the congregation's history, traditions, and values, but concurrently articulates a robust hope for what yet will be and must be to advance the mission.*

A church board gives full attention to the future, but also expresses full appreciation for the history and heritage of the ministry agency as it cultivates the congregation's story and fosters its memory. Board members recognize that they do not operate in a vacuum, but have responsibility to respect and preserve the mission and values that shape the agency, while simultaneously reshaping a vision that defines how they intend to contextualize the mission and values effectively and efficiently into the future. The horizon of board members cannot be the immediate week or month, but must be at least twelve or twenty-four months in the future, as well as the previous twenty-four months. They must discern and anticipate as best they can opportunities and threats that will affect the spiritual health of the congregation and influence its ability to achieve the mission. Effective church boards give adequate attention to solving the immediate, pressing issues, but they devote the majority of their energies to future priorities, not affairs of the moment. The board acts as an effective change-agent under the Spirit's direction.

The board establishes the foundation for its work by complete commitment to the mission and the values that attend that mission. Every board member needs to be convinced that the mission of the ministry agency is of great importance and so is ready to devote prayer, time, energy, finances, and competence to fulfill the mission. Within the agency, the board collectively becomes the greatest champion of the mission. It respects and upholds the constitution and bylaws and only seeks change through the processes defined in those documents. It stewards the trust placed in its hands by the congregation with all due diligence.

Evaluative Questions:

a. During church board meetings held over the past twelve months, how much time has been devoted to discussing future direction?
b. In its decision-making, how does the board reflect upon the ministry agency's story and enable it to influence the process? Does the board ever rehearse and reflect upon this story? How does the board ensure that its various constituencies know the story?
c. Does your board ever discuss questions such as: What core values define this ministry? What is the primary thing this ministry agency does? Who benefits?

d. In its decision-making process, how much consideration is devoted to discerning alignment with the mission, vision, and values? When was the last time the board said no to a proposal because it was not aligned with the mission?

   e. How does the board define excellence in relation to this ministry's operations? What might be some of the key benchmarks that demonstrate excellence?

2. *Vigilantly safeguard the board's ability to do its work effectively and tend to its capacity to govern well.*

A board-developed statement of board responsibilities guides the board members in discerning the key aspects of their work. This includes an appropriate understanding of governance within the context of a church, and the model of board governance that currently is being used. The chairperson has a position description that defines the nature of his or her leadership within the board, including the nature and limits of the chairperson's authority. The board clearly defines the principles it will use to guide its work—good agendas, clear procedures, carefully written minutes, authorized leadership, defined priorities, effective decision-making processes, and continual education to improve its collaborative work. In developing the board agendas, the chairperson ensures that only items pertinent to the board's mandate are included, but that all such items are in fact included.

The board has developed a code of conduct that defines expectations for board members. Robust, honest discussion based upon mutual trust and respect is fostered within the board so that it becomes a venue in which diverse points of view regarding various issues can be expressed and examined carefully in light of biblical and theological values. After the board comes to a decision, it speaks with one voice. In all of this the board takes full advantage of the benefit of the diverse experience and expertise that each board member contributes. The board leadership is careful to orient new board members so that they can quickly participate knowledgeably and effectively.

The board recognizes that other groups in the congregation will have a legitimate voice in various decisions. It organizes its work to ensure that these voices have the opportunity to give input appropriately and in a timely manner.

The board conducts an annual evaluation of its performance and also evaluates the chairperson's leadership. Board officers, board members, standing committees, and ad hoc committees receive appointment appropriately and the board holds them accountable for the tasks assigned. Board members participate in meetings informed, with worshipful hearts, and are committed to the mission. When inappropriate conduct occurs, the board acts to discipline itself. Board members understand what constitutes a conflict of interest and act with integrity in all such matters. Some form of annual board evaluation occurs consistently. The board uses the results from an annual board evaluation process to discern how to improve their governance in the coming year.

The board actively pursues its own education so that it can continually develop its capacity to govern well and ensure that it meets all legal and ethical standards in board and staff operations. It budgets funding for this educational work.

The board understands that all of its work is spiritual work and ensures that its collaborative operations reflect God's values and advance his kingdom purposes. Good leadership exercised in the context of well-defined governance will result in vital ministry agencies.

Evaluative questions:

a. Do you agree with the concept of governance expressed in this section? Why? Why not? What is the relationship between good governance and effective board operations?

b. Can you identify specific actions taken by your church board in the last twelve months to educate itself regarding critical issues or strategic development? Is there a plan for future educational activities? What does the board need to learn in order to fulfill its responsibilities with excellence?

c. When the board has invested in self-care, what benefits have resulted from these actions?

d. How does your board seek to set all of its work within a spiritual frame of reference?

e. How do current policies enhance the board's work? How do they impede it? What needs to change?

f. Is the board able to identify three of the most significant issues it faces in the next two years? Is the board actively addressing any of those issues?

g. Are all board members supporting this ministry?

3. *Give attention to the appointment, caring support, and evaluation of the lead pastor.*

Discerning and appointing good leaders forms a most significant part of good governance. Within the church context, this relates to the appointment of the lead pastor. Each congregation in its bylaws will define and oversee the process by which this selection occurs, but the board has to have a strong voice in such process. Once the appointment has occurred, the board is responsible to ensure that the appointee is cared for, supported, and consistently receives a fair annual evaluation.

In the appointment phase, the board will oversee the revision of the position description, as well as give attention to defining the search process. However, normally it will not serve as the search committee except perhaps in smaller congregations. The board will also have to define the employment package, i.e., salaries, benefits, and expectations. It will also need to determine what financial assistance will be available for relocation costs. The official letter of appointment should come from the board, including a copy of the official position description. Once the appointment process is completed, then the concern of the board shifts to ensuring that the lead pastor is cared for well. It conducts annual evaluations in ways that support and advance the pastor's leadership capacity. The primary issue in the evaluation will be the degree to which the lead pastor has enabled the congregation to achieve the annual ministry plan (which relates to the ends that board has set). There should be provision for professional development regarding any issues discerned in the evaluation process.

The board will work with the lead pastor to develop a code of conduct for all employees, which they sign when hired and for which they indicate continued support by re-signing a copy during their annual performance evaluation. They also sign a copy of the church statement of faith, indicating continued agreement with its contents. The board will want to ensure that employees realize the consequences if serious violations of the code of conduct or significant changes in personal belief contrary to the congregation's statement of faith occur, i.e., that these will be grounds for dismissal.

The board will develop policies that define the limits of the lead pastor's authority, but then give full authorization for the pastor to lead within those boundaries. The board will define the chairperson's role in such a way that it does not interfere with the responsibilities of the lead pastor. Both roles are accountable to the board, but for different functions.

When it is time for the lead pastor to conclude employment, the board will have a policy in place to define the process so that, as far as possible, the change enables relationships to remain positive. This will include transition and succession plans.

In this relationship, the board will want to minimize surprises and build mutual trust.

Evaluative questions:

> a. Does your board have a leadership succession policy/plan in place? If the lead pastor/CEO is incapacitated, who is the designated interim leader for the first ninety days?
>
> b. In what ways has the board defined for the lead pastor/CEO the limits of authority? To what extent has the board defined its performance expectations for the lead pastor/CEO and is this the basis for the annual evaluation?
>
> c. To what extent has the board developed an annual performance review process for the lead pastor/CEO position? Based on the evaluation, how does the board ensure that real change occurs?
>
> d. How does the board ensure that it is providing appropriate care and support for the lead pastor/CEO?

4. *Be proactive in pursuit of the congregation's mission, but with attentive regard to fostering and preserving financial integrity and vitality.*

The primary responsibility of the church board is to ensure that the congregation's mission is being achieved in accord with its stated values and related to the resources available. If this is not occurring, then no matter how well the board may think it is doing its work, it is failing. For the board to discern this it must define its vision (based on the stated mission and the congregation's context) and the key ends that the board must reach if the vision is to become reality. The board will only know if it is achieving its defined ends if it has reviewed and approved an annual ministry plan, with measurable objectives having been expressed, has defined accountability for those objectives, and has implemented assessments in order to discern whether it has met the objectives. This is part of the board's spiritual discipline. One of the key tools for the board to develop will be indicators of congregational health and tracking these indicators. The lead pastor's reports to the board will include data related to these indicators.

The board also must determine the resources necessary to sustain the mission and ensure that they are available and being stewarded well. If the board cannot identify the resources, then it will have to modify the desired timeline and/or the activities/services proposed in order to achieve the mission. Risk management then also becomes a central board responsibility. The board is concerned with preserving all resources (i.e., financial, physical, and human) for the advancement of the mission. Competent reporting is required if the board is to exercise appropriate risk management.

Evaluative questions:

    a. In what concrete ways does the board use the mission, values, and vision statements to shape its decisions?

    b. What does the board do annually to evaluate progress toward mission achievement? How does it measure the contribution of its own performance to mission advancement?

    c. Has the board defined what congregational health looks like and defined ways to measure it on a consistent basis?

    d. What process does the board have for developing, reviewing, and implementing an annual ministry plan?

    e. How does the board exercise risk management on behalf of the congregation?

    f. In what ways does the board seek to balance its focus on mission advancement with appropriate concern for financial viability?

    g. If the ministry agency has debt, do the board members understand its extent and whether they are managing it appropriately?

    h. What training do board members receive to understand the financial issues and financial reports?

5. *Promote a congregational ethos that encourages and facilitates personnel to do their best work.*

The strategic leadership of the congregation lies with the board. It will delegate components of this, but it cannot delegate its responsibility. Ultimately, the board is responsible for the advancement of the congregation's mission. As noted in the previous section (number four) much of this leadership comes through intentional, strategic planning and assessment. However, equally important is the encouragement of a positive, spiritual ethos within the faith community among staff, volunteer leaders, and members in general, i.e., ensuring that the gospel is being lived within the total fabric of that community.

Key elements that foster congregational health include good communications, clear direction, transparent processes, trust in the integrity of the board, willingness to try new ideas even if some fail, empowering leadership, open accountability, servants' hearts, and forward thinking. It ensures that the board celebrates key wins and recognizes the committed service of others within the congregation. It invites the congregation to share its wisdom when the congregation faces crucial decisions. When the board has made a wrong decision, it acknowledges it and acts to remedy the problem.

Where the congregation has a denominational linkage, the board will ensure that it tends these relationships well for the benefit of the congregation.

Evaluative questions:

a. When you review the minutes from the last twelve meetings of the board, what evidence is there that the board is providing strategic leadership for the congregation?

b. In making decisions, how does the board allow appropriate groups in the congregation to speak into that decision?

c. Does the board in fact give oversight to the management of external, congregational relations? How?

d. As the number of staff increases, how will the board ensure that its role remains strong and that appropriate support for the staff in their ministries is also provided?

e. To what degree is the board responsible to nurture unity within the ministry agency and to model it by its own behavior?

6. *Create a culture that expects and respects collaborative establishment of goals, constant attention to strategic planning and implementation, and rigorous evaluation of programs and other operations.*

The relationship between the board and the staff forms a most critical element in the overall ability of the congregation to achieve its mission, i.e., making disciples (Matt 28:19–20). The chairperson and lead pastor give leadership to the oversight of this relationship. Tensions often arise around two questions: How is strategic direction set, and how is the accomplishment of mission-centered goals or ends assessed? The board ultimately is accountable for both, but it has to build processes that enable the wisdom of the staff and other ministry leaders within the congregation to shape the results.

In terms of strategic direction, the board oversees its definition, assigns resources, and authorizes staff to ensure its implementation. The lead pastor is part of the board so staff have a voice in these discussions at the highest level. Also, a wise board will invite staff to consult on these matters and share their best insights so that the board can make well-informed decisions on these critical matters. Once the board makes its decision about a strategic direction, then in consultation with the lead pastor it will assign responsibility for its implementation. Such assignment carries with it the responsibility to ensure that evaluation occurs at set points to measure whether or not the program is achieving the goal(s) intended by the board.

The board will also ensure that it is reviewing and revising policies regularly.

Evaluative questions:

a. Where in the annual cycle of the board's work does it give attention to providing and defining strategic direction (based on specified ends), i.e., developing or reviewing strategic plans or an annual ministry plan?

b. When the board approves new initiatives or requires specific action, how does it assign responsibility? How does it ensure accountability?

c. How do the minutes of board meetings enable the board to keep track of assigned accountability?

d. Does the board have an ordered collection of board policies that guide its work? Are these available to all board members?

e. What recent innovation in ministry has had the greatest impact on congregational/agency life? Why?

7. *Determined commitment to value all its work as worshipful work, i.e., the spiritual oversight necessary for the proper care of the entire congregation.*

A church board is primarily a ministry team composed of several mature, spiritual leaders appointed by and from the congregation, along with the lead pastor. While much of its work focuses upon policy, evaluation, and strategic leadership, all of this occurs with a view to advancing the mission of the congregation and enhancing its spiritual health. The mission is linked essentially to the command of Jesus Christ in Matthew 28:19–20: to make disciples. Congregational and organizational health is a matter of spiritual care. When Paul defines the qualifications of church leaders in 1 Timothy 3, a primary issue is whether or not such people have demonstrated good care for their households. First Peter 5:1–4 speaks of this by using the shepherd/sheep analogy, and in 1 Peter 4:17 he calls it "the household of God." These images result in the characterization of congregational leaders as "shepherds" and "parents" who have responsibility to care for the respective organization.

Board members pursue their ministry together as an expression of their calling in Christ to discipleship and they form a significant ministry team within the congregation. Their mutual relationships, their methods of decision-making, their faith in divine provision, and their processes for resolving conflict all reflect the values Jesus taught in the New Testament, and which the Holy Spirit enables through his empowerment. Scriptural truth informs the strategic leadership of the board and prayer envelops it. Primary measurements of missional advance include decisions made by people to follow Jesus, baptisms, the investment of people's lives in service, the use of financial resources, etc.

Board work at its root is worship-filled work. To be worshipful, it has to be redemptive, expressive of stewardship, filled with integrity, relentlessly evaluative, and in step with God's mission.

Evaluative questions:

a. What practices does the board employ to ensure that it intentionally operates within a framework of spiritual values?

b. In what ways does the board agenda demonstrate that it regards its work as an act of worship to God?

c. Where do board operations give space for prayer, reflection upon Scripture, listening to the Holy Spirit?

d. Does the board demonstrate in its work and relationships a passion for Jesus Christ and his church?

e. Who is responsible to nurture the spiritual life and work of the board?

Appendix: Who is Assigned Governance Authority within the Congregation?

A common question raised with respect to congregational governance is: What is the definition of the group of people to whom the congregation entrusts its governance? The exercise of governance in many congregations is quite fragmented and when they have to discuss and decide significant issues, the questions of process often become more debated than the issue at hand.

In most congregationally led churches, there is one board, composed of individuals appointed by the congregation and the lead pastor. This group constitutes the governing board and exercises certain authority on behalf of the congregation as defined in the agency's bylaws. Other church groups possess a different polity that distributes governance authority for different aspects of congregational life among various groups. For example, in some Christian Reformed congregations, the corporate members (the consistory and the deaconate combined) appoint a board of directors and its authority is focused upon matters of business and property. A consistory formed of elders and ministers oversees spiritual and strategic ministry matters. Another group, sometimes called the deaconate, looks after benevolence ministries and attends to responsibilities associated with directors, e.g., finances, facilities, etc. The ministers, elders, and deacons form the council that deals with any matters not assigned in the bylaws to the board of directors, the consistory, or the deaconate.

However the governance responsibilities are assigned in the bylaws of a respective congregation, the group, i.e., board, that carries out those responsibilities on behalf of the congregation needs to understand its role, its authority, and its mandate as defined by the congregation.

Case Study: "Culture Wars" in the Church Board[1]

Dover Community Church (DCC) was approaching its fortieth anniversary. Some great ministry had made a significant impact within the local community during these years. In some periods, more than three hundred people had attended Sunday services and regarded DCC as their church.

Ten years ago, some leadership issues had created serious division within the congregation. The board worked hard to provide direction and good oversight at that time, but was not able to prevent about one hundred people from leaving. This event also led the lead pastor to resign. The credibility of the church board came under serious scrutiny.

After several years without a lead pastor, God directed the congregation and board to a new lead pastor. They extended the call and he accepted. For two years, people worked with enthusiasm and they made progress in healing relationships. At the beginning of the third year of this pastor's mandate, the board thought it would be wise to sell the manse that the church had purchased thirty-five years earlier. No lead pastor had used it for twenty-five years. It produced modest rental income, but did not really contribute toward any program of the church in a meaningful way. Several board members felt it would be wise to sell the property that had appreciated significantly in value and use the funds to repay some minor debts and

---

1. Although the story in this case study may seem to resemble a real situation, the names, places, and actual circumstances do not describe any actual church, church board, pastor, or chairperson.

support some struggling programs. They would invest the remainder and use the income to support a youth pastor's position.

People in the congregation accepted the board's recommendation and the sale proceeded well. The board used the funds as planned and the investment grew (about $300,000). Unfortunately, the investment instrument chosen by the board did not perform as expected and in the previous six months the principal had lost half its value and the expected income did not materialize. When the congregation learned about this, it damaged the credibility of the board and relationships became so difficult among the leaders that the lead pastor resigned.

For two more years, the board struggled to provide leadership as the search for a new pastor proceeded. A year into this process a group in the congregation lost faith in the congregation's leadership and the ability of the board to move the church forward. The result was that ten families left. The financial impact was severe. They could no longer sustain the salary for the youth pastor, board members were getting frustrated and some resigned, and the search committee became fearful that the congregation would not have the resources necessary to support the salary required for a new lead pastor. In the midst of all of these challenges, the board chairperson had to resign because he was transferred by his company to another city.

Because of these events, several board members were losing confidence in their ability to discern direction and make good decisions. A spirit of timidity and discouragement was evident. When faced with major decisions, the board became indecisive and debates were becoming more fractious. Some thought the solutions were spiritual and urged the board members to examine themselves and repent. Others traced the difficulties to the board's unwillingness to manage well the leadership responsibility the congregation had entrusted to them. The board was unsure what its operational culture was or should be.

Now the board has approached you to serve as the new chairperson. You filled this role a number of years ago at another church, but you are wondering, given this board's history, whether the board's culture can be renewed and refreshed and the confidence of the congregation be restored in its leadership. If so, how can this be done and what kind of board culture should you attempt to nurture?

1. Church board cultures become entrenched and they often incorporate unhealthy features. Changing and renewing a church board culture are daunting tasks, often related to changing the composition of the board. I suspect that every church board needs to be evaluating and reshaping its culture consistently, lest its ethos become toxic to the life

of the congregation. "Can a leopard change its spots?" asks the prophet Jeremiah (13:23), as he wonders whether those accustomed to evil can learn to act righteously. I think in the case of church board culture that answer has to be yes as we trust in the power of the Holy Spirit.

2. What are some indicators that suggest to a chairperson that some culture adjustments may be necessary? Fractious debate about key elements on every agenda might provide some evidence. Lack of enthusiasm for and commitment to the mission and vision probably would be another signal. Loss of credibility with the congregation or key segments of it may point to the need for some board culture revision. An inability to recruit good people to the board probably is another indicator—word gets around! Maybe the board just keeps making the wrong decisions! Or maybe you sense that the board is just too compliant and has no courage to ask the hard questions.

3. Changing a board's culture, i.e., the way it does things, will take time. However, as chairperson, you are in a particularly critical role to act as a catalyst. Your first step is to analyze what aspects of the board's culture need to change and whether these changes in fact will increase the ability of the board to provide strategic spiritual leadership in your congregation. If you do not know the what and the why, then when people challenge your proposals, you may not be able to respond convincingly. Of course, this analysis also assumes that you have a good sense in your own mind about what a better board culture will look like. Your plan also should relate as clearly as possible to improved effectiveness of the board in its strategic, spiritual leadership.

4. Then there is the question of process: How will you lead the board from its current culture into an era of improved board effectiveness? I would suggest you begin with making small changes that are within the scope of your authority. You do not need the board's permission for doing these, because they have already given you the authority to make such changes. For example, when the next idea for ministry development comes to the board and it does not address several critical issues, suggest that the board return it and ask that the proposer provide the critical information before the board makes a decision. This does two things. First, it informs the board that it has to do its due diligence in making decisions. Second, it tells the church administration that proposals coming to the board have to include all necessary information that enables the board to make good decisions.

5. When you think the board has done a good job in its work, give them due praise. You can encourage such celebration by ending some meetings with a short evaluation period. Perhaps ask one of the board members prior to the meeting quietly to observe the board's operations during the meeting. Then, at the end of the meeting invite the board member to share these observations about what worked well and what may not have been helpful. This process encourages that individual board member to become more reflective about board practice, and signals to the whole board that improvement is possible. The current culture is a choice and can be changed.

Questions for Reflection

a. Take one set of evaluative questions provided in this chapter and work through them diligently. What ideas do your responses generate for enhancing your church board's effectiveness?
b. If you agree that these seven areas comprise for the most part the key responsibilities of a church board, how does this inform your role as chairperson?
c. Compare your current description of the board's responsibilities with these seven principles. Does this description require adjustment?

Suggested Resources

a. John and Miriam Carver, *Reinventing Your Board: A Step-by-Step Guide to Implementing Policy Governance.*
b. Larry Perkins, "Seven Habits of Effective Church Boards."
c. Cathy A. Trower, *Govern More, Manage Less: Harnessing the Power of Your Nonprofit Board.*

Chapter 3

Models of Church Board Governance

Part I: Which Governance Model and Why

THE WAY THE CHURCH board operates in many churches reflects traditional and pragmatic factors, and demonstrates considerable eclecticism. If a church has extensive history, then the governance model, whether implied or explicit, will show the influence of different chairpersons and pastoral leaders over time, as well as developments in response to crisis. If a church is only recently established, then its governance model may be borrowed from its mother church or denomination, or reflect the way the founding pastor liked to lead, or may have developed without much intentionality at all. However it has come into being, each church board has a governance model or a culture of operation—some set of principles or traditions, whether implicit or explicit, that guides its operations. Often the congregation will embed several of the key principles in the bylaws, but often the church board is building the bridge as they walk on it.

You might question whether it is really that important to understand various governance models, purposefully select one, and then develop board operating principles and practices accordingly. Does it matter how a church board operates so long as it gets the job done? Do the ends of ministry accomplishment justify any means of board governance?

It must be admitted that a governance model is only a means to an end, but I would add that the means, if deliberately and purposely chosen and discerned as compatible with scriptural values, will significantly facilitate the work of a church board. When you prepare for a family vacation, you probably have some idea of your destination. Usually, you can select many different routes to reach the vacation spot, as well as choose several different modes of travel. However, through some process, you select the route and mode of travel that enables you to accomplish your goals, i.e., travel as quickly as possible, travel as frugally as possible, include in the journey as many points of interest as possible, visit Aunt Jane on the way, etc. Your goals determine your means. Similarly, but in a more complex fashion, the mission (purposes), goals, and values that a church board, together with the congregation, adopts should determine the governance model the board will use to shape its operations. Of course, if the mission, goals, and values change, then it might also be appropriate to select a different governance model.

In chapter 1 we proposed that governance involves *the processes by which the leadership group, entrusted by a congregation with specific authority and spiritual care, discerns, plans, and makes decisions that enable that congregation to fulfill its mission, with due regard for its values, bylaws, resources, reputation, and stakeholders.* The model of governance that your church board and congregation selects then has to enable the board to discern, plan, and make decisions for the purpose of fulfilling the congregation's mission in ways that are consistent with its biblical values and nature as the Messiah's community. Some key questions you might use to help a board make an informed choice would include:

a. Does the size of the congregation require the board to be both a working/management board and policy-making board, or only a policy-making board?

b. What do the congregational documents state concerning qualifications for people who constitute the church board?

c. What governance model will enable the church board to exercise spiritual care, advance the mission, and manage risk most ably?

d. What governance model will develop the best alignment of resources to fulfill the mission?

e. What governance model will enable the congregation to grow?

f. Are there cultural factors within the congregation which indicate that one particular governance model is more appropriate than another?

g. What governance model brings the greatest clarity to issues of accountability?

Congregations are dynamic entities. Growth, as well as reduction in size, will probably require some adjustments in the governance model. Discerning when such transitions need to happen and managing them well form a significant part of a church board chairperson's responsibility.

Another dynamic that frequently motivates changes in the governance model is dissatisfaction among the board members over the board's mode of operation. When a church board is not able to arrive at good decisions, or is unable to manage crisis, or functions merely as an advisory committee, board members who are eager to see the congregation's mission advance under the strategic leadership of the board will become disenchanted and begin to disengage from the board. They are not willing to expend time and energy in a board that is dysfunctional.

I would suggest there are five primary responsibilities that a church board must perform well: 1) To create and establish policies (for itself, for employees, and for the congregation), 2) discern congregational vision and ensure its strategic accomplishment, 3) ensure that all aspects of congregational life are managed well (includes strategic planning and assessment), 4) provide spiritual care for the entire congregation (including employees), and 5) gather and conserve resources (stewardship). All five aspects, exercised in a disciplined manner, are essential for fulfillment of the congregation's mission. How the board members desire to carry out these responsibilities effectively, efficiently, and with spiritual integrity will determine which model or adaptation of models they will select.

Chait, Ryan, and Taylor suggest there are "three types of governance," but I think their types reflect three primary functions that nonprofit boards must perform. Using their terms, these functions would be fiduciary, strategic, and generative.[1] In the same order, they define the "board's principal role" as "sentinel," "strategist," or "sense maker."[2] It seems to me that every church board, to some degree or other, must fill each of these roles. However, they are correct in their observation that some nonprofit boards, and this includes church boards, tend to function primarily in a fiduciary mode, with some attention to the strategic mode. However, for a church board to act as "the source of leadership for the organization"[3] would require a fundamental change of perception, particularly on the part of many pastoral leaders. In the previous chapter we used the phrases "redemptive ministry," "strategic leadership," and "fiduciary stewardship" to describe a church board's primary functions.

Although the literature on nonprofit board governance discerns several different governance models, I would propose that three models most frequently find adaptation in church board contexts, depending upon the various factors defined previously.

1. *Advisory Board.* In a church-planting situation, or where the lead pastor is the founding father, the influence of the leader is paramount. Trust is so high in the lead pastor that the board serves essentially in an advisory capacity. The lead pastor forms the agenda

---

1. Chait et al., *Governance as Leadership*, 132.
2. Chait et al., *Governance as Leadership*, 132.
3. Chait et al., *Governance as Leadership*, 132.

and calls the meetings, which tend to be rather informal. The focus is upon the immediate tasks—just keeping everything going. If this model persists for too long within the ministry agency, several dangers may emerge. Once the leadership registers the congregation as a nonprofit charity, then the board has to be in a superior position of authority to any employee and that includes the lead pastor. An advisory board cannot meet this test. Second, the board members run the risk of significant liability if things go awry, because they did not act prudently and with due diligence. Third, there is little or no accountability that the board can require from the lead pastor. Compliance too often becomes complicity.

2. *Management Board.*[4] Traditionally, many churches that follow congregational polity create management boards. In essence, the board takes responsibility to manage the entire ministry agency, primarily through a series of committee structures. This model builds upon the assumption that board members have to lead ministries in order to exercise their spiritual leadership. Further, the assumption is that the pastor preaches, teaches, and offers spiritual guidance. The board members should then relieve the pastor from responsibility for more mundane tasks.

Congregations adopt this kind of board model as well for a very pragmatic reason: many churches do not have enough administrative staff to implement the ministry plan and so board members have to function voluntarily as the administrative staff in many cases. The board committees tend to parallel church administrative functions, i.e., youth ministry committee, children's ministry committee, worship committee, visitation committee, facility committee, finance committee, etc. Each board member chairs or leads a committee and is responsible to the board for administrating this aspect of congregational life through the committee. In essence, the board functions as the collective CEO in this model. A lead pastor is involved, but he in essence leads a pastoral

---

4. A subcategory of the management board model could be called a cooperative or consensus model. In this arrangement, the board collectively is the CEO, with no person having authority over another. While democratic in essence, it is very fragile because it depends upon the willingness of each person to exercise consistent, significant commitment. For a time those participating may sense wonderful camaraderie, but at some point decision-making will become frozen because compromise will not occur and accountability will deteriorate because no one has specific authority to require accountability. The model of leadership proposed by Hirsch and Frost (Apostle, Prophet, Evangelist, Pastor, and Teacher) would, in my view, follow the cooperative or consensus model of governance. It probably would be limited by church size in terms of functionality (Cf., Alan Hirsch and Michael Frost, *Shaping of Things to Come*).

relations committee that oversees the Sunday services and general pastoral work. A large part of this would include the preaching and counseling ministry in the congregation.

When a church board functions according to this model, the members tend to be appointed because of some professional capacity that they bring to the management of the congregation or perhaps they have particular interest in one of the congregation's key ministries.

This model works somewhat effectively in small organizations where volunteers have to carry the majority of the leadership tasks.

Three problems frequently arise in the application of this model. First, the board tends to micromanage everything. The leaders of the various committees often become unsure about the level of authority they have and so almost every decision comes back to the board for resolution. The board's agenda becomes so full of management decisions that it has little time or energy for developing policy, strategic planning, or generative leadership activities. Secondly, board members are never sure what hat they are wearing—management or governance. Board members become confused about the relationship between their role as leaders of ministries and their role as church board member. Thirdly, the focus in the board meetings tends to be upon fiduciary responsibilities, i.e., monitoring, rather than leadership. The big picture gets lost in the myriad details. Board members frequently find the meetings long and not very productive because the board is constantly acting as a committee of the whole.

In churches that have less than 150 in attendance (which includes the vast majority of protestant churches in North America) the management board model is probably necessary as the initial model. There simply is not enough paid staff to fill the primary administrative leadership roles. Given this reality, how can the chair help such a board function well?

a. Education: make sure that board members using this model realize the extent and diversity of their responsibilities, i.e., both the governance and management functions. Suggest to the board members that in-depth discussion and decision briefs on key theological issues, significant ministry opportunities, or potential threats will enable them to function in a governance mode more effectively.

b. Meeting agendas: distinguish in the agenda items that are governance/policy issues and those that are administrative. You may even want to go so far as having two different agendas to help the board members understand the very different roles they are filling.

Such a strategy also prepares the board members for the day when the growth of the congregation requires full and formal transition to a governance/policy board model.

c. Clarify accountability: wherever possible, have ministry committees report to the lead pastor, not the board, so that the lead pastor is able to create alignment among the ministries to advance the mission. In other words, create a paid/volunteer staff team that is responsible for ministry implementation. Have the lead pastor develop and lead this team and designate this person as the primary channel for ministry reports. The board can handle some responsibilities such as finances and facilities through standing committees accountable to the board. Some individuals may serve as a board member and as a ministry staff member.

Transitioning to this kind of structure will be resisted, perhaps by the lead pastor who sees more work being required, or perhaps by board members who think that the board will lose control or their roles will in some way be reduced. However, if done properly, neither has to be the outcome.

d. Policy development: even though the board may follow a management model, it will still have to develop policies. When the board makes decisions about various matters, it is following, revising, or creating policy. The more a church board understands this and consciously articulates its policies, the more effective it will become in its work. Policies are also great time-savers in board work.

e. Strategic development: build into the annual agenda space in which the board can give sustained time to pray, discuss, and discern future strategic leadership direction.

3. *Policy Board.* This governance model assumes that a nonprofit board's primary job is to ensure that the organization has effective, high-level policies that guide its development, define and delegate the appropriate authority to those it appoints to enact such policies, ensure that the organization is acting in compliance with these policies, and hold staff and board accountable for their performance as defined by these policies. These policies provide the framework within which all of the work of the organization occurs and enables every person involved in the organization to perform effectively and efficiently in advancing the mission. The entire set of guiding policies relates specifically to the accomplishment of the mission, the values

held by the agency, and the vision it has for its service, because they focus upon the achievement of key ends.

Some forms of this model locate strategic planning and fundraising within the purview of the board, whereas others delegate these functions to the administrative leadership. In this model, committees are few and exist only to serve the specific needs of the board. Most are ad hoc committees, rather than standing committees (e.g., audit and finance committee).

One of the criticisms of this model of board governance is that it may distance the board members from the actual work of the organization. Because the information about the organization reaches the board through the lead pastor, the board has to vest considerable trust in this employee. Further, the board gives the lead pastor very wide latitude, within specific boundaries, to fulfill the mission. To prevent the board from meeting only to hear reports of compliance, this model often focuses on the future, shaping its work to include strategic planning and fundraising. Board education becomes critical because the board members have to be sufficiently aware of the organization and its broader environment in order to assess whether or not the lead pastor is in fact leading the organization well. Whistle-blower protection for paid and volunteer employees becomes an important tool to prevent the lead pastor from hiding inappropriate behavior from the board members.

The policy board model works well with larger churches (two hundred-plus members) who have or are developing multiple staff leadership teams. This model does require the lead pastor to understand the vocational role in a different manner from the traditional pastoral model, i.e., that he is the primary organizational leader, not just the agency's chaplain. It also requires a significant shift in the way board members understand their roles. However, in my opinion, the principles that define the policy board model fit well within the theological values that guide congregational polity.

Part II: Reflections on Carver's Model in the Context of Church Governance: A Specific Definition of a Policy Board Model

One person whose research and writings have reshaped the contours of nonprofit board governance is John Carver. His book *Boards that Make a Difference: A New Design for Leadership in Nonprofit and Public Organizations* offers a critique of various models and argues for what he terms "Policy Governance" as the most appropriate way for nonprofit agency boards to organize themselves.[5] However, many question whether Carver's model of board governance is suitable for a local church board to use.

1. *Carver, Governance, Policy, and Local Church Governance—Are They Compatible?*

What is the essential principle or presupposition that guides the Carver Policy Governance model? A volunteer board in a nonprofit institution must "provide strategic leadership, it must clarify policies and expect organizational activities to give them life."[6] The key questions the board must answer, according to Carver, are these: What human needs are satisfied by our institution, for whom, and at what cost? Or to put it another way, what is lost if our institution ceases to exist? Carver's desire in developing this model is very basic—to enable the board to address the most significant issues that define and affect the institution and then to lead. It is all about acting concertedly to make a difference.

What is the essential function of the Elders Team, or the Deacons Board, or the Leadership Council that acts as the board in a local church?[7] When you strip away all of the stuff, what is its primary responsibility? I would suggest *job one* is keeping the church spiritually focused on fulfilling the Great Commission, which is its primary mission. It seeks to ensure that the local church stewards all of its resources so that human beings in that local faith community connect with God and live in sacrificial obedience to Jesus as Lord, forming a healthy kingdom community. You might define it somewhat differently, but the church board ensures that the local church keeps focused on the main thing and thus enables that church to make a difference for God in its community.

Church boards committed to being missional for God can use policy governance as the means to discipline themselves to act missionally. Because the board is entrusted and authorized by the congregation (within the boundaries of its constitution, bylaws, and statement of faith) to fulfill the congregation's mission, all of the board's work in a policy governance framework is theologically centered and grounded. There does not seem to

---

5. Carver, *Boards that Make a Difference*; Carver and Carver, *Reinventing Your Board*.

6. Carver, *Boards that Make a Difference*, 26.

7. Regardless of the term a congregation employs to describe the governance body, it nonetheless must fulfill the responsibilities of a board if the congregation is established as a nonprofit charity.

be any essential incompatibility between policy governance as defined by Carver and the essential function that a church board must fulfill for a local church to be healthy. This is not to say that policy governance is the only model that will achieve it. However, it can be an extremely effective model for a church board to use.

2. Carver, Governance, Policy, and Local Church Governance—Can the Board Chairperson Handle it?

According to John and Miriam Carver, the person who chairs the board "ensures the integrity of the board's process and, occasionally represents the board to outside parties."[8] Within the context of a local church, the board chairperson usually has very few specifications to provide guidance in discharging this role. The bylaws may have one or two general statements about the number of times the board meets, required numbers for a board quorum, the essential responsibilities of the board, and what key decisions the congregation has to approve. They may also refer to *Robert's Rules of Order*[9] as the basis for conducting the board's operations, but rarely do people read it and no copy exists in the church.

Within Carver's model, the chairperson (or "chief governance officer" as Carver names this role[10]) is responsible to the board for "the integrity of the board's process,"[11] i.e., to ensure that the board has decided and described how it will manage itself (operational policies) and is following its own prescriptions. In other words, the board knows what its job is and the chairperson exercises on behalf of the board the discipline needed to keep the board in compliance with its own guidelines.

Two elements are critical for the chairperson to fulfill this role. First, the board must understand its collective role and define its own governance processes, i.e., how it will function and make decisions. The board articulates these policies in specific documents. The internal governance processes aid the board in accomplishing its responsibilities with excellence. The board must have some clarity about itself and its responsibilities for the chairperson to provide good leadership. Second, the board must be clear about the way it wants its chairperson to lead. This will require the board to consider such issues as: board evaluation processes, agenda construction, board committees,

---

8. Carver and Carver, *Reinventing Your Board*, 110.

9. Robert, *Robert's Rules of Order* can be accessed free of charge at https://robertsrules.org/.

10. Carver and Carver, *Reinventing Your Board*, 19.

11. Carver and Carver, *Reinventing Your Board*, 19.

discipline of board meetings, decision-making protocols, board education, and orientation of new members. So two policies are essential—the board's job description and the chairperson's job description.

Regardless of whether a church board adopts the Carver policy governance model, it is important for a board to have clarity on these two matters. In the absence of written policy and position description, the board lacks ground rules to guide its decision-making and the chairperson's actions are subject to accusations of favoritism or inconsistency. The fact that most church boards get some things done without such policies probably speaks to the high level of trust that often is found within the group. However, when difficult issues arise or conflict emerges, then the lack of such policy and position description leaves the board and the chairperson vulnerable to a whole range of dysfunctions.

People who accept the role of board chair must also realize that the good functioning of the board depends upon their commitment to good process, good communication, and good governance. This requires humor, patience, and great persistence, but at the end of the day, if this role is fulfilled well and carried forward with integrity and care, then that church will be blessed (along with all of the board members and pastoral leaders).

3. *Carver, Governance, Policy, and Local Church Governance: Can the Board Handle it?*

According to John Carver, "policy governance offers not a mere improvement in board leadership, but a revolution in boardroom behavior." [12] These are strong words. Any church board that might consider adopting policy governance as its framework for governance leadership must discern very carefully whether it wants to embrace such a revolution. To put it baldly, if a church board is not willing to accept responsibility for ensuring that the faith community is achieving its stated mission, then it should avoid policy governance.

Carver argues that boards (and I might add here lead pastors and ministry teams) up for the challenge of vigorous, governance leadership must accept this reality: "the board is accountable [to the congregation] for everything that goes on in the organization."[13] Kind of daunting! This kind of governance leadership is not for the faint-hearted, muddle-headed, or the spiritually uncommitted. To define outcomes unambiguously, to assign their

---

12. Carver and Carver, *Reinventing Your Board*, 17.
13. Carver and Carver, *Reinventing Your Board*, 43.

accomplishment to someone clearly, and then to make sure the outcomes are being achieved effectively—this is hard, soul-filled work.

A church board only grabs hold of policy governance because it wants the congregation to be more effective for Jesus, because it yearns for the rule of Christ to be demonstrated throughout its ministry, and because it desires people in the community to hear and respond to the good news. But then, this board will have to change in order to work within this framework. If there is no commitment to change and to engage in the disciplined, intentional, unremitting focus on mission achievement, then the church board should not adopt policy governance .

So if your church board is evaluating policy governance as a preferred mode for exercising its leadership, then make sure each board member counts the cost for getting the congregation on target. Board members must prepare to be more engaged in thinking strategically, more educated about significant issues, more willing to hold themselves and their primary leadership accountable, and more rigorous in pursuing their agreed outcomes. It may mean a significant change in the composition of your board, but the rewards are great:

- No more frustrating board meetings where the discussions result in no direction and nothing seems to change!
- No more acceptance of mediocrity within the board or among the key leadership!
- No more paralyzing uncertainty as to who is responsible and who is accountable!

For church board members who discern their roles as a significant part of their Christian stewardship, such change is welcome, because they passionately want to serve Jesus well. They hold the trust invested in them by their congregation with humble seriousness. They know it is the Holy Spirit who must give wisdom, must empower, and must encourage, but they stand ready to move as he directs, indeed, ready to suffer as he requires.

If you truly desire your church board to lead, "to see that tomorrow is created in a better image,"[14] and not to let tradition eat strategy, then take a very careful look at the policy governance mode of governance leadership. Carefully count the cost of embracing it—but also evaluate the price of ignoring it and choosing not to change.

---

14. Carver and Carver, *Reinventing Your Board*, 229.

4. *Carver, Governance, Policy, and Local Church Governance—Can the Pastor Handle it?*

One of the key principles embedded in policy governance is that the board holds one person accountable for implementing its policies and achieving the institutional ends—the Chief Executive Officer.[15] For the CEO, this is a double-edged sword because on the one hand it gives tremendous flexibility within well-defined boundaries, but on the other hand puts great responsibility on the CEO for achieving the mission. Is this principle compatible with the pastoral role, and if so, are pastoral leaders up to the challenge, and willing for the board to hold them accountable for organizational leadership? (If a lead pastor does not function as the key person executing the decisions of a church board, then who fills this role?) Perhaps more importantly, are church boards willing to give the pastoral leader the authority necessary to achieve the discerned outcomes?

According to Carver's model, the board focuses upon developing policy consistent with the mission, values, and ends of the organization. Once the board defines these policies, it empowers the CEO (lead pastor), within specific limitations, to ensure that the organizational resources are focused upon accomplishing the desired ends. In the context of a local church, the board (which most often includes the lead pastor) would establish the policies, including the key ends they want the church to achieve. It then hands off to the lead pastor the chief responsibility to employ all of the resources of the local church to accomplish these outcomes, i.e., to execute them within specific boundaries. This model creates significant clarity for the lead pastor and the board as to their respective responsibilities. So long as the lead pastor is guiding the local church to achieve the outcomes within the limitations specified, the board supports the lead pastor in his role. Reporting lines are clear. The accountability of all other paid (and volunteer) staff is to the lead pastor, not the board.

Does this mean that other church board members have no role in ministry leadership? Not at all! However, if they are assigned a ministry role in the church (i.e., small-group leader, facility oversight, member care, etc.), they are accountable to the lead pastor for that role, not the board. They do not report to the board, but to the lead pastor (or to one of the members of the administrative team who has oversight for this responsibility). It may also be the case that the board assigns them a specific board responsibility (i.e., audit oversight, personnel matters, etc.) and in this case they are accountable directly to the board. So the members of the church board need

---

15. This title often generates criticism from pastors. However, it serves to designate who executes the decisions of the board. And in this model, it is the lead pastor.

to be clear as to the nature of their responsibilities and to whom they are accountable for the accomplishment of said responsibilities.

The board must address several key questions if it plans to adopt policy governance as their model of leadership. First, are they prepared to empower the lead pastor (church CEO) to accomplish the outcomes the board specifies? Second, is the lead pastor prepared to accept this responsibility and run with it? Third, is the church board chairperson prepared to work in a disciplined way with the church board to follow these principles? Fourth, is the lead pastor prepared to let the church board chairperson lead the church board? Fifth, is the lead pastor willing to embrace accountability and annual performance evaluations? If the answer to these questions is yes, then the local church may be prepared to embrace the Carver policy governance model and make it work for the benefit of the congregation. If not, then the board should consider some other model.

Do these elements of the Carver policy governance model contravene scriptural principles? I am not aware that this would be case. In fact, they may assist the local church in consistently and fairly applying the biblical principles of accountability, empowerment, stewardship, and good order. Whatever model the local church may adopt, it should understand it clearly and work it consistently. Much frustration and tension arises because leaders do not agree on the model, apply it inconsistently, or act with accountability.

Some pastoral leaders may bristle at the suggestion that they function as a CEO, serving as the primary organizational leader. In their view, this defines the church as a corporation, not a community. Of course, no one desires a local church to function as a business. However, the model proposed by John Carver specifically addresses nonprofit agencies, so it is not built upon a business model per se. Second, someone in the local church has to be given authority to lead responsibly, i.e., to execute decisions, and the lead pastor normally is the professional leader hired to fill this role.

5. *Carver, Governance, Policy, and the Local Church Board: Can the Board Chair and Lead Pastor Relationship Sustain it?*

The Carver policy governance model requires both the church board chairperson and the lead pastor to understand their respective roles clearly and be supportive of each other in those roles. This is especially important when a local church seeks to implement the policy governance model.

Carver argues that the board chair's primary role is to ensure that the board disciplines itself to govern according to its stated policies.[16] Such responsibility includes overseeing board planning, ensuring educational development is occurring, conducting board evaluation, and working with the primary leader in the organization to advise and support him. The primary organizational leader simultaneously takes responsibility for the same kinds of functions within the organization so that the organization is achieving the vision and the ends established by the board within the board's stated limitations. This person advises and supports the board chairperson.

As in most social entities, good relationships and trust are critical for healthy and sustained development. Within the context of a local church, whether or not the board operates according to Carver policy governance, the relationship between the board chairperson and the lead pastor must be marked by:

  a. Deep, mutual trust;
  b. Mutual acknowledgement of their different but necessary roles and responsibilities;
  c. Sustained and growing respect for the wisdom and gifts God provides to each;
  d. Constant, clear communication on all significant issues;
  e. Commitment to the success of the other in their ministry;
  f. Consistent spiritual awareness and accountability;
  g. The ability to keep confidences and maintain confidences.

Well-defined role descriptions can bring great assistance, but will not in themselves guarantee good relationships. The mutual support required will go far beyond words written on a page. Their respective leadership within the church puts them at the very center of the spiritual warfare they constantly engage as Jesus' representatives, advancing his rule in this world.

To sustain and enhance this relationship takes time, prayer, patience, humility, a teachable spirit, a forgiving spirit, and continual interaction. Some simple, but consistent practices will go a long way toward preventing disruption, dysfunction, and conflict:[17]

  a. The board chairperson should always invite the lead pastor's input into the development of the board's agendas well in advance of the meeting. There should be no surprises for either leader at the board

---

16. Carver, *Reinventing Your Board*, 110–11.
17. Basinger, "Board Chair-CEO Relationship."

meeting. Similarly, the board chairperson should not be hearing about a new ministry initiative from a church member, but directly from the lead pastor before it comes to the board for review.

b. There should be formal agreement not to contradict one another in public, or to introduce new developments or ministry initiatives until there has been some private discussion.

c. If differences do arise, there should be a deep commitment to pray, interact and find resolution in healthy ways, but to keep such discussions confidential as much as possible.

d. They should find time to share with each other their respective visions for the church's ministry, with freedom to disagree and interact in love, without feeling defensive.

e. When an offense, either real or perceived, is experienced, deal with it immediately, one to one.[18] The board chairperson must take responsibility to ensure that the board deals with employment issues fairly, in a principled manner, and as expeditiously as possible.

f. Exercise a lively, loving concern for the welfare of each other.

Each working partnership will develop uniquely because of the personalities, gifting, and competencies that each brings into the relationship. A good part of the ministry energy sparking the church's development should come from the generative thinking, passionate praying, and mutual care these two individuals enjoy together. Trust gets built over time and incrementally. Give it time, work at it, support it with prayer, listen well, and think the best of the other. The Holy Spirit can work some amazing things.

6. *Carver, Governance, and Policy: Can the Congregation Handle It?*

If the church leadership discerns that Carver policy governance would provide a more adequate and beneficial governance model for their local church, how does it prepare the congregation for this shift? Or is the congregation unaffected by such a change in governance modality?

Some communication with the congregation is advisable. In our current Evangelical culture, many are suspicious about methods or technologies which are developed in society and then adopted by the church community. These are legitimate concerns because methods and means used by the

---

18. There may be situations in which it would be prudent for a chairperson to have a third party present when acting to resolve a conflict with the lead pastor or deal with an offense. If the chair meets privately and alone with the other party, then no independent witness can confirm what transpired should that become necessary.

church must be compatible with the values espoused by the faith community. If a church board desires to adopt policy governance, then it has a duty to demonstrate to the congregation that this mode of board governance is compatible with the kingdom values embraced by the church. But perhaps even more importantly it needs to show that this change will enhance the community's life—improving excellence, enabling better decisions, implementing better accountability, and enhancing the board's capacity to devote its time to the critical things that promote church health.

The congregation should also understand that this shift in governance requires a change in the way pastoral staff exercises its leadership. In terms of policy governance, the board will be empowering the pastoral leaders to implement the ministry initiatives (following appropriate decision-making protocols) necessary for the congregation to achieve its vision. Pastors will be empowered to lead, not only to provide spiritual care. In some congregations, this requires a major change in perspective.

Policy governance, if it is working properly, elevates the level of accountability throughout the institution. This holds true for the faith community. Because churches rely on a significant level of volunteer leadership, those in these positions of leadership will need some encouragement and mentoring to understand and accept this new level of accountability. The other side of this coin, however, is that policy governance also empowers, granting permission to use whatever means are legal—consistent with the institution's values, and within the financial and other resources of the entity—to achieve the vision. If the leaders are not achieving the outcomes established, then the board will evaluate and expect changes to be made.

The congregation should also expect a change in the level of decisions they will be making. Some may feel this is a loss of democracy; others may claim that this represents a power grab; still others will suggest that the board is no longer sensitive to the needs of the congregation. Again, good explanation well in advance and continually reinforced by exemplary actions will go a long way toward eliminating such fears. On the positive side, the congregation should expect to be engaged in making decisions on those things that really matter (i.e., how can we plant another church or how can we reach the youth in our community?) rather than debating the color of the new carpets or approving the contract for garbage collection. The result should be a congregation more engaged, rather than less, because they are dealing with matters of kingdom significance.

When church boards are considering policy governance, they should take time to explain well to the congregation why the board is recommending this direction, what the benefits should be, and how roles will change. As implementation occurs, continue to point out how it is working in beneficial ways. Do not expect the congregation to be able to discern this on their own. Be proactive, anticipate difficulties, and be transparent throughout the change process.

Policy, Governance, and Biblical Principles

Phillip Jenkins has defined boards as "the well-intentioned in full pursuit of the irrelevant."[19] While this is a rather pessimistic and cynical evaluation, church boards often fall into this mode of operation. Church boards tend to operate by functioning as advisors and rubber stamps or by meddling and micromanaging. Although the intention of board members in operating in such ways might be good, the results fall far short of the potential such boards could have in advancing their congregation's mission. These realities that historically have been endemic among nonprofit agency boards led John Carver to develop and advance his ideas now known as policy governance. However, because Carver developed his ideas outside of the framework of Christian communities and church boards, some wonder whether they are compatible with biblical principles and congregational forms of church governance in particular.

Richard Biery[20] argues that the fit between Carver's principles and biblical values is very close. He defines linkages with four primary Carver principles—the servant leadership role of the board in stewardship, accountability, empowerment within policy guidelines, and clarity of values. He shows how values such as integrity, the use of words, and excellence, as well as the concept of covenant and the wise use of resources, similarly are harmonious with biblical perspectives. I would add several, broader categories of biblical concern that Carver's model addresses.

1. *Ensuring the appropriate location of authority.*

   Applying the principles developed by Carver requires a nonprofit agency to sort out the question of authority. In the context of a congregation, the implementation of his ideas enables the church board to discern its role, to clearly define the role of the pastoral staff, and to articulate how other stakeholders in that context speak into respective decisions. The writers of the New Testament were careful to control the use of authority within a congregation and quick to condemn its abuse. In the cultural setting of the Roman Empire, where authoritarian modes of control were dominant, the principles of kingdom living

---

19. Jenikins, in Malphurs, *Leading Leaders*, 14.
20. Biery, *What is Biblical?*

that Jesus taught created a community in which authority, while present, was to be expressed within the more significant values of mutual submission,[21] sacrifice, equity, service, love, and grace. Leaders exercise authority in the congregation in trust for the good of the body and not for selfish reasons. Carver's principles enable a congregation to assign appropriate authority but also implement checks and balances so that leaders employ their authority for advancing the mission in ways that are consistent with the values of the congregation. This model requires both the church board and pastoral staff to submit to the distribution of authority as defined by the congregation.

2. *Providing an effective and efficient leadership structure.*

Jesus, Paul, and Peter addressed matters of leadership within the church. Jesus talked about values and vision primarily, but Paul and Peter also treated matters specific to leadership principles and structure. The metaphor of body that Paul invoked to illustrate the nature of the Christian church has concepts of structure embedded within it. When he expanded the metaphor in Ephesians 4:11–16, he described the body as joined together and working well because every part is restored to its created order and obediently fulfilling its function for the good of the body. The result is that all believers in church contribute to the growth of the whole body of Christ, i.e., the church (Eph 4:16). Christ empowers them and restores them for this purpose by providing people who are gifted to teach, mentor, train, and encourage. In 1 Corinthians 14:40, Paul again urged that everything be done "decently and in order." In Acts we see how the Holy Spirit guided the church through various crises (e.g., Acts 6, 15) to develop new structures to facilitate its mission and ministry. Although structure and leadership patterns are diverse, there are many places where early church leaders address both. Carver's principles take up this concern for clear, effective, and efficient leadership structures, and enable a church to define and implement such structures. In particular, the clarity his principles require for the board's leadership, the pastoral leadership, and the congregational leadership enable each to work coherently together, sharing governance appropriately, because they understand their respective contributions to the leadership of the congregation. Yet Carver's principles provide considerable flexibility in their implementation.

3. *Keeping the church board on mission.*

---

21. Consider Ephesians 5:21.

A key element in Carver's philosophy of board operations is the definition of the primary end or outcome that the agency was created to accomplish. Once the board discerns, defines, and decides this, then all of the board's work must achieve this end. This singularity of focus brings discipline to the board and its operations. It also fosters unity and requires alignment of purpose within the roles of the staff. People know the direction, resources are applied to pursuing that direction, and evaluations are related to progress made toward achieving the goal. Within a congregational context, this requires the board to keep its decisions in step with the fulfillment of God's mission for his people.

4. *Elevating the role of church board members.*

    The New Testament writers denounced the pursuit of leadership in a congregation for purposes of personal status and ambition. Yet the writers encouraged the proper recognition of those who give their time, energy, and gifting to serve the people of God well. Enabling believers to live out their calling in Christ in meaningful ways is also valued. Carver's principles enable the board itself and the stakeholders in and related to the congregation to recognize appropriately, and to respect, the important role that the church board fulfills. Too often within the congregation the board is regarded as a committee doing some kind of administrative work, rather than the energized, Spirit-directed ministry team that is giving its full attention to the accomplishment of that church's mission. When church board members discern how directly connected their work is to the achievement of the congregation's mission, this has the capacity to transform their sense of service.

5. *Enabling voices to be heard.*

    The belief in biblical principles such as the priesthood of believers, the equal relationship that all believers have with and in Christ, the role of the Holy Spirit in every believer's life, and the concept of the giftedness and empowerment for ministry, contributes to the importance that a church board must place upon enabling voices within the congregation to be heard respectfully and prayerfully. Carver's principles allow for, encourage, and enable church boards to develop and adhere to appropriate mechanisms that support shared governance. This means that the board knows and values the ways and means that the bylaws provide for congregational input and decisions. Similarly, the board understands the appropriate involvement of staff in its decisions and values that input. Too often church conflict arises because church boards do not enable or value the input of appropriate congregational segments into the decision-making progress.

What does all this mean for a church board chairperson when considering ways to enhance the development of his or her board? Is the Carver model of board governance an appropriate means for a church board to define its role? Does it cohere with biblical principles and values? I think the answers to these questions are yes, provided the board demonstrates integrity in proposing such a transition. All systems can be abused, even the Carver model. However, if the board implements well, with good understanding, and with a view to enhancing cherished theological principles and being accountable to other values that the church embraces, then it can be a very productive and energizing church board development. As chairperson, you would play a significant role in introducing such a proposed change, helping the board educate itself about this model of governance so that it discerns its value, and then working carefully and transparently to implement it if the board decides to proceed. Recognize that implementation will take about two years. Seek external guidance to educate the board members first and to discern whether this model of governance will be helpful for your church. These advisors might also assist you in the implementation process. This will be time and money well spent.

Case Study: The Accountability Vacuum[22]

Bob pondered the proposed agenda for the next church board meeting. The congregation would hold their annual general meeting in six weeks. The past year had gone relatively smoothly with no wrenching decisions and most ministries seemed to be functioning well. Yet Bob, in his second term as board chairperson, sensed that things were not as rosy as they appeared to be. He wondered what would happen if a serious matter arose that challenged the board.

At the last several board meetings, two of the board members through their comments indicated that they had not read the reports circulated prior to the meeting. As a result, they came unprepared. Were they capable of evaluating potential risks when they made uninformed decisions? Jerry, completing his third term as a board member, was encountering some serious marital difficulties. Bob wondered about the spiritual tone of the board. Of course, board

---

22. Although the story in this case study may seem to resemble a real situation, the names, places, and actual circumstances do not describe any actual church, church board, pastor, or chairperson.

meetings began with a short devotional and prayer time, but it seemed rather perfunctory at times. His recent attempt to encourage the board to develop a code of conduct for board members had met with a lukewarm reception. These diverse events were significant indicators that some board members were becoming complacent and losing their sense of accountability for the important work they did together. To his knowledge, the board members had never evaluated their effectiveness as a board.

Bob's mind skipped back to a recent conversation he had with his pastor. He valued his relationship with Pastor Ed and looked forward to these monthly meetings when they talked about the health and welfare of the congregation. However, Bob knew that the board had no policy that defined an annual performance evaluation of the lead pastor. Bob had no reason to doubt that Pastor Ed worked hard, but his observations of how the various church staff operated led him to the inevitable conclusion that they received little direction. Each did his or her own thing—often with tremendous creativity and commitment—but with little awareness of the larger mission to which all of their collective work should be contributing. Bob was afraid that sooner or later this rather lax method of leadership was going to generate serious problems. Yet without a regular performance evaluation of the lead pastor and his work with the staff, the board could not address this issue naturally and effectively.

Bob also knew that the board had no policy that required regular performance evaluations for any other paid staff. At several meetings through the year, some board members had shared concerns about the activities of one of the paid staff. However, the board did not know how to process the information because it had no mechanism by which to implement a review. The board had asked Pastor Ed to investigate, but so far he had not reported back.

The board's reports to the congregation in the annual general meeting, although comprehensive in their content, did not communicate the sense that the board considered itself accountable to the congregation for its work. At the most recent congregational meeting, several astute members had posed some probing questions to Bob as board chairperson, and they were not very satisfied with his responses. He knew that more questions would be coming to him at the annual general meeting (AGM) and he wondered how well he could respond on behalf of the board.

Bob knew that one key way the board could grasp its responsibilities for the health and development of the congregation would be to become more accountable itself. It also needed to develop a culture of accountability within the pastoral staff. However, how could the board do this given the current state of things and the lack of any strong tradition of accountability within the agency?

Reflections

1. How would you advise Bob as board chair to lead this board strategically in the next twelve months to develop a culture of accountability? What essential rationale (including biblical principles) would you suggest Bob use to persuade the board members and lead pastor that such a development is a necessary and responsible step to enhance the board's capacity to function effectively as the strategic ministry leadership team in that congregation?

2. What are the risks to Bob as chairperson, the lead pastor, and the board collectively if Bob is unsuccessful in leading the board to develop and implement necessary policies of accountability?

3. Whose support does Bob need to have and maintain in order to help the board members step up to the challenge? What possible changes does Bob as chairperson have to face if only some of the board members support him and the lead pastor refuses to see the need for annual performance evaluations?

4. What message is the board sending throughout the congregation if it cannot develop a culture of accountability? How will this message impede the board's ability to advance the congregation's mission?

Questions for Reflection

a. As you reflect upon the way your church board works and how it relates to other authorities within the congregation, what model of governance is your board using for the most part?

b. How important is it for the board to distinguish between governance decisions and management decisions? If your lead pastor is used to the board making management decisions, how can you gradually, but firmly, help him adjust to a greater leadership role in the management of the ministry? Will this require a reorientation of the position description?

Suggested Resources

a. John Carver, *Boards that Make a Difference: A New Design for Leadership in Nonprofit and Public Organizations*.

b. Dan Hotchkiss, *Governance and Ministry: Rethinking Board Leadership*.

Chapter 4

Discerning and Building Your Leadership Character as a Church Board Chairperson

Part I: The Key Ministry Role of a Church Board Chairperson

IN A CHURCH COMMITTED to congregational polity the path to becoming a church board chairperson normally follows one of two directions. One is that the bylaws may require the congregation to appoint the chairperson. In this case, a nominating committee will seek someone among the membership who will be willing to serve in the role of board chairperson as a member of the church board. Other churches leave this decision to the church board and expect the board to appoint a chairperson from among the board members whom the congregation appoints. A third option is sometimes dictated by denominational practice, namely that the lead pastor will function as board chairperson.[1]

Frequently in none of these three options for selection and appointment is there any specific training offered to prepare a person to fill this chairing role, and more often than not there exists no formal role description to assist the candidate in understanding what is required. The church board probably has a list of the basic qualifications for candidates to serve as a board member (usually described as "elder" or "deacon" role) and may even have a rudimentary position description for the board chair, if this is a congregational appointment. 1 Timothy 3, Titus 1, and sometimes 1 Peter 5 most often serve as the source for these qualifications. Where no position description for a church board member or church board chairperson exists,

---

1. In such cases, the lead pastor may choose to delegate this role to someone else within the board. While there may be some reason for a lead pastor, i.e., an employee, to lead a church board, it inevitably involves serious conflicts of interest that the board has to manage very carefully.

the board can easily remedy this deficit. You can find a sample church board chairperson role description in *Appendix A*.

The encouragement is that the Holy Spirit does operate through these processes to call people to fill this role, even though they may not feel qualified, competent, or capable. If God's people discern within you some ability and giftedness, as well as the integrity, to fill the role well, then the question is this: Will you step out in faith and obedience to help the church of God? Although you may have accepted the invitation to fill this role with great reluctance, can you move from grudging hesitancy to a passionate yes? This is possible with the Spirit's help, a willing, humble disposition to learn, commitment to give the role the time it deserves, and confidence that God can do something wonderful through you, enabling you to have a remarkable kingdom impact. Sometimes the previous chairperson will be willing to mentor you. As well, the lead pastor may have resources to assist you. You will find other resources at the churchboardchair.ca website.

Getting to a passionate yes requires first that you understand the two central realities that define a church board and thus the role of its chairperson. First, *a church board forms one of the most significant ministry teams in a community of faith, i.e., a local church*. Whether the board members are called elders or deacons or some other title, in every case a church board is first and foremost a ministry team. A local church simultaneously is a faith community and a ministry organization/agency. It is a seedbed of kingdom reality growing in "this present evil age" (Gal 1:4). The board oversees the development of this special, divinely created community called a church, under the direction of God's Holy Spirit.[2] Everything the board does in its governing role is worshipful, spiritual leadership, devoted to advancing the spiritual health of a community of believers, demonstrating good faith governance.

Does God's Spirit give this ministry team (i.e., the church board) the capacity to achieve the desired results (i.e., build a healthy church)? If you answer this question with a yes, then you believe that God has given his church the capacities it needs to be both a faith community and a ministry agency. It does not depend upon you as board chairperson, but upon the willingness and ability of the Holy Spirit to empower and resource his church. The primary responsibilities of a church board and its chairperson are to discern, develop, and steward all of those capacities so that the church can achieve its divine mission and be a thriving spiritual community.

---

2. Consider Paul's comments in Acts 20:27–31, which he addresses to the elders of the church in Ephesus. The Holy Spirit "has made you overseers" so that you can "shepherd the flock of God, which he bought with his own blood." He warns them of "wolves" who will come "and will not spare the flock."

This fundamental premise gives to the board and its chairperson hope (i.e., confidence that things operate according to a deep, divine sense, even though the current experience may be chaotic) and responsibility for the healthy growth and development of this local church, exceeding what any other group in the church may perceive.[3] The board must give its full and constant attention to this primary responsibility. A church board chairperson facilitates the capacity of the board to accomplish this fundamental spiritual activity. A chairperson is then a spiritual leader in the church and within the board.

The second reality is that *the church is a ministry organization/agency, i.e., a nonprofit society fulfilling a mission of service and promoting the life of a specific, cultural community.* The primary group that guides this nonprofit society and ensures mission fulfillment is the board who acts with accountability to the members of that ministry agency/nonprofit society. This reality sets the board within a legal framework and a context of public accountability that the chairperson needs to understand well so that the board functions appropriately within this framework. There are things that the board must do in order to fulfill and sustain this legal status.[4] The chairperson helps the board to accomplish these legal responsibilities in a timely, ethical, and effective manner. Whether this has to do with fiscal integrity, preserving resources, employee welfare, liability issues, truthful communication, board evaluation, or annual general meetings, a board chairperson has to keep an eye on these matters, lest the board forget or overlook its legal and ethical obligations and put the entire ministry agency in jeopardy.

These various ministry and legal aspects constitute the two significant realities of church board life. The congregation trusts that the board and its chairperson will give appropriate care and attention to both, but especially to the ministry aspect, otherwise the church community will suffer. This is where spiritual wisdom and creativity on the part of the chairperson become critical factors. Learning how to carry forward both the spiritual and legal mandates in an integrated and appropriately balanced manner requires skill, insight, awareness of the future, and a deep sense of the church's mission. The legal and ethical elements nestle within the context of the spiritual values established by the church. However, the ministry mandate always has

---

3. This assumes that the lead pastor is part of the board and thus involved intimately in achieving this result.

4. The exact nuances of the legal requirements vary from province to province and country to country. Denominational leaders can help church board chairpersons understand the specific requirements that may apply in their regions or countries.

priority and the legal aspects serve as means to help the board advance the ministry mandate.

A chairperson's role can be one of the most exciting ministry opportunities that a person ever experiences. The challenges are great, but so too is the Spirit within. As you realize the scope of what a chairperson oversees and facilitates, you can appreciate the need for a passionate yes to fill the role. It is not for the timid. As Peter says in 1 Peter 5:1–4, candidates should embrace this role with a willing heart, with zeal for God, and with a deep desire to serve as an example to the "flock of God." Understanding the dimensions of the role helps a person get to the passionate yes.

If people in your local church are asking you to consider serving as the chairperson of the board, this may be one of the ways God wants you to live out your calling[5] as a Christian for the next period of your life. It would be wise to seek some affirmation of this by following your usual method of discerning God's direction in your life. Pray about it. Talk to one or two people whose wisdom you respect and who will give you some honest input. Ask to meet with the current chairperson and get some perspective on what the role entails and some of the current challenges that your church board is facing. Consult with your lead pastor. Then pray some more.

Reflect on the following questions:

1. Has the course of my life prepared me to fill the role of board chairperson?
2. Do I have a passion for Jesus and his church that motivates me to give time and energy to serve in this way?
3. Do I have the leadership capacity to facilitate the board?
4. Are my motives pure in this matter?
5. Am I willing to be held accountable in this role?
6. Am I prepared to carry the burden of this leadership role?
7. Are my communication skills sufficient to help me succeed in this role?

5. When a person repents and accepts Jesus as Lord and Savior, that individual is responding to God's "call" and thus "is called." In Romans 1:7, Paul describes Christians as people who "are loved by God and called to be saints." Similarly, Peter defines believers as people "called by God" (1 Pet 1:15; 2:21; 5:10). The way a particular believer lives out that calling as a Christian depends upon gifting, circumstances, the Spirit's direction, opportunity, and obedience to kingdom values. While people in the church tend to value some roles in the kingdom more than others, God enables every believer to live missionally no matter the situation, and the Spirit's presence in the believer makes each one equally precious in God's sight. God may give diverse gifting to individuals, but every Christian is equally a disciple and kingdom agent (1 Cor 12:18, 24–27; Rom 12:3–8). Galatians 3:28–29 leaves no doubt that we are all "sons of God" in Christ.

8. Am I willing to study and learn what it means to serve as chairperson so that I serve as effectively as possible?

If you can sincerely say yes to most of these questions, then you should consider saying yes to the request to serve.

Part II: The Role of a Church Board Chairperson

What attitudes and spiritual commitments will be necessary?

Paul makes it very clear that ministry leadership, whether volunteer or vocational, requires spiritual maturity. Take a few minutes and review carefully the qualifications for ministry managers/stewards (overseers/supervisors) and assisting agents (deacons) (1Tim 3:1–10; Titus 1:6–9). The majority of these qualifications have to do with character and only a few relate to competence.

Reference	Character	Competence
1 Tim 3:2; Titus 1:6	Above reproach; blameless within and without the congregation	
1 Tim 3:2; Titus 1:6	Husband of one wife	
1 Tim 3:2	Temperate	
1 Tim 3:2	Sensible	
1 Tim 3:2, 8	Respectable	
1 Tim 3:2; Titus 1:8		Hospitable
1 Tim 3:2		Apt to teach
1 Tim 3:3, 8; Titus 1:7	Not given to drunkenness	
1 Tim 3:3	Not violent, but gentle	
1 Tim 3:3	Not quarrelsome	
1 Tim 3:3	Not a lover of money	
1 Tim 3:4; Titus 1:6		Cares for his own family well
1 Tim 3:6	Not a recent convert	
1 Tim 3:6	Good reputation with outsiders	
1 Tim 3:8	Sincere	

Reference	Character	Competence
1 Tim 3:8; Titus 1:7	Not pursuing dishonest gain	
1 Tim 3:9		Preserves the deep truths of the faith
1 Tim 3:9	Tested	Tested
Titus 1:7	Not overbearing	
Titus 1:7	Not quick-tempered	
Titus 1:8	Loves what is good	
Titus 1:8	Self-controlled	
Titus 1:8	Upright, holy	

In effect, Paul required ministry leaders—and this includes a person who fills the role of board chairperson—to be mature disciples of Jesus and to have a track record of caring for others well.

One of Paul's instructions to Timothy is "not to lay hands quickly on anyone" (1 Tim 5:22). Those entrusted with the spiritual care of the Messiah's people require tested faith and evident obedience to Jesus. Maturity in following Jesus arises because of consistent attention paid to the guiding presence of the Holy Spirit. Presumably, your fellow believers are asking you to consider the role of board chairperson because you demonstrate this level of maturity and have a strong appetite to learn more of the ways of God. Probably no one feels entirely ready to fill this role, but as God directs, accept it with humility and eager anticipation because the Spirit will help you.

A significant mark of spiritual maturity will be your track record of caring for others well. When Paul says that someone suitable for the role of overseer "manages his household well" (1 Tim 3:4), I think he focuses attention upon the ability of the individual to care well for people for whom he has responsibility. So when they approach you to fill this role, can you say that you have a heart that truly cares for the congregation? Will you invest yourself in this role because you want them to have the best possible spiritual care in their journey with Jesus? A person accepts the chairperson's role not because it gives any authority or power over people, but rather because it enables a person to serve people well. Much of this caregiving will find expression in mentoring others. Sometimes protection will be required, as false teaching may enter the congregation. On other occasions, the care will be quite practical, i.e., ensuring that the congregation has means to provide food to a needy church family. Then there is the care for the spiritual growth of people, ensuring that the leaders are teaching God's word well and completely. A board chair is not responsible to do this alone, but the chairperson must help the board give these matters serious and constant attention.

If you ask current board chairs what critical capacities and competencies a new chairperson requires the most, you will receive diverse answers. Consider the following:

1. *A capacity for visionary leadership.* The phrase "visionary leadership" undoubtedly is overused today and people define it in many different ways. If leadership essentially is the ability to influence people toward a specific goal, then visionary leadership in a church context would entail possessing a deep sense of what God desires a particular congregation to be in their context, confidence in God's ability to enable the congregation to fill out that vision, and the ability to influence people toward the achievement of that vision. There has to be an unrelenting obedience to impact the community for Christ and discernment as to how best the congregation will accomplish this. It will require a commitment to continually develop your leadership capacity and to apply your leadership and facilitating skills for the good of the board and its members.

2. *An intentional embrace of spiritual discipline is necessary.* I think the most radical change in perspective about this role that you may have to embrace relates to its spiritual character. A congregation appoints church board members because they evidence spiritual maturity. The board members appoint you as chairperson because among themselves they have discerned within you the spiritual intelligence necessary to lead them. If the lead pastor is speaking in favor as well, then you also have his evaluation of your spiritual wisdom to consider. (If he is not, then in such cases it is probably best to decline the invitation to fill the role.)

    What does this spiritual discipline entail? I would suggest three key elements. As chairperson, you must act with *complete integrity*. You cannot manipulate decisions by withholding information, nor can you play favorites. Your leadership in the board must be above reproach in following policy, process, and any other principles that the board has adopted. Self-interest cannot factor into this role. Second, you must carry forward the duties associated with the role *faithfully*. This has two parts. First, you will need to devote the time necessary to learn the role, prepare yourself and the board for good meetings, and diligently seek to advance the board's work effectively. Second, you will need to lead with evident trust in God, i.e., faith-filled leadership. Knowing where the line is between acting presumptuously and acting faithfully will form a key part of your leadership. Third, you will need to embrace the *spiritual care* of the congregation as a primary value in all that you do. This includes a ministry of prayer, a willingness to suffer with the burden of such leadership, and walking with a sense of deep dependence upon the Holy Spirit.

3. *A grasp of essential board functions and duties.* If you are new to the role of board chairperson, then you will need to study the nature of this role and its craft. Much of it involves sustaining the board's routines, i.e., agenda preparation, writing of appropriate minutes, reception of standard reports, preparing for the annual general meeting, etc. If you do not know how to read and analyze a financial statement, you will need to develop this skill. Some aspects of this role require you to help the board discern future direction for the congregation and designing ministry roles that will help it realize its future. Other aspects involve learning the ethical and legal standards that enable the board to function well and sustain the trust of the congregation. For example, through an organization such as the Canadian Council of Christian Charities, you may need to become conversant with government regulations regarding charitable agency financing. Finally, you will need to think deeply about how the board through its actions can develop the congregation's capacity to succeed. If your church has experienced considerable leadership turnover recently, you will have to help the board discern why this has happened and what the board must do to create a healthier leadership climate and to foster good employment relations. Or, maybe your congregation has struggled to gather the financial resources to sustain ministry growth and this becomes a key issue that the board must solve if the church is to move into a healthier space.

4. *Learn how to get the job done.* Essentially what a church board does is steward the church's resources so that its mission is accomplished. The word "steward" comes from two Anglo-Saxon words: the lord's great house was his *sti* and the individuals responsible for its well-being were his *weard*, the keepers or wardens.[6] So *sti-weard*-ship involves the act of entrusting (being put in charge of what belongs to another), faithful management (all affairs managed for the owner's welfare), and accountability (return of the property in good or improved condition to the owner). All board members have to act consciously as stewards of what the congregation (and God) has placed in their care. The chairperson helps the board to exercise faithful stewardship.

6. Heclo, *On Thinking Institutionally*, 143.

Good stewardship only happens when those responsible remain focused in a disciplined way on achieving progress and following good process. For the chairperson, this will mean developing and circulating agendas for board meetings at least a week in advance of the meetings, along with necessary reports so that board members have time to read, pray about, and reflect upon the decisions before them. No one else within the board can manage this other than the chairperson.

When key decisions are being made, the chairperson has to facilitate the board's deliberations ensuring that all board members are speaking to the question, that motions are being made in an orderly fashion, and that the board is exercising due diligence in these deliberations, i.e., ensuring that it has the required information to make informed choices. The chairperson needs to know what specific professional or experiential expertise various board members bring to the table and how to enable them to speak to the question out of that expertise, whether that is financial, theological, ministry leadership, human resource management, legal wisdom, or facility management.

This means that a board chairperson's relationship with the lead pastor must be cultivated carefully. If that relationship becomes dysfunctional, then the ability of the chairperson to lead the board becomes seriously compromised because the lead pastor normally will be a member of the board. The next chapter gives attention to this issue.

5. *Evaluating your leadership potential.* Whatever your perspective, entering into the role of board chairperson can be a daunting prospect, as is the case with any position of major ministry leadership. Peter (1 Pet 5:1–4) offers three criteria that individuals can use for self-evaluation when considering this role: willingness before God, proper motivation, and commitment to lead through personal example. While initially you may conclude that you do not understand the role very well, are you willing to study it and acquire the skills and competence necessary to serve as an effective board chairperson? None of us has achieved spiritual perfection and so for persons considering the role of board chair they must consider their relationship with God and whether anything they currently are doing or have done would eliminate them from serving in this role. Finally, we have to check our motivation. There is some authority residual in this role, as well as honor and respect in the congregation. It is a public role, as you may have to represent the congregation in the broader community for various reasons. Your motivation has to be sincere love for the church, the

bride of Christ, and your willingness to use the gifts and wisdom the Holy Spirit has given to you to advance his kingdom.

6. *Willing to accept the burden of leadership.* The work of a church board chairperson requires a spirit of courageous endurance. The weight of the responsibility can be significant, particularly when crisis occurs. Without a sense that in this role you are exercising your calling in Christ at all times, it will be easy to give up or take the easy road, to the detriment of the congregation. Be prepared to carry the burden of this leadership assisted by the Holy Spirit. It may entail some suffering, but this is the norm for followers of Jesus. However, as chairperson, please realize that you can do a lot to minimize the suffering through your wise leadership.

Serving as a church board chairperson is not rocket science, and neither is it simply a function of chairing a committee. With prayerful diligence, you can fulfill this role in ways that will sustain and deepen the health of the congregation within which the Lord Jesus has called you to serve.

Case Study: Decision Time[7]

Frank was in his third year of serving as church board chairperson for Community Bible Church. During this time, the congregation had grown steadily under the consistent guidance of the lead pastor and Sunday attendance was pushing three hundred. Finances were reasonably healthy and they had just completed a project to replace the roof on their twenty-year-old facility. Pastor Bob was in his fourth year as lead pastor and well respected in the congregation. Frank was enjoying the ministry of being a board member and chairperson, even though it had its challenging moments.

At the previous board meeting, Pastor Bob had proposed the creation of a new ministry staff position. Bob had undoubtedly been thinking about this staffing issue for a while, but had not communicated his concerns or his intent to Frank, the board chairperson, or to any of the other board members. So when he brought forward his proposal at the last board meeting, it caught everyone by surprise. Without question, Pastor Bob's workload had increased because the church was growing. Yet, when the congregation passed the budget for this new fiscal year three months ago, he had not raised this issue at all. In the modest strategic ministry plan the board was developing,

---

7. Although the story in this case study may seem to resemble a real situation, the names, places, and actual circumstances do not describe any actual church, church board, pastor, or chairperson.

the lead pastor had proposed no new staff additions for at least a year. To add further complication, the Sunday offerings were starting to reflect the influence of the recent economic downturn because five key congregational members had become unemployed in the past month.

As chairperson, Frank had done his best to facilitate a fair, but thorough discussion of Pastor Bob's proposal. Even though Pastor Bob had overlooked some key issues in his proposal (e.g., how the congregation would fund it, where and how they would secure the required office space and equipment, and a clear statement of this new staff member's responsibilities), the board members wanted to be supportive because they respected Pastor Bob and wanted to encourage him.

A year ago Frank had worked with the board to initiate a procedure that major decision items would be introduced for discussion and prayer at one meeting, but then voted on at the next scheduled meeting. Accordingly, he had put Pastor Bob's proposal at the top of the board's agenda for this meeting. He did not know how the board finally would respond to the proposal. Because Frank had been away on a business trip, he had had no time to discuss the proposal further with Pastor Bob.

When the board engaged in their second discussion, the interaction was robust to say the least. Several wanted to forge ahead and trust God for the finances. Others felt that the financial situation of the church just could not sustain a new salary at this point. And two others were quite unsure, now speaking for it and then a few moments later apparently opposing it. After an hour of discussion, Frank decided to call things to a close because no new points were being raised and there were several other items on the agenda that needed attention. One board member put forward a motion to approve Pastor Bob's proposal and immediately it received support. Taking a deep breath and making a silent prayer, Frank called for the vote. As he feared four voted in favor, including Pastor Bob, three voted against, and two abstained. Technically the board approved the proposal, but over half the board had in fact registered lack of support.

As chairperson of the board, what was he going to advise the board to do in the light of this decision? If Frank had called you the next day for advice, what would you say to him?

Observations

a. Church boards generally should not permit the inclusion of significant proposals in their agendas without prior notice. If a board person wants to bring forward a proposal for which the board chairperson has not received prior notice, then the board member should bring it forward as an item of concern. The chairperson would note it and then defer discussion to the next meeting. Rarely is any matter so urgent that the board must attend to it immediately. If this board had employed this procedural principle, then it would have given some time for the chairperson or some other board person to guide Pastor Bob in the development of his proposal so that it addressed some key issues otherwise omitted.

b. It is good that this board had in place the principle that in major decisions they had discussion at one meeting and then made the decision at the next meeting, allowing time for prayer, further interaction, and reflection. Normally this procedure would give time for Frank to work with Pastor Bob to address some of the deficiencies in the proposal. When Frank knew this could not happen because of his business travel, he could have asked the vice-chair of the board to work with Pastor Bob to address some of the key questions raised in the board discussion before it came to decision at that following board meeting. Alternatively, the board might ask the finance committee to collaborate with Pastor Bob to find a solution to the funding question and recommend a way to move forward without jeopardizing the congregation's financial stability.

c. Although Pastor Bob obviously felt strongly about this matter, he did not exercise good leadership in forcing this issue in this way. He probably lost some of his credibility as a leader by bringing the proposal to the board like this.

Options

a. If the chairperson had a clear indication from the discussion that the board members had not achieved consensus, he could have advised them to table the motion before the board voted and then asked two board members to work with Pastor Bob to address serious concerns. The board would review the revised proposal at the next meeting.

b. Just because the board has voted, it can still defer action on the motion. At this point Frank needs to discern whether retaining unity within the board is more important than approving Pastor Bob's proposal. Pastor Bob also should be sensitive to this issue of unity. A divided board ultimately will be unhealthy for the congregation. If board unity is a priority, then the chairperson could advise the board to defer action until it has better information or a more adequate proposal around which to develop stronger consensus.

c. If finances are the issue, then it may be advisable to build this proposed staff position into the strategic plan, but defer implementation until the board senses the congregation is able to support it financially. In this way the board supports Pastor Bob, signals its concern about the issue, but exercises good risk management regarding the financial stability of the congregation.

d. Pastor Bob's action may signal that he does not feel the board is aware of the situation the ministry staff is facing and is ignoring the pressures that are building because of recent growth. If this is the case, then perhaps the board needs to develop a personnel committee and take greater responsibility to ensure that they are caring for the needs of the staff.

Questions for reflection

a. Evaluate how much time you are giving on a weekly or monthly basis to serve as chairperson. Is it enough to help the board operate effectively? What aspects need more time and how can you organize your personal life to devote that time?

b. What spiritual discipline do you need to pursue and develop in order to enhance your effectiveness as chairperson? Do you need to commit time in prayer for the board members? Do you need to meet personally with the board members to encourage them in their service?

c. What keeps you awake at night as chairperson? What can you do to deal with these anxieties?

Suggested Resources

a. T. J. Addington, *High Impact Church Boards*.
b. Aubrey Malphurs, *Leading Leaders: Empowering Church Boards for Ministry Excellence*.

Chapter 5

Church Board Chairperson and Lead Pastor Relations

WE KNOW ENOUGH ABOUT church culture to realize that tradition, social context, personal perspectives, church size, and leadership gifting shape the relationship that develops between a church board chairperson and the lead pastor. Without a doubt, this relationship is critical to the health of a congregation and its ability to pursue God's mission with singular focus, deep passion, and sustained energy. However, it is also the case that church leaders have few resources to which they can turn to guide them in fostering this significant relationship. Yet, if the lead pastor and board chairperson fail to develop a working relationship that is robust and demonstrates spiritual maturity, the whole congregation surely walks with a limp. They must work together like a pair of chopsticks in order to accomplish their respective responsibilities well.

I readily acknowledge that the model of the chairperson and lead pastor relationship that I propose in this chapter runs counter to several strongly-held perceptions of the role of the lead pastor in congregational life. These perceptions elevate the authority of the lead pastor and often place this person beyond accountability to the church board. Some consequences of these perceptions for chairpersons would include: a) the lead pastor believes that he controls the board and that the chairperson is merely the facilitator of a committee; b) the lead pastor establishes the vision, which is then communicated to the board; c) the lead pastor is not accountable to the church board and so the board cannot require any kind of performance review; d) the pastoral staff form the strategic ministry leadership team in the church, not the board. In my view, these perceptions ignore the role of board members as key ministry leaders in the congregation, potentially create opportunities for the abuse of power by a lead pastor, relegate the board to being merely an advisory group to the lead pastor, and create excessive and dangerous conflict of interest patterns on the part of the lead pastor.

The lead pastor and chairperson each lead an influential ministry team—the lead pastor leads the staff and volunteers to implement ministry and the chairperson leads the church board to discern vision ends and policy. Both of these ministry teams contribute to a local church's ability and capacity to function as a community of faith. In new churches and smaller churches, often the church board and the ministry team are the same or overlap to a large degree, because there is only one or two paid employee positions. In such cases, the roles of the board chairperson and lead pastor can easily get confused because it is unclear when the leadership team is functioning as the church board or as the ministry staff. The paid ministry staff in larger churches become more numerous and it is easier to distinguish the respective roles of the board and the staff. However, new challenges arise because one group may contest the authority and role of the other group. Further, the board may struggle to understand and define its voice as a ministry team responsible for the spiritual health of the congregation.[1]

Both board chairpersons and lead pastors get involved in their roles for limited periods of time in a particular congregation. A lead pastor who serves a church for twenty years may have to learn to work with four or five different board chairpersons during his tenure—not an easy task. If a board chairperson continues in his role for several terms, he may find himself giving leadership to a pastorless church, as well as managing the delicate task of discerning the preferred way a new lead pastor desires to relate to the board chairperson. If the individuals in either role do not exercise spiritual wisdom, patience, mutual respect, and humility, the relationship can easily become confused and strained, i.e., essentially dysfunctional. In cases where the board chairperson is female and the lead pastor male, or vice versa, they will need to exercise care lest their interaction itself become a matter of criticism.

Congregational size does matter in this relationship. Some variables arise because of the stage of church development and size.[2] To use some commonly accepted categories:

---

[1]. A church board is responsible for the spiritual health of a congregation in the sense that developing a healthy congregation will be one of the key elements of the church's vision. The board will express this in its ends policy, the position description of the lead pastor, its monitoring function, its evaluation of programs, and its various decisions.

[2]. Church leadership literature proposes various paradigms. See McIntosh, *One Size Doesn't Fit All*, 13–24, for one example.

1. *Family church: active membership/attendees fifty or less*

   Less formal structure; decisions taken mostly by consensus; pastoral influence shared with other key family leaders; board agendas shorter and board meetings conducted with less formality.

2. *Pastoral church: active membership/attendees fifty-one to one hundred fifty*

   The lead pastor is more central to the church's leadership. The board is hands-on or a working board. It sets direction and assists the lead pastor to manage and implement. The board needs more formal processes, because governance becomes more complex and accountability has to be exercised carefully. The pastor is the board's primary resource who develops the board's capacity to enable the congregation to grow. Volunteers lead most ministry projects and some of them also serve as board members.

3. *Program church: active membership/attendees one hundred fifty-one to three hundred fifty*

   The lead pastor becomes more central to the execution of ministry. Lay leaders accomplish more ministry functions and the church staff also is growing. Building and maintaining alignment around vision is critical. The lead pastor tends to wield more influence than the board and the board tends to remain more like a working board while starting to shift to a policy-making board. It shifts from micromanaging to empowerment and accountability. A chairperson must construct the board agendas carefully so that the work of the board is appropriate and managed well, distinguished from that of the pastoral team. Committee structure will become more complex. Most churches in this category function with three or more staff people. Activity and structure often expand faster than the available resources.

4. *Corporate church: active membership/attendees three hundred fifty-one or more*

   The lead pastor pastors the staff, who in turn oversee ministry. The lead pastor spends considerable time hiring the right staff and generating alignment around vision. The lead pastor must hone skills in organizational leadership, including communication, team-building, and oversight. The board tends to become dependent on the knowledge base of the lead pastor, as well as the ministry staff. The board governs mostly by policy, while setting direction for ministry and establishing outcomes for which it holds the lead pastor accountable.

The board relates primarily to the lead pastor and the authority and power of the lead pastor will be balanced with accountability to the board. Board members need more training in boardmanship and specific aspects of governance.

Most evangelical, congregational churches in Canada would fit in the first three categories. The lead pastor and board chairperson must understand how the size of the congregation shapes their roles and the working relationships that they both have. Failure to grasp this will result in wrong expectations, improper interventions, and frustrations. The larger the church the more significant leadership succession issues become. In larger churches, ministry is done by many, but policy is discerned by few. In smaller churches, ministry is done by few, but policy is decided by all. Communication in a larger church must be more repetitive and intentional. In larger churches, the staff needs to be more continuous, because volunteers tend to change more often. Concurrently the board needs to employ the concept of shared governance more intentionally, so that groups or individuals do not feel disenfranchised in decision-making.

The potential personal variables that exist between a church board chairperson and a lead pastor can be quite substantial: age, leadership experience and ability, spiritual maturity, amount of theological training, cultural expectations, gifting, personality differences, risk aversion, gender, job expectations, beliefs about the nature of the church, fiscal approach, and degree of confidence. Institutionally, the church rarely has developed a set of principles that it desires these individuals to follow in managing their relationship. The bylaws may have a paragraph or two that defines with more or less clarity their respective roles, but the bylaws normally say little if anything about how their relationship should proceed. If it does get off-track, who in the church has the status or experience to intercede and help them develop it properly?

The board chairperson and lead pastor form a unique ministry duo in the local church. They are not accountable to one another, because both are accountable in different ways to the entire board[3] to fulfill their respective responsibilities. The board requires that the individuals in these roles work together wisely, respectfully, and consistently, because this interaction is necessary for them to fulfill their respective roles. Their attitudes toward

---

3. Some pastors may challenge the principle that they are accountable to the church board, because in their perspective it is the congregation that has called them. There is some truth to this, but it disregards the fact that congregations generally delegate to the board the responsibility to govern on their behalf. This normally includes caring for the pastoral staff and ensuring that the ministry leadership is accomplishing its responsibilities well.

one another are significant and both must engage the relationship with humility and mutual support. Their interaction must be highly relational so that they can discuss any congregational or ministry matter together without one or the other feeling threatened. Together they seek before God the best wisdom that will generate mission-focused solutions and recommendations for the congregation. Their discussions will proceed within the context of prayer. Each should know well the roles and responsibilities of the other so that each understands the respective authority that their differing roles possess.

Some of the following principles would be basic to fostering and sustaining the kind of relationship between a board chair and lead pastor that contributes to a healthy church:[4]

1. Create clarity about the respective roles, responsibilities, and accountability to the entire board.

2. Keep your focus on advancing the mission and fulfilling the vision of the congregation. This is the main thing, and developing a strong, effective board is a key part of this.

3. Foster deep trust that grows out of the spiritual commitment you each have to Christ, the church, and one another. This includes sustained prayer for one another.

4. Operate with humility that arises from a heart that desires to serve, and recognition that you both can learn from the other even if large differences exist in personal gifting, experience, or expertise.

5. Maintain mutual respect for each other, the job that you each must do, and your respective authority.

6. Have a commitment to enable each to succeed. This means the avoidance of any territorial tendencies.

7. Agree that your roles must be interactive and collaborative.

8. Schedule regular interactions that are relational, candid, and confidential, and which are capable of sustaining fierce conversations, but always keep your emotions under control. This requires spiritual maturity and a professional attitude.

9. Sustain the confidence to discuss any matter and hold one another accountable, not for specific responsibilities, but for the integrity of the relationship.

---

[4]. For additional perspective on the chair-lead pastor/CEO relationship, see Naufal, "Chair-CEO Relationship."

10. Work toward adaptive change, constantly seeking innovative responses to common problems, supporting one another when it is appropriate to take risks.

When this relationship is working well, the two major ministry teams in the church (i.e., church board and ministry staff) can focus appropriately and collaboratively on their respective work.

One of the growing pains that churches experience is that pastoral leaders do not always know what to do with the board. In the analysis of church size referred to in this chapter, you will note that churches tend to be group-centered or pastor-centered. However, pastors frequently misunderstand the changing role of a board as a church grows.

Both the lead pastor and board chairperson have distinctive, but related roles. I realize that in some denominational settings the lead pastor also serves as the board chairperson. However, in this publication I assume that the board chairperson is a different person than the lead pastor and that this individual probably is a lay person, i.e., does not have professional theological education. Further, in some denominational settings churches have both councils and boards, with the council providing discernment and leadership in spiritual matters, which may include the performance evaluation of the lead pastor.

So, one of the critical aspects of the lead pastor-board chairperson relationship concerns the management of their respective boundaries. It is normal for a lead pastor to have a position description that defines core responsibilities and aspects of accountability, especially to the church board and through the board to the congregation. As I have noted previously, this is not always the case for a board chairperson. In many churches the only direction a board chairperson has to guide him/her in fulfilling this role will be a few statements in the congregation's bylaws and these in turn will probably relate to matters of appointment, term, and general board responsibilities. The absence of such a position description for a board chairperson creates considerable opportunity for misunderstanding in the management of the boundaries that these respective roles entail.

If you are just beginning to serve as a board chairperson and there is no position description, then make it one of your first priorities to work with the board to create such a description, even if it is only a series of key principles. Because you are accountable to the board, it is the board that must decide what it is they desire you to do for them as their leader. With your respective position descriptions in hand you both are in a position to discuss how the two of you can work together to advance the congregation's mission and help the board fulfill its essential work.

As noted earlier, the lead pastor gives oversight to the leadership team responsible for implementing ministry (paid staff and volunteers). This leadership team is accountable to the church board through the lead pastor and includes the lead pastor. The board chairperson is accountable to the board and facilitates the life of the church board, helping it to establish policies, oversee key employees, manage risk, and bring recommendations to the congregation that enable its vision to be accomplished. The church board, however, is accountable for its actions to the congregation, not the lead pastor. The lead pastor may seek the advice of the board chairperson on diverse matters and the chairperson may do the same.[5]

The lead pastor usually is a member of the church board, but the board chairperson is not a member of the ministry staff team. This arrangement can become problematic if the lead pastor does not keep the board chairperson informed of key ministry issues that the ministry staff team is engaging. It is important not to allow the boundaries, as important as they are, to hinder clear and open communication between these two leaders. These two ministry teams cannot operate as completely independent, closed silos. Rather, the lead pastor and church board chairperson form the primary communications linkage between these two teams. For example, when the board makes decisions about employment issues, it may be wise and helpful for the church board chairperson to communicate these decisions directly to the ministry staff team. It creates a bit of space within which the lead pastor can work with the staff, if the decision is a difficult one.

When the church board chairperson also has ministry responsibilities over and above his or her board involvement, he or she will be accountable to one of the pastoral staff for such ministry leadership. For instance, the chair may also lead a small group in the church. In fulfilling that responsibility, the chairperson is not accountable to the board, but rather to the pastoral staff person who is overseeing small groups in that congregation. Conversely, in the board, the lead pastor has to recognize when he is speaking as lead pastor, i.e., employee, or as a board member. While it is difficult for the lead pastor and the board members to segregate these two roles, it is important to do so. All board members, for example, must exercise their vote in ways that advance the whole ministry of the congregation. When ministry proposals come to the board from the ministry staff, the lead pastor may initially present the proposal, but when it comes to a board decision, the lead pastor must vote on the matter from

---

5. In the case of a bicameral governance system, e.g., council and board, the relationship and respective jurisdictions must be defined clearly in order to avoid harmful power struggles.

the standpoint of the board, not from the standpoint of the ministry staff, otherwise a conflict of interest exists.[6]

As noted earlier, a lead pastor and board chairperson may come into their roles possessing very different levels of experience and expertise. This may particularly be evident in their respective understanding of governance[7] as it operates within a congregational setting. It is important that both leaders be on the same page on this issue as much as possible. For example, some lead pastors may regard governance processes as an impediment to their leadership. Alternatively, some board chairpersons use governing processes inappropriately as devices to control the lead pastor. As a congregation grows and moves from being smaller to larger, the matter of governance will become more important to the congregation's health. Both leaders will need to discern the implications of growth for the governance process, their respective roles, and the best ways to facilitate the board members in managing these changes well. Sorting these matters out becomes especially critical during periods when pastoral leadership is changing. A chairperson would do well to schedule personal time with a primary pastoral candidate to explore this issue in depth. Unless there is clarity and basic agreement about how the candidate and chairperson discern the relationship between the church board and lead pastor, conflict will inevitably occur in the future should the congregation affirm the candidate as lead pastor.

As a congregation becomes larger and more complex to lead, the board may desire to move toward a policy style of governance, which will require the lead pastor to give more attention to ministry oversight and implementation, staff development, and communication within the congregation. However, if the board does not carefully work with the lead pastor in making such changes, the ability of the lead pastor to accomplish assigned responsibilities will suffer because expectations will become too diverse. Further, the board may need to plan to establish and fund additional staff positions to assist the lead pastor to work effectively with the new governance processes (i.e., executive pastor).

6. Ministry staff often do not understand the twofold role that a lead pastor fills within a board. They expect that any proposal that lead pastors take to the church board for decision will automatically have their support. After all, they are present in the board to advocate for the dreams and issues of the ministry staff. It is incumbent on lead pastors to explain to the staff their perspective on this matter and be transparent with a particular staff person whether they will or will not support a ministry proposal. Sometimes lead pastors will not permit a proposal to go forward to a church board unless it has their approval. Here again, lead pastors need to explain to the other staff what their mode of operation is in such matters.

7. You may want to review the discussion about church governance provided in chapter 1.

If you do not want to be dancing on eggshells or stomping on toes, then sorting out this relationship will be an important priority for you as chair.

Governance becomes an issue when defining vision and developing strategic ministry plans. Who bears the responsibility to develop the vision and the strategy? If the board is responsible in governance for establishing ends policy, then the board will have to have some voice in both the discernment of vision and the final definition of the strategic plan. If, however, lead pastors consider that they alone have the responsibility (and prerogative) to discern the congregation's vision and develop the strategic plan to accomplish it, but the board believes is has authority to define key ends, then board chairpersons will have to work very hard to avoid constant conflict between lead pastors and church boards as each jockeys for jurisdiction.

Understanding governance responsibility can also become critical when serious problems arise (e.g., a lawsuit arising over the injury of a child during a church-sponsored function) and dispute occurs internally as to which body should provide the leadership necessary to resolve the issue. Is it a staff issue or a board issue? Who has the authority to decide? In my view, the board always has the last word where bylaws do not provide clarity. Frequently, a lack of clarity in governance will surface when significant financial matters are in play. Who has control of the budget, or who can bring to the congregation recommendations concerning amendments to the budget or for extraordinary expenditures? What happens when the lead pastor and the board are at odds regarding such matters and the lead pastor decides to speak in opposition to the board's recommendation at a public meeting?

Such situations do happen and this is why the lead pastor and church board chairperson need to have a common understanding of governance within their respective congregation. If you as board chairperson discern that a major difference of opinion does exist, then with the support of the lead pastor bring it forward to the board for discussion and resolution before a major crisis ensues. It is very hard to sort out such matters in the midst of public conflict. The key focus of the board in such matters would be:

i. What understanding of governance is congruent with the current bylaws?

ii. What understanding will help the lead pastor fulfill assigned responsibilities without violating board policy? Does policy have to change in order to resolve the impasse, and is such change wise?

iii. What understanding will enable the board to advance the mission of the congregation most effectively?

In the end, good governance will be congruent with the "best interests"[8] of the congregation, which the board and the lead pastor hold in trust together. While it is always possible for egos to distort good, sensible processes, spiritually mature leaders who serve on the board will listen carefully to God's Holy Spirit. The best interests of the congregation will not necessarily be what the lead pastor deems is in the best interest of the pastoral staff or what a particular board member regards as the best interest of the congregation.

One of the ways in which a lead pastor and church board chairperson can find common understanding about governance is to learn how to think institutionally. Hugo Heclo, in a recent book entitled *On Thinking Institutionally*,[9] challenges the current primary focus on the self as the sole determiner of value and meaning. He explains and argues for the value of institutions such as the legal system, health services, education, government, family and marriage, and philanthropy. They can be "*enabling* constraints that make it possible for us to live out and further develop our humanity."[10] Human beings as moral agents have to consider "what it is to think as moral agents within a framework of institutional values."[11]

Thinking institutionally requires the following mindset:

i. To "be committed to the ends for which the organization occurs rather than to an organization as such."[12] The mission and values of the institution require the loyalty of those involved, not necessarily its current forms and functions;

ii. To live and act "mindful[ly] in certain ways, exercising a particular form of attentiveness to meaning in the world."[13] Decisions and actions reflect the organization's vision and values, accumulating to habitual responses demonstrating a certain kind of intelligence;

iii. To be "in a position primarily of receiving rather than of inventing or creating."[14] There is a sense of rootedness in the legacy received which has thus shaped the institution. An indebtedness to carry forward the

---

8. "Best interests" include supporting the stated theological values of the congregation and its mission.
9. Heclo, *On Thinking Institutionally*.
10. Heclo, *On Thinking Institutionally*, 43.
11. Heclo, *On Thinking Institutionally*, 79; italics his.
12. Heclo, *On Thinking Institutionally*, 90.
13. Heclo, *On Thinking Institutionally*, 97.
14. Heclo, *On Thinking Institutionally*, 98.

vision and values in faithful reception shapes the consciousness of those involved;

iv. To embrace "value diffusion as well as infusion. Institutions diffuse values by connecting a person to something that goes beyond the self-life."[15] People are shaped personally by these values and the life of the organization in turn more or less incarnates those values;

v. To attend to precedent and "to stretch your time horizon backward and forward so that the shadows from both past and future lengthen into the present."[16] We work with what belongs "to predecessors and successors,"[17] guided by a deep sense of stewardship.

Sometimes leaders in the church shy away from regarding it as an institution because many voices urge us to see it only as family or community. The word institution reeks of hierarchy, authority, bureaucracy, and rigidity. However, if we apply Heclo's definition of institution to the church, we can agree that the church does constitute "*enabling* constraints that make it possible for us to live out and further develop our humanity." Of course, it is more than this, embodying as it does the mission and values of the Messiah himself. However, it demonstrates institutional traits and so it is important for its leaders to be able to think institutionally about the church.

The board chairperson is one of those leaders. What might be some of the implications of thinking institutionally about the church as Heclo would enjoin? I would suggest the following:

i. The current shape of the church as institution is only an imperfect representation of its vision and values as defined by the Holy Spirit in Scripture. While there may be culturally conditioned reasons for doing certain things certain ways in a particular congregational setting, a board chair must be able to think more fundamentally, i.e., to be asking how the vision and values embraced by the congregation can best be expressed in policies, systems, programs, facilities, use of resources, etc. The means are important, but not as important as the ends. For example, the fact that your board has never required an annual evaluation of the lead pastor does not mean the board should not decide to implement it. The more important question is whether such an evaluation will enable the board to achieve the ends or goals that the congregation has established in accordance with its values. If the

---

15. Heclo, *On Thinking Institutionally*, 102.
16. Heclo, *On Thinking Institutionally*, 109.
17. Heclo, *On Thinking Institutionally*, 110.

board does not require this, will it be delinquent in its stewardship of the congregation's resources and fail to fulfill its vision?

ii. Church board chairpersons have the responsibility to be so imbued with the congregation's vision and values that they intuitively guide the board to make decisions that advance and exemplify them. The exercise of this spiritual intelligence consistently shapes the congregation's life. Not every proposal brought to a church board aligns with its mission or its vision or its values and so the chairperson will help the board members to discern this and act accordingly.

iii. Church board chairpersons realize that they steward a legacy, one created by predecessors and faithful stewardship. They must attend to this heritage. This does not mean that tradition rules, but rather that significant change occurs carefully and prayerfully, so that the essence of the church continues even as its forms and functions ebb and flow. One practical application of this principle would be the realization that the vision and values of the congregation are more important than the desires of any particular individual or small group. As much as we desire in Christian organizations to be sensitive to the needs and desires of individuals, at the end of the day, no one person is more important than the whole. As board chairperson, you must model this principle.

iv. The life of a church board represents the continual diffusion and infusion of values. The board chairperson and the other board members are moral agents acting individually and collectively to carry forward the congregational mission. The values of the congregation must diffuse through their deliberations and decisions and in turn infuse the life of the congregation. In this sense, everything a church board does has spiritual implications because it reflects the values of the congregation.

v. Church board chairpersons lead with a deep consciousness of time—both past and future, as well as present. Church boards make decisions not just for present stakeholders, but for the congregation as it will be in five or ten years. Often this becomes evident when planning a new facility or renovating and expanding current facilities. The planning has to consider what the congregation will require in ten years, not in the next twelve months. This long-term vision should be operating in the case of all major decisions.

At the beginning of this chapter, I proposed that the relationship between the lead pastor and the church board chairperson is the most significant relationship in the congregation. Having reviewed this matter in some detail, I trust that you will agree, and that as board chairperson you will give your fullest attention to enabling this relationship to flourish.

Yet I must also state some caveats that have to be avoided or at least carefully managed:

1. As chairperson of the board, you are still only a board member and have no authority to do anything more than speak on behalf of the board. It is not that the lead pastor and board chairperson run the church; rather, the board chairperson enables the board to function well and in order to do this, a good working relationship with the lead pastor is an important element. If you as chairperson seek to usurp the role of the board, then you prevent the board from stewarding the trust given to it by the congregation. Beware of the power that personality can wield, both positively and negatively. The board cannot let its voice be diminished or cowed by the chairperson or the lead pastor or both together. While the board should be able to trust your respective leadership and relationship, they cannot trust too much lest they abdicate their responsibility. Boards need to be board-centric, not chairperson-centric or pastor-centric, to coin some expressions.

2. Be careful in how you present ideas promoted by the chairperson and the lead pastor together to the board. In such instances the chairperson will have to work hard to ensure that the board does not feel it has been steamrolled into a decision that it does not fully support just because board members do not want to be obstructionists.

Case Study: Stepping in or Stepping Out as Chairperson[18]

John was partway through his third term (a two-year stint) as the chairperson of the Brighton Community Church board. He had six months to go. During his first two terms, the board responded well to his leadership and he felt good about the progress they were making together. Participants worked energetically, pulled together, and were willing to tackle some tough stuff—and they did it with prayerful courage. However, John also was entering a new phase of life as he was enjoying semi-retirement and making plans for some new adventures, including a few short-term mission opportunities. Recently he was diagnosed with high blood pressure and his physician had advised him to

---

18. Although the story in this case study may seem to resemble a real situation, the names, places, and actual circumstances do not describe any actual church, church board, pastor, or chairperson.

lower his stress level, lose weight, and begin a disciplined diet. He now took a prescribed drug daily to deal with his blood pressure.

The composition of the board changed at the last annual general meeting. Two of the members whom he had relied upon for wisdom and leadership in the board had stepped off, even though they could have continued. John had sought to encourage several people to serve, but none had agreed. The nominating committee worked hard to select good nominees. In the election at the annual general meeting, the congregation appointed to the board a person who had never served on a church board before and the other appointee, although she had some prior experience, did not have a good reputation as a collaborator. The total number of board members at this time was five, including himself. One of the other seasoned board members was signaling he wanted a change as well.

The lead pastor, a solid, caring leader, turned sixty-five last week and John knew that retirement was imminent. In the next year or so, the board would probably be leading the search for a replacement. In addition, the church facility would require considerable upgrades in the next year or two, namely a new roof, internal and external paint jobs, and a heating system replacement. The church had few financial reserves and the costs for this would be several hundred thousand dollars. The last time the church had to raise funds for facility maintenance things had not gone well and memories were still rather raw for some. The pastor had also revealed confidentially to John that a serious matter of membership misconduct was about to become public. This event would send some shock waves through the congregation.

The chairperson of the board's nominating committee had asked John to meet him for coffee and John knew he would ask him to let his name stand for another term as a church board member. Without doubt, if he did, the board members would support the recommendation from the nominating committee. John was also aware that one of the current board members had the capacity to become chairperson, but John was uncertain whether he would agree.

So how should John respond to the nominating committee chair? Should he step in and continue to provide significant leadership for the church and its board? Or, should he step out, having served faithfully for six years? What would you advise John to do? What factors should he consider as he makes his decision?

1. Obviously, given the circumstances, the church board will be doing some heavy lifting in the next two years. The chairperson will be a critical player in the board's ability to lead the congregation effectively through these institutional changes. So John has to be willing to give

considerable time and attention to this role. John needs to evaluate whether he has the heart to devote this kind of care to the role, especially as he moves into semi-retirement. Will he be able to accomplish the plans he has in this new phase of life and still lead the board as chairperson? If not, is he willing to sacrifice some of his personal goals (which include short-term mission opportunities) in order to enable the congregation to flourish?

2. When institutions experience significant change, the leaders experience stress. Given the new situation with his health, John has to evaluate whether another term as chair of the board will create serious health risk.

3. The leadership vacuum is also a concern. Perhaps one of the negotiations that John needs to engage in with the board is the question of leadership succession. He may be able to manage another term if the board will identify and appoint a successor to serve as vice-chair. This would allow for a period of mentoring, but if John's personal situation warranted it, the opportunity to resign as chairperson before his term was completed could also be considered.

4. There is also the pastoral leadership succession issue that is looming. Perhaps John needs to have a private conversation with one of the people who recently completed work on the board to see whether he/she would be willing to chair the anticipated search committee. If one of these individuals committed to this, it would give John confidence that this process would go well, alleviating a significant worry point. Similarly, he might need to have some conversation with the chair of the board's finance committee to consider what strategies the committee might propose in order to secure the funding for the necessary facility upgrades. If the board can discern a clear path in this matter, again it will shift some of the leadership burden. In other words, John can serve another term if he is to plan carefully and gather around himself two or three key leaders who will help him lead the congregation through this period.

Questions for Reflection

a. How frequently do you as chairperson meet with your lead pastor? Who usually calls those meetings? What do you discuss? What are two or three things you can do as chairperson to improve the effectiveness of these interactions and thus enhance your relationship with your lead pastor?

b. When your congregation experiences a change in lead pastor, what questions will you as chairperson be asking the next primary candidate about his perception of church boards and the relationship that the candidate might want with the chairperson?

c. If your relationship as chairperson with the lead pastor is not going well, what steps can you take to improve it? How risky is this? Whom might you ask to help you in this process? If it does not improve, what will be your response?

Suggested Resources

a. *The Board Chair and President Relationship.*

b. Rebekah Basinger, "The Board Chair-CEO Relationship Is Like a Pair of Chopsticks."

Chapter 6

Leading the Church Board as a Ministry Team

THE TERM "BOARD," WHEN used to describe a group of people entrusted with governing authority, arises from the mercantile practices of the later Renaissance. The term itself historically referred to a large table usually used to serve food, but which often served as a gathering place for conversation. A person leading the conversation often sat in a chair at the table around which investors and other principals gathered to discuss matters related to a particular endeavor. It is important within the church setting that the term "board," as applied legitimately to the group which is entrusted with governing authority, does not conceal or dominate the more strategic and essential role that this primary ministry team of senior spiritual leaders plays within the congregation.

When people accept the role of church *board* chairperson, often they do not perceive initially the board's collective, strategic, spiritual leadership. A church *board* is first and foremost a *ministry team*, i.e., a group of mature spiritual leaders entrusted by the church with the care of the congregation such that in its identity and action it truly becomes the church of God. Although Evangelical congregations in Canada usually are constituted as nonprofit charities, that is not essential to their purpose but a convenient mode of operation in the Canadian legal reality. This group of spiritual leaders does function as a *board*, but this is just a means to accomplish some of its spiritual care for the congregation. It is the linkage of this spiritual responsibility with specific legal responsibilities that forms the unique stewardship of this ministry leadership team/church board.

As a ministry leadership team, the church board's focus is not the micromanagement of ministry and its implementation, but rather it gives attention to the big-picture issues of vision, values, and strategic planning necessary to advance the mission of the congregation. In giving attention to vision, this ministry team seeks to discern the best way for this congregation to incarnate the Great Commission in its community, given the resources that God provides. When defining values, a church board is providing spiritual guidance to the congregation regarding its theological framework and its response to culturally significant questions (i.e., the nature of worship, an understanding of marriage and divorce, etc.). As the church board embodies biblical values, it proclaims the gospel. As it engages in strategic planning with the lead pastor, this ministry leadership team ensures that it attends to the spiritual and other needs of the congregation, conserves and uses resources appropriately, and identifies and manages risks diligently and prudently. It acts missionally, pursuing ends and using means that are biblically consistent. Through these actions, this ministry leadership team enables the church to suffer for the name of Christ energetically, presents a good witness for the gospel in the community, and encourages each believer to faithfully live out the calling of Jesus in their life.

The chairperson of this ministry leadership team facilitates and develops the capacity of this leadership group, the *church board*, to serve the congregation well and contribute to its spiritual health and growth. This spiritual reality requires the chairperson of this ministry team and the lead pastor to develop an effective working relationship. However, chairpersons, more than any other board members, have to understand this spiritual stewardship and embrace it if they are going to help the board fulfill its stewardship. Perhaps one challenge that a chairperson has to face is the temptation to reduce the operations of the board to that of a committee. Teams are more than committees because the responsibility of each member for the success of the whole becomes more explicit and active, and personal accountability becomes a more serious issue. A wise chairperson can blend the diverse character of this leadership group as board and as ministry team and take good advantage of this diversity to encourage individual board members to a higher standard of engagement.

Patrick Lencioni,[1] writing primarily for the business world, examines systemic practices and attitudes that prohibit a business leadership team from achieving its best results and consequently hindering the corporation's development. He identifies five key dysfunctions:

> Absence of Trust > Sense of Invulnerability
>
> Fear of Conflict > Artificial Harmony
>
> Lack of Commitment > Ambiguous Engagement
>
> Avoidance of Accountability > Low Standards
>
> Inattention to Results > Status and Ego.[2]

---

1. Lencioni, *Five Dysfunctions of a Team*.
2. Lencioni, *Five Dysfunctions of a Team*, 185–220.

Each of these elements, when present within a team, is sufficient in and of itself, Lencioni claims, to make a team dysfunctional. Addressing them, initiating lasting change, and dealing with failure to implement become in his view the most important things that a CEO must manage. All of these elements apply to a chairperson's leadership of a church board as ministry leadership *team*. Much of this can be addressed in a code of conduct for a church board, but if and when they manifest themselves, then the chairperson needs to help the board as a team recognize what is happening, discern the threat, and have the courage to deal with it.

A key action by a chairperson would be to help the board members understand and develop three core capacities/competencies which a church board uses to exercise primary care in the church body.[3]

Table 1: Core Competencies for a Church Board

Core Capacity	Competency:	Core Issues
Redemptive Ministry	The church board discerns and defines the spiritual foundations/values that align and integrate relational leadership and ministry partnership within a local church.	*Personal Calling of Board Members*: individual spiritual discipline, intelligence, and preparation, as well as orientation to ministry *Ministry Structure*: size/ministry dynamics of the local church, identifying an appropriate leadership structure to meet the size requirements *Ministry Team Relationships*: between pastor/chairperson and between board and staff as primary ministry teams in a local church *Spiritual Community Development*: retreats, congregational communication, the spiritual community of board and church

---

3. I am indebted to Dr. Lyle Schrag for the development of the basic framework that I have adapted in some details.

Core Capacity	Competency:	Core Issues
Strategic Leadership	The church board discerns the strategic dynamics necessary to sustain the health and advance the mission of a church in full compliance with stated values [the alignment and integration of mission and ministry]	*Values Definition, Vision Development, and Strategic Planning*: discern missional mandate and ends: mission, values, vision—active implementation *Decision-Making*: strategies to form wise, God-honoring decisions *Conflict Management*: abilities to discern points of tension and discern solutions that sustain unity
Fiduciary Stewardship	The church board ensures faithful accounting in the functioning of a church	*Meeting Stewardship*: effective meeting strategies *Ministry Advancement:* • *Pastoral Development*—elevating pastoral evaluation to a higher purpose • *Board Development*—the continuing education of the board • *Congregational Vocation*—discipling and training all in the congregation to fulfill personal and collective vocation *Resource Allocation*: demonstrates responsible preservation and use of all resources for purposes specified *Legal and Ethical Responsibilities*: complies with government regulations and with all additional ethical standards consistent with the congregational mission and values *Risk Management*: exercises due diligence to minimize risk to the ministry agency

Redemptive Ministry describes the spiritual dynamics and operations necessary to develop good church boardmanship, to sustain grace-filled relationships, and to ensure effective alignment among church leadership. It is ministry because ultimately it requires a servant's heart and attitude, working to enable others to fulfill their calling in Christ. As the board members give attention to this competency, they spread a redemptive dynamic throughout the congregation, restoring and enhancing Christian lives and relationships. In this way, the board attends to the spiritual care and leadership the congregation requires.

Strategic Leadership refers to aspects of governance that are oriented to the future and the accomplishment of the vision. It requires a church board to develop conflict management and effective decision-making skills so that the board members can sustain in a united way the priorities necessary to advance the mission. This kind of leadership is more concerned with future stakeholders and beneficiaries, rather than current ones, because it focuses upon the congregation and local community as they may be in three, five, or ten years, as God permits. Some kind of annual planning document integrates these major priorities and has the agreement of the board and staff, providing alignment of efforts and resources toward the mission. It will define goals or ends that all agree are crucial, thereby enabling the board members to make coherent and united decisions because they have consensus about the overall direction of the congregation's life.

Sometimes strategic leadership will require the board to discern emerging theological or ethical issues about which it will need to ponder and provide wise, biblically-grounded guidance to the congregation because the statement of faith and bylaws do not address them, or if they do, the manner in which they do is no longer adequate. For example, many congregations continue to struggle over worship patterns and church boards are not sure how to sustain unity without requiring unanimity on all matters. It might be wise for a church board to develop—first for itself, and then for the congregation to consider—a statement that defines biblical principles of worship (a brief practical theology of worship, if you will) along with key implications for designing and leading contemporary worship that will guide congregational worship leaders. Although you will not get agreement on every single issue, it is quite probable that the vast majority of the congregation will agree on most of the issues, which will allow the board then to provide biblically-grounded counsel to the pastoral staff on these matters.

Fiduciary Stewardship expresses a church board's responsibility to ensure that all resources within the congregation are being valued, preserved, and employed for the advancement of the mission. Usually we think in terms of financial and facility resources, but I would suggest that the more important resources are the people—the paid staff, volunteer leaders, and other members within the congregation. The people are the church's most significant resource. One of the key elements then for the board to oversee will be the processes by which the leadership disciple people in the congregation to understand their calling in Christ, their gifting, and the application of these as kingdom agents in their families, the marketplace, the community, and the congregation. The church board must also give attention to regular pastoral evaluation so that they can assist the lead pastor and other staff to become all they can be in ministry by God's grace and power. This will also apply to the evaluation of specific ministry programs on a regular basis (perhaps a three-year cycle) to ensure that they are accomplishing their intended goals and that there is agreement about future direction and development. In other words, quality control and improvement are part of fiduciary stewardship.

One aspect of this that board members often overlook is their responsibility for their own collective evaluation, education, and development. A board will only improve its ability to serve well if it is attending to these matters. For example, for the chairperson to ask at the end of board meeting "In what ways have we advanced the church's mission in this meeting" keeps the key purpose of their collective ministry front and center for each board member. Watching a short video together about an aspect of church board operation and then discussing its implications for board meetings or actions is another effective evaluation and education tool.

Another significant aspect of fiduciary stewardship is risk management. While this has a financial component (e.g., annual audit or financial review), it encompasses much more. What are the potential hazards or threats that, if they occur, will severely hinder the congregation from achieving its mission? Does the board know what these are and has the board taken all reasonable steps to protect the congregation and its resources and people served by the congregation from harm? Whether these relate to physical safety, harassment on the job, misuse of funds, or immoral behavior—the board must do what it can to mitigate such risks. Risk management is a function of due diligence. A whistleblower policy may be part of the actions the board takes to ensure that it knows about risks and can act responsibly to avert them.

This discussion about church board competencies could have occurred in chapter one or two, but I purposely included it in this chapter because I wanted to emphasize the spiritual ethos within which all of these competencies must be developed and exercised. An effective board chair will possess some or all of these competencies and thus be able to tutor the board to some degree in the collective development of their capacity to govern well. Knowing the importance of each competency and the issues they address will enable a wise chairperson to suggest to the board areas in which it would be important to educate themselves, perhaps at a retreat or through attending a workshop or seminar together.

If your church board does not have a written statement of its collective purpose and responsibilities within the life of the congregation, this definition of capacities and competencies could serve as the foundation for the development of such a document. As chairperson, you might take some initiative here and propose a draft for the board to discuss. It will take a bit of work, but in the end, it might be one of the most useful contributions you make to the spiritual life and effective governance of the board.[4] With this in hand you can then create a simple evaluation survey that the board members might complete annually, giving them opportunity to reflect on how well they are governing and specific areas that might need some work. By doing it collectively, it is non-threatening to any one board member, but requires board members to think about their own contribution to the board and its work.

While it is a daunting prospect for someone new to the task, a church board chairperson (with the assistance of the lead pastor) facilitates the life of the board as a ministry team. A concept developed by Charles Olson[5] suggests one way that a chairperson expresses this kind of leadership. He coined the expression "worshipful work" to describe the life of a church board as a spiritual community (or, in my terms, ministry team). All that a church board does is worship, because all of its energies are in service to God for the church, and board members work together in worship to God and in some small way for the enhancement of his glory. No part of a church board's agenda escapes this characterization—if so, it does not belong on that agenda. The chairperson is constantly affirming this critical reality for a church board—all their work is worship given to God, no matter how mundane, because it is contributing to the local church's mission. So in essence, a chairperson is the worship leader for this ministry leadership team. The agenda will always be including times for prayer, scriptural reflection, and praise so that this dimension of board life remains a conscious reality in the minds of board members.

A second element that enables a board chair to provide this leadership is cultivating spiritual intelligence, i.e., discerning the work of God's Spirit in the life of Jesus' followers. God sends his Spirit into our lives, renewing our minds, so that we can grasp God's ways, program, and values, and have the passion and courage to get in step with God's Spirit. This capacity enables human beings to exercise kingdom leadership. What you yearn for in this regard is something you should covet for every board member. Personally, you are committed to working out God's values in your life and demonstrating progress in doing this. You grasp the principles of spiritual formation that help believers advance in their discipleship. You know how to share the gospel perceptively and seize opportunities to do this. You are theologically astute so that you can identify destructive teaching.

4. Appendix A provides a sample.
5. Olsen, *Transforming Church Boards Into Communities*.

You respect people and demonstrate capacity to work collaboratively with others to accomplish God's work. You understand the nature of grace and forgiveness, practicing both within your relationships. You are producing a wonderful harvest of spiritual fruit. You demonstrate capacity to motivate others to embrace kingdom vision.

One of your goals then is to cultivate spiritual intelligence within the board through worship. This includes the corporate study of God's word to discern direction on specific issues, and the use of biblical, spiritually sensitive decision-making processes in the board and in all other church contexts. You encourage a culture of learning, ensuring that the church body is a transformative instrument for kingdom advancement in the larger community. You hold fast to the conviction that people are ends, not means, and must be recognized and cared for as the holy ones of God.

Third, you approach your leadership of this church board team confident that God's Spirit gives it the capacity to fulfill its stewardship well. You believe that God has given his church the resources it needs to be both faith community and ministry organization/agency. This fundamental premise helps you guide the board to sustain the healthy growth and development of this local church. This is the primary responsibility to which the board must give its full and constant attention. You are the conductor of this small chamber orchestra devoted to producing the music of ministry. A church board is responsible to develop all necessary capacities so that the congregation can achieve its divine mission.

The board chairperson plays a very important role, enabling the board to develop the relationships of trust and systems of working together necessary to nurture this identity and accomplish its spiritual work in exemplary ways. Every board member has responsibility to promote good internal dynamics—trustful relationships, effective decision-making processes, maintaining good records, keeping the focus on what is most important, doing only what the board should be doing. However, the chairperson is the one that keeps calling the board to this work and its accomplishment with spiritual maturity. When the board perceives itself as a ministry team, prayer becomes more important in the activity of the board. The spiritual formation of the board members assumes a larger place in the board's work. How the board makes decisions will change.

A fourth element in a church board chairperson's leadership toolkit will be a consciousness that the board is overseeing a ministry organization/agency which, in order to flourish, must be both a learning organization (i.e., teaching itself God's will and contextualizing that truth faithfully), and an adaptive agency (i.e., constantly inquiring how it should be developing to fulfill its mission). How does a church board chairperson help this ministry team ensure that this congregation remains or becomes an adaptive agency, able to flourish as external and internal environments change? We might use the analogy of a person driving a car and the various competencies that this person requires to reach his or her destination safely. Four competencies are necessary:

a. adaptive capacity—the ability to monitor, assess, respond to, and stimulate internal and external changes; (driver's proficiency in making adjustments when weather, traffic, or fuel availability change)

b. leadership capacity—the ability of staff, board leaders, and other volunteer leaders to inspire, prioritize, make decisions, provide direction, and innovate (driver's ability to determine where he wants to go and to set a course to get there safely)

c. management capacity—ensure the effective and efficient use of organizational resources (driver's ability to address problems as they arise, such as running low on gas, fixing a flat tire)

d. technical capacity—the ability to implement all of the key organizational functions and deliver programs and services as defined by the agency's mission, vision, and values (driver's ability to be licensed and to know the rules of the road, as well as some mechanical skill to diagnose and respond to vehicle failure)

The term "competency" includes the wide range of capabilities, knowledge, and resources that the congregation as ministry agency needs within its leadership teams in order to be vital and effective in mission fulfillment. Competency has to keep developing in order to keep pace with the congregation's growth, and to enable the agency to flourish. If a church board's capacity to lead is not growing, then that local church will struggle to grow. Adaptation and competency development are the hallmarks of successful ministry agencies that deliver quality programs, fulfill their missions, and make a kingdom impact in their communities.

A chairperson understands the necessity for the church board to grasp the importance of these four competencies for healthy congregational life. If one competency is out-of-sync with the others, it will create stress and disturbance. A chairperson aligns all of these competencies if the local church is to fulfill its vision efficiently and effectively.

I think that adaptive capacity is the most important one for the church board to cultivate because:

a. it enables the agency to be innovative, flexible, and resilient;

b. as the agency is attuned to its external environment, it identifies changes and opportunities, generates new ideas, and modifies or initiates strategies in response to changes;

c. expanding adaptive capacity is critical as the pace of change increases and the results you desire become more defined.

In your role as chairperson, you personally need to develop adaptive capacity and slowly but incessantly help the church board learn and exercise this competency consistently. This applies particularly in the expression of its strategic leadership.

Lastly, I would suggest that as the leader of the church board ministry team, the chairperson needs to have some understanding of what factors contribute to a healthy congregation. This does not require you to be an expert in church growth, but it does mean knowing basic principles that will be helpful as you facilitate the board's work. Every church possesses an organizational culture—how things traditionally operate. You find it embedded in its history of decision-making, its language, rituals, values, and organizational structure (both formal and informal). It may or may not be particularly healthy, but this culture is the context within which the board seeks to express its leadership and help the church as ministry agency define, assess, and improve its various competencies. A healthy church culture will demonstrate at least three things:

a. Unity—engender open and honest communication across all levels of the agency, leading to a deep sense of cohesion and group identity focused around its mission, values, and vision;

b. Validation—support and celebrate the successes of individuals (staff, volunteers, groups) and of the organization as a whole, as it evaluates its ministries and progress in achieving its mission;

c. Continuing renewal—allow and encourage staff, volunteer leaders, members and board members to reflect on their work, to build deep relationships in service together, and to reconnect with their original motivations to become involved in this agency and its mission.

The board is critical to the development and nurturing of a healthy church culture. Attention paid to this and its sustainability is time wisely invested. You need to become a student of your church's culture so that you know what its needs might be and how to encourage the church board to respond to those needs. A lead pastor should address these key elements in monthly reports to the board.

Case Study: "Relative" Interest in a Church Board Member[6]

At the annual general meeting of Popkum Community Church, the nominating committee presented two current church board members as nominees for an additional term on the church board, and the congregation appointed them. However, because three positions were vacant, the board chair had asked several congregational members whom he perceived could make a good contribution to consider a nomination, but none had felt they could let their name stand. The new board terms did not start for several months and so the board chair still had time to recruit an additional candidate and make a recommendation to the nominating committee.

One Sunday, the chair felt led to talk with a person whom he had not really considered previously about letting his name stand as a board member. During the conversation, the person disclosed that he had thought about this possibility but was uncertain whether it would be wise. He was a cousin of the lead pastor. The individual was concerned about conflicts of interest and the impact such an appointment might have on family relations. The chair respected the concern, but suggested that there were ways to deal with this on a case-by-case basis. There was an opportunity to serve and make decisions in the best interests of the congregation.

The person agreed to give it further thought. Undoubtedly, he would have further conversation with the lead pastor about this. A few weeks later, the chairperson discovered that this person had scheduled a conversation with a current board member to discern whether he should let his name stand. The chairperson was encouraged at this and continued to pray that God would give wisdom to all concerned.

After several weeks, the person agreed to let his name be placed in nomination. Another board member made the recommendation to the nominating committee and asked that they consider the person for the role of board member. At the next membership meeting, the committee brought forward his name and the congregation appointed him.

So now the chairperson had to consider how best to orient the new member to the work of the board and what advice he should provide in the matter of conflicts of interest.

1. Navigating the world of kinship relationships within congregations can be tricky, particularly when it comes to board roles. In some

---

6. Although the story in this case study may seem to resemble a real situation, the names, places, and actual circumstances do not describe any actual church, church board, pastor, or chairperson.

cases the bylaws speak to the issue and strictly limit the number of board members serving at one time who have family relationships—a good idea by the way. From time to time, however, well-qualified board candidates may be reluctant to serve because they have heard about some bad experiences in churches where related parties have become members of the board. Sometimes congregational members become suspicious that too much power is being concentrated in one family group. This will be particularly relevant in the case of smaller churches. Or, there is concern that the board members may not make decisions in the best interests of the congregation particularly when the issues affect people they are directly related to. Given the nature of church congregations, it is quite probable that you as a chairperson will face this situation.

2. Church boards should develop guidelines for board members regarding conflicts of interest, i.e., where a board member has a direct interest in the decision because they might be affected financially, positionally, or relationally. The policy should stipulate what constitutes a conflict of interest, the responsibility of the board member to be proactive in bringing a conflict of interest to the board's attention, and normal responses when the board discerns a conflict of interest. The board itself needs to deal with such situations carefully and seriously. For example, if the church board is discussing a matter of church member discipline that involves a person related to one of the board members, that board member should excuse themselves from the meeting for that discussion, with the minutes clearly showing that this was the case.

3. If your church board has a conflict of interest policy, then it would be wise in the orientation meeting to review its stipulations carefully with new board members in this situation. You can discuss with them possible scenarios in which conflicts of interest could arise and how you suggest they handle it. Seek to work at this collaboratively and let the board members know that you will seek to indicate where they may need to take appropriate action.

4. It would also be helpful to have a similar discussion with the lead pastor. He may also experience additional conflicts of interest, particularly if new, related board members encounter difficulties.

5. Finally, this occasion may provide you with an opportunity to review with the entire board the issue of conflicts of interest. If your board has a policy in this regard, take time to review it with the board and ask whether they need to revise it. Be transparent with the board

members about this matter, because not all board members may realize that kinship relationships exist among board members or among board members and staff.

Questions for Reflection

a. Church board members often discern the board either to be only a legal entity or only a spiritual leadership group. What can you do as a chairperson to help board members embrace both aspects as critical to their effective governance?

b. If the lead pastor does not consider the church board to be a "ministry team" exercising spiritual leadership in the congregation and collaborating with the staff ministry team, what rationale can you develop to change his mind and perspective? What are the implications for the board in its relationship to the lead pastor if you are not successful in changing his or her perspective?

c. As you analyze the capacities of your current church board, where do you discern its greatest need for development—redemptive, strategic, or fiduciary competence?

d. Sometimes board members place greater value on what they regard as the real spiritual ministry of the board and do not value what they perceive to be the business activities of the board. What action might you take as chairperson to help such members value all of the work of the board as spiritual work?

Suggested Resources

a. John Carver, *Carver Guide No. 4: The Chairperson's Role as the Servant Leader to the Board.*

b. Charles Olsen, *Transforming Church Boards Into Communities of Spiritual Leaders.*

c. Larry Osborne, *Sticky Teams: Keeping Your Leadership Team and Staff on the Same Page.*

Chapter 7

Developing and Sustaining Church Board Effectiveness

As BOARD CHAIRPERSON, YOU desire the church board you serve to excel in its leadership through spiritually focused, missional governance. After all, you did not accept this role in God's kingdom to endure or mandate mediocrity. You may have served in this role for several years and are wondering what legacy you can leave that will help this church board to become even more effective in its governance leadership. However, where do you start to try and measure your board's effectiveness? What profile or standard should you use? Because it is a church board, you feel compelled to keep the spiritual context central to your measure of its effectiveness. This adds to the complexity. Boardsource published a small pamphlet recently entitled *Govern More, Manage Less*, written by Cathy A. Trower.[1] The last chapter suggests "six characteristics of effective boards."[2] In this chapter, I reflect on Trower's proposals and evaluate them particularly in light of a church board context and from the standpoint of a board chair's role and responsibility. The goal is to discern several measures by which to assess your church board.

1. *Contextual Understanding*

An effective church board is *a student of its internal context*. A church board will only discern its future clearly if it has a firm understanding of its past and present, and this requires knowledge of context. As board chairperson, do you know the story, the commonly embraced narrative of your church's origins, key struggles, remarkable faith victories, and the significant turning points involved in its planting and development? Taking the time to ensure

---

1. Trower, *Govern More, Manage Less*, 29–36.
2. Trower, *Govern More, Manage Less*, 30.

that you and each of the board members and ministry employees knows this narrative is an important step in creating strategic alignment and appreciation for how the vision of the church has taken shape. Rehearsing this story from time to time in the board meeting and in other public meetings of the congregation helps everyone to keep in step with one another and develop confidence in the emerging vision.

    a. *Effective church boards know their church's story, both past and present, and share it often.*

    Discerning the internal context enables a board to have its finger on the pulse of the congregational heart, the issues that may be causing strain, and matters that the board must address to sustain church health. The board will not know whether the decisions it is making are the right ones if they have little or no awareness about the connection between these decisions and matters of concern percolating within the congregation. If the board members know that significant numbers of people in the congregation have a passion to participate in short-term mission experiences, but does nothing to encourage and support this, it could erode confidence in the board's leadership. Or, if there is a theological issue emerging in various congregational venues (e.g., extent to which members of both genders can be involved in church leadership), but does nothing to give spiritual direction in this matter, then strategic governance is sadly lacking. The church employees may have a grievance over vacation policy, but despite several communications the board takes no action. This again would display a lack of awareness of the internal context that in turn prevents the board from demonstrating effective leadership.

    b. *Effective church boards know the congregation's concerns and act to sustain and develop church health.*

    The internal context relates to the congregation's values and vision. New board members need specific orientation to these core elements in order to help them participate in informed decision-making. A church board chairperson carries some responsibility to ensure that new board members understand these matters. One way to accomplish this over the first few months of the new board members' terms is to link them with board veterans and encourage them to meet occasionally for coffee. During these conversations, the new board members can orient themselves quickly to the congregation's values and vision, hear and reflect on their story and appreciate the guidance it provides for the future, and learn how the board calibrates its decisions in light of these essential features.

c. *Effective church boards work intentionally to develop a board culture that is dynamic, relational, and future-oriented.*

Another aspect of the internal context is the life of the board itself—its traditions, methods of decision-making, relational ethos, etc. An effective board will be intentional and self-conscious in its development of these internal processes to help it lead with excellence. Regular reviews of these processes will help new and continuing board members keep themselves on track and even find ways to improve how they work together. Just as the congregation has a narrative that highlights its journey, so does a church board. Rehearsing this will help board members sense the dynamic reality of church board life.

d. *Effective church boards regularly review their internal processes to ensure that they are working well together and making good decisions.*

The church board chairperson ensures that the board is giving attention to this internal context. This person helps the board to articulate the values it uses to organize its operational life, relationships, decisions, and communications. Perhaps a term that might bring these various aspects together is the concept of "collegiality"—the desire, mutual trust, commitment, and processes that enable a board to work together, respect its diversity, and achieve deep consensus in its governance. Annual board retreats become important occasions for building and sustaining this collegiality.

e. *Effective church boards have chairpersons who give attention to developing social relationships within the board and a deep spiritual trust.*

Church board members are already part of a congregational family. Depending upon the size of that congregation, the members will already know one another to some degree and some may even have kinship relations. Regardless, the chairperson needs to give attention to the development of good relations among the board members. You begin by asking different board members to share their personal Christian journeys or the way they relate their employment to their Christian calling. In other words, intentionally give some space in the board's agenda to develop member relationships. Consider hosting an evening with board members and spouses at your home once a year to foster these social relationships. It will help when the going gets tough.

In my opinion, church board chairpersons demonstrate spiritual intelligence as they are awake to these actions, processes, and attitudes, with the result that the church board appreciates and is attuned to the institution's internal context.

2. Continual Learning

Effective church boards keep challenging their collective boardmanship, i.e., they intentionally educate themselves about their organization, their role within the organization, and their performance in that role. When was the last time in your church board experience that your board reflected upon how well they were doing or studied an article about board practice that might help them accomplish their work for the congregation more excellently? Does your church board have an annual retreat where they focus on improving their serve? Do you muddle along despite your frustrations about the process and its constant tedium and lack of direction? Effective boards are not satisfied with their current level of operations—they have a passion to serve Jesus better in their role.

   a. People on the board may not know who is responsible for board learning and so the board does not know how to help itself. Chairpersons may view their role merely as the meeting facilitator. Individual board members probably give little thought to the question. The lead pastor may desire the church board to work more effectively, but shies away from offering suggestions in case board members perceive him to be meddling or trying to change the board to suit his agenda, or being overly critical. The result is that nothing changes and poor habits of boardmanship persist because no one has the energy, motivation, mandate, or spiritual wisdom to lead change. Then there is the matter of turnover in board leadership and board members. Such discontinuity makes it difficult to improve board operations over the long term. I am probably a little harsh and judgmental in my assessment, but I suspect I am not far off the mark in many cases. Someone has to seize the moment and find a way to help the church board discern effective ways of operating.

   b. One place to begin is for the church board chairperson to suggest that the board take a few minutes at the end of a meeting to evaluate how well the meeting went. Initially the comments might be somewhat disjointed or disconnected because there are no common assumptions upon which to evaluate the meeting. This may be the first experience in which members of the church board have reflected on the way the board operates collectively, how the chairperson manages the meeting, or how individual board members have helped or hindered the board's progress. A chairperson may need to model humility because some board members may comment upon the way the chairperson has led the meeting. It will be important to create a safe environment in which people can share their criticism in a gracious manner. As the board members become more comfortable with the process and small changes and improvements in board operations become observable, it may set the stage for considering other elements of good boardmanship.

c. Another aspect of this focus on boardmanship would be the orientation of new board members to board operations. Again, you might discover that your board has no intentional means to accomplish this. If you are a board chair serving in this situation, consider adding this to one of the agendas as an item for discussion. Perhaps you could phrase it as a question: "When you started on the board, what information would have helped you begin to serve more effectively? What do you know now that you wished you knew then?" Compile the responses and then at a subsequent board meeting propose that the board establish a simple process for orienting new board members. You, as board chairperson, may have to volunteer your services, along with those of the lead pastor, as the team to develop and lead the orientation session. You might plan to do it over coffee with the newly elected board members prior to their first meeting. Informality will prompt questions and interaction.

d. I have always considered it important to encourage board members to come to the meetings prepared, having read the materials circulated in advance. This means that I, as board chairperson, have to ensure that the agenda, minutes, reports, and decision/discussion briefs are prepared and circulated electronically at least a week in advance of the meeting. If I, as board chairperson, am not prepared myself to facilitate the board's work in this disciplined manner, then I cannot expect the board to improve their game too. Leading by example is biblical and extremely motivating. Excellence can be caught and taught.

e. Governance is all about process, planning, and purpose, undergirded with an appropriate understanding of entrusted authority. One area that church boards often overlook in their boardmanship is defining the appropriate process for a particular decision. For example, if the need for an extraordinary expenditure of funds occurs mid-year and exceeds the budget parameters approved by the congregation at the annual general meeting, then the board members must decide how to process a decision regarding this item. If they decide to reject the recommended expenditure, then no further action is probably necessary, except to explain the rationale for the decision to those affected (e.g., perhaps employees whose salaries might be affected). However, if the board decides to support the recommendation, then it must determine whether according to its bylaws it has the authority in itself to make such a decision. If the board believes the bylaws authorize it, the board members may still have to explain why they made the decision at the next congregational meeting. If the bylaws require the board to gain congregational approval, then the board has the responsibility to ensure that the congregation formally approves the expenditure. It is the board's responsibility to manage the decision-making process so that it hears the voices of those groups in the organization who have important knowledge. Understanding what processes are required is part of boardmanship.

3. Cultivate the Board's Collective Welfare

Church boards are fragile things. The constant change in personnel, the personal involvement of members within the congregation, managing the inherent and constant conflicts of interest, and dealing with many diverse issues can easily rend the relational fabric. When strife happens within the board, the church board's effectiveness diminishes significantly and quickly. Effective church boards carefully cultivate internal relationships and consciously reflect on ways to improve their internal operation. They know how to resolve conflicts. Perhaps company boards or boards leading other kinds of nonprofit agencies might be able to do a reasonable job without fostering good internal relations, but the spiritual dynamics of congregational life and the calling that Jesus Christ gives to his followers do not permit church boards to overlook such matters. Church boards form an essential ministry team in a local church, and how they model Christian leadership, integrity, and unity impacts everything within that congregation.

A church board should foster cohesiveness, inclusiveness, and intentional peer quality and respect if it is to become an effective working group. As I suggested in the previous chapter, Lencioni's *Five Dysfunctions of a Team*[3]—namely absence of trust, fear of conflict, lack of commitment,

3. Lencioni, *Five Dysfunctions of a Team*, 185–202.

avoidance of accountability, and inattention to results—are frequently resident within a church board's life and each in its own way corrodes good working relationships. Board chairs must give attention to these matters if they are to help the board operate effectively and embrace the trust given to it by the congregation.

Boards can implement several specific strategies as part of their normal meetings and annual schedule. If followed consistently, they can help a board take a quantum leap in effectiveness and, at the same time, build greater motivation among the board members for the ministry work they are doing.

a. *Require courtesy and respect in all board member interactions.* Paul identifies "kindness, goodness and self-control" (Gal 5:22–23) as fruits of the Spirit. The spiritual maturity that characterizes ministry leaders (1 Tim 3) should enable a church board chair to facilitate meetings with the expectation that board members will demonstrate mutual goodwill and respect. The board's ability to engage in worshipful work depends upon this, lest rancor and strife debilitate its ability to function as a key ministry team in the congregation. Helping the board observe common norms of constructive discourse, engage in spiritually mature conflict and resolution, and complete the meeting in a spirit of genuine unity in Christ sits high on a board chair's agenda.

b. *Ensure that all board members have equal chances to engage questions and equal access to all information.* When a church board chairperson ensures that all board members know they have equal voice in all discussions, this goes a long way toward developing a cohesive, effective board. Inevitably, some board members will speak more than others because this is how they process decisions—they have to talk them through. Others will process information and reach decisions with less need for group interaction. However, all members need to be engaging at some level in the decision-making process. Sometimes the chairperson must deliberately go around the table and require board members to declare their position. Equal voice requires equal access to all information. If some in the board have information related to a critical matter that others do not, this inequality will distort and disturb the board's trust quotient. While some board members are more attuned to congregational dynamics than others might be, at the board table all members must be able to make decisions having had access to the same pertinent information.

c. *Foster relationships through occasional, but consistent social gatherings for the board members and their spouses.* One of the best ways a board chairperson can facilitate effective board operations focuses upon fostering good, social relationships among the board members. The more board members know each other, usually the better the board is able to function collectively. Occasional social gatherings become important means to open up communications within the board, develop friendships, and nurture trust. Including spouses in these events signals that the board is thankful for the time and energy the board members are giving to their tasks and the cost this represents to the family. During these events, the chairperson can share the vision of the board's work, invite prayer support, and build the team dynamics which are so essential to effective board work. An annual board retreat can provide a significant context for building such relationships. New surroundings can create fresh opportunities.

d. *Encourage a worshipful spirit, but also an atmosphere of friendly repartee.* The work of a church board involves serious issues, affects people's lives, and, most importantly, carries divine accountability. It is serious, but worshipful business. The chairperson, however, would be wise to moderate the intensity of discussions and help board members deal with the emotions that inevitably become engaged by using humor and other means, such as storytelling. Allowing some friendly repartee among the board members during discussions and in between agenda items can be a wonderful way to grease the board's machinery. This will be important particularly during board retreats. In a completely different way, calling the board to prayer as a significant discussion is reaching its conclusion, provides an opportunity for board members to center their minds and hearts on Christ as they come to a decision. It becomes a significant reminder of the sacred context of their discourse and interaction.

e. *Build a sense of group identity.* As board members work together, advancing the congregation's mission, God's Spirit can nurture an amazing, productive group identity. Within a congregation, a board does not want to create an us-versus-them dynamic. However, a church board needs to cultivate a significant group identity and trust it if it is to weather the severe storms of congregational life that inevitably come. Group identity requires unity, even as diverse opinions and perspectives are valued. The ministry staff often develops a very creative synergy that enriches the congregation's life and nurtures its vision. The same thing needs to develop within the board so that it can reap full benefit from the giftedness God has placed within it and be able together to achieve what none of the members individually could accomplish. When the chairperson speaks within the congregation and is able to say without hesitation that the board has unity in recommending a course of action, this speaks volumes to the people and models the kind of unity that Christ expects within his body, the church.

If you are a church board chairperson and reflecting upon these things, you probably are wondering how you possibly can keep all of these things in mind so that you facilitate your board's effectiveness. Perhaps I can suggest some ideas to help you:

1. Have the board appoint a vice-chairperson, if it has not done so, and work with this person to assist you in monitoring and implementing some of these things. As chairperson, you sometimes get caught up in the moment and another person can observe things happening and suggest a course of action to help the board achieve resolution. Involve your vice-chairperson so they can assist you.

2. Some advance planning can assist. For example, as you prepare the agenda, make some notes on your copy as to when in the flow of the meeting you will seek to foster this or that element of board life, or pause for a specific moment of worship. Preparation in advance can help you be intentional. Perhaps as the board reaches a decision on each discussion item, have one of the board members pray for its implementation.

3. Ask the board for some evaluation at the end of each meeting. Such brief discussions, led by wise questions on your part, can help the board members to become more conscious of their work together and to increase their effectiveness in working collaboratively.

4. Celebrate when things go really well. Positive reinforcement of great moments encourages their repetition.

5. Above all, spend personal time in prayer before each meeting, asking God's Spirit to keep you attentive to the board dynamics.

4. *A Spirit-Informed Discernment*

A church board's ability to accomplish its role well reflects its capacity for Spirit-led discernment. Possessing the right information, analyzing it well, understanding internal and external congregational dynamics, and engaging in critical discussion, all enveloped with prayer, become characteristic practices of such a board. If a board chairperson fails to grasp this dimension of an effective board, then the board will be unable to make good, sensible, spiritually wise decisions, and church board work is all about making decisions.

Take a look at the last church board agenda that you used. What key decisions were you asked to make? Did you possess the right information sufficiently in advance to consider the issue prayerfully? When the board members discussed it, did they come prepared? Was there serious, analytic engagement with the issue? Was it clear how the decision achieved would advance the church's vision? Did board members feel safe to express different views? When the meeting ended, was there some time given to review the board's work and to consider whether it was done well? If the board meeting only included one or two of these elements, then perhaps your church board needs a tune-up in its decision-making process.

What can a board chairperson do to help their board operate at a high level of spiritual discernment?

a. Always give time at the beginning of a church board meeting for prayer and Bible study. Surprisingly, giving at least thirty minutes at the front of the meeting to worship enables the board to process the agenda more effectively.

b. Give adequate time in the first part of the agenda for the board to engage those decisions that are most critical. Conversation with the lead pastor will help you to assess the items. You will have to exercise some judgment in this, but you probably are well aware of the relative importance of the issues coming to the board meeting.

c. Ensure that whoever is responsible for gathering the information that explains the issue and possible outcomes and their implications has put that material together at least a week before the board meeting. Make sure that the discussion paper incorporates several options and not just one selected outcome. Circulate it to the board members so they have enough time to read, reflect, and even do some additional research about the issue. As chairperson, you might adopt a simple rule—nothing comes to the church board for decision that does not have appropriate documentation and that the board has not seen in advance of the meeting. Poor board discussions and decisions sometimes occur because the board members have not received the information in advance and they feel rushed into making a decision. A church board has to make the time to process key decisions well. It is violating its trust with the congregation if it fails in this duty.

d. As chairperson, you can stimulate effective discussion by using various techniques. For example, if there are three options from which it is proposed the board choose a direction, then divide the board into three groups and have each group prepare the best case of one option. Have them present it to the board. Then switch the groups and have each group take an option and outline the risks and downside to that option. Such a process will engage the whole board, require the members to look at all options very closely, and have clarity about the possible risks that each option entails. With this information in hand, the board then can debate and discuss, arriving at a very informed decision.

e. Sometimes a board faces an issue about which it has very little understanding. In such cases, a good strategy is to locate a trusted resource person who would come and give the board a short (perhaps forty to sixty minutes) introduction to the issue and its implications for a congregation. This accomplishes several things:

   i. it adds another informed voice to the discussion who will have some objectivity;

   ii. it educates the board in ways that a one- or two-page report could never do;

   iii. it helps board members discern that big issues are complex, filled with ambiguity and uncertainty;

   iv. it gives board members an opportunity to ask their questions in a less pressured context.

f. A church board's ability to exercise spiritual discernment will require each board member to be spiritually mature and living in obedience to the Holy Spirit. Key decisions will be a matter for personal prayer, as well as prayer with the entire board. Sometimes reading and reflecting upon a biblical story will reveal some commonalities with the current issue. Occasionally it is helpful to refer to board documents that define the congregation's theological values and vision, helping the board to orient itself to the decision appropriately.

5. *Respect for the People*

The term "politics" generally does not have good press within church life. When others accuse a person of playing politics, it means this person's activities connote manipulation, coercion, or even guile to achieve a goal that has some personal benefit or favors a particular group in the congregation.

Church boards have to give due regard for developing and sustaining Christ-honoring relationships among a wide array of constituencies. When significant constituencies perceive that a church board is playing politics and not relating to them in healthy ways, then it compromises that board's ability to lead and erodes trust. Suspicion replaces confidence. Transparency, continuing and clear communications, respect for legitimate process, and rejecting a win-lose mentality become important values and means to encourage respectful, empowered relationships. The chairperson tutors, facilitates, and helps the board discipline itself so that it handles all of its relationships in ways that will advance the congregation's mission.

A helpful, simple exercise for church board chairpersons to do is to list the various internal and external constituencies that their boards deal with in the course of a twelve-month period. Internally, this would include the entire group of people that constitute the congregation, the members of the society specifically, the lead pastor, the employees, the volunteer leaders, and specific committees. Externally, these constituencies probably would be denominational leadership, other churches, parachurch agencies, civic entities (government or otherwise), groups that use the facility, businesses, etc. Obviously some of these relationships will be more significant or more frequently engaged and so some prioritization is helpful. Select the top three in the internal and external categories. Then ask yourself how the board currently is interacting with these various constituencies and whether the board members can enhance this engagement so that the board and the congregation together can advance the mission more effectively.

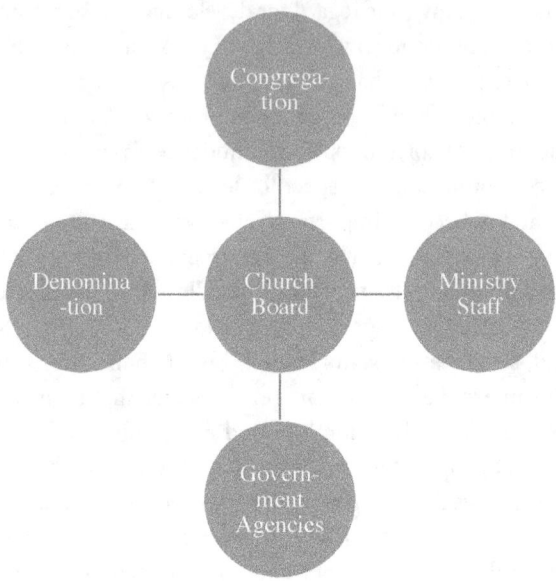

Let's consider the internal category of "staff" as a significant constituency that a church board has to manage well, whether your congregation has one or ten paid employees. In a small church with one or two paid employees, the tendency is to manage this relationship quite informally. The pastor may not have a job description or even a formal letter that has invited him to fill the role and under what terms. Rather the board may have done all of this verbally and think it is understood. While this informality might work for the first few months of employment, at some point issues will arise that will require greater formality and a more precise definition of the relationship. Why not do it properly from the very beginning? A ministry leader will welcome this definition and clear communication. It demonstrates the church board's determination to do things properly, it expresses the value that the board places upon the person and the relationship, and it enables a good relationship. Similarly, in matters dealing with vacation, benefits, use of office equipment (i.e., cell phone costs), travel costs, etc., careful attention by the board will reduce sources of irritation, avoid misunderstandings, and demonstrate care and concern for the employee's well-being.

If your church has multiple employees, then the importance of developing and sustaining good relationships with them becomes even more critical for the church's success. How does the board ensure that the church is an excellent employer? Should this be a corporate value? How do you communicate this verbally and through specific actions? When issues arise, do you deal with them promptly and seriously? If an employee is failing, how does the board ensure that the church leadership is doing what is necessary to turn the situation around? Does the church board have a fair process for releasing employees? When conflicts occur within the staff, does the board have mechanisms that inform it appropriately and ensure that staff leadership is dealing with the issues fairly and carefully? In such contexts, the church board normally will work with and through the lead pastor for resolution. However, what if the conflict is between the lead pastor and another staff person? How does the staff person know that the board will handle his or her situation fairly?

An example of an important external relationship is the one your church has with local civic leadership. Take the case of a church that has received a letter from the local city council informing it that it is in violation of parking bylaws on Sundays because its parking lot is too small to accommodate the growing congregational attendance. Neighbors have complained about people parking too close to their driveways and the local mall that is adjacent to the church property has objected to church attenders using their lot for parking. How will the church board handle such matters? How will the board receive information about this matter? What outcome does the church board desire to achieve in resolving the situation? Is it important for the church board that the church's relationship with the local government be courteous, respectful, and congenial, living out Romans 13?

The church board is not an island unto itself. It operates within a wide network of relationships. Ignoring or mishandling these relationships generates needless conflict, saps the energy of the board members, and prevents a church board from stewarding the trust it has received from the congregation as well as it should. A church board chairperson will be alert to these dynamics, helping the board make and communicate its decisions with wise discernment about this political dimension of board life. When managed well, these relationships will promote and nurture the congregation's mission.

6. *Commitment to Strategic Priorities*

Keeping a church board on task has to be one of the most challenging and frustrating responsibilities that a church board chairperson manages. It seems that many individuals and issues conspire to derail a church board from its primary purposes and diffuse its energy, resulting in wasted time, dissatisfied board members, and loss of ministry momentum. Church board effectiveness relates directly to the ability and discipline of the board to keep focused upon strategic priorities—whether these are defined in spiritual or in other terms. A board chairperson has to discern with the board what these strategic priorities are for a specific year and then through determined leadership assist the board to move toward addressing those priorities. Doing this requires hard work, humor, and no small degree of holy dissatisfaction, i.e., the conviction that God is at work in the congregation and he wants it to make a God-honoring impact in its community.

So the first question a church board chairperson must ask is this—do you know what the strategic priorities of your board (that is, the congregation) are? Has the board defined these in general or specific terms so that after twelve months of work the board can evaluate its progress? If it has, are these priorities in fact strategic, i.e., the priorities that if advanced will help the congregation achieve its mission? If your answer to one or both questions is no, then the effectiveness of the board you chair may be compromised by lack of direction. The board needs to address this so that you as chairperson know how to guide the board in achieving its priorities. Perhaps at the next board retreat, you, as chairperson, should challenge the board to establish in its collective understanding what strategic priorities it should choose in the next twelve months in order to advance the church's mission. If your board already has done this, then make sure the board reviews and revises this list annually. Involving the lead pastor in discerning these strategic priorities will be critical to success.

What does the establishment of strategic priorities contribute to board effectiveness?

a. Requires the board to *discern direction*. As already mentioned, the board has to set some direction in order to guide its work through the year. If the board sets no goals, then it will probably fail to advance the church's mission in any substantial way. Board members may complete the agenda, but they will feel increasingly that it is busy work. At the end of meetings, board members will sense that they have not used their time, energies, and wisdom to full advantage because no progress is discernible. Priorities only become clear when the board has clarity about vision and values. The absence of clear strategic priorities indicates that the board lacks clarity about the congregation's vision. If this is so, then it must remedy this. The board could initiate action by asking the pastor and ministry staff to recommend a set of strategic priorities that will advance the vision, providing rationale for each priority proposed. The board can review this set of recommendations and adjust them, or add to or revise them as they see fit. If a priority needs several years to be achieved, then the board should have a clear pathway to completion. Once the board has adopted a set of strategic priorities, it can then set agendas that will focus upon those priorities.

b. Requires the board to *function in a disciplined manner*. How does a church board determine what business it should be conducting? Too often external influences set the agenda and the board finds itself in reactionary mode, rather than giving its attention to the things it regards as critical. No board can escape entirely the need to deal with surprises, but having clear priorities enables the board to be disciplined with its time and keep itself on track with respect to the most important things. Boards in smaller congregations are particularly susceptible to these external pressures. There is a spiritual aspect to this discipline as well and that is the prayer agenda of the board members. Once the board identifies its strategic priorities, these become the prayer list for the board. Achievements of the strategic priorities become answered prayers.

c. It *builds accountability*. How does a board hold itself accountable for exercising responsible leadership within the congregation? At the end of the day, it is the board itself that must define its agenda and hold itself accountable for achieving that agenda. The more clearly the board can articulate its strategic priorities, the better it is able to sustain and demonstrate good accountability. Both the chairperson and the individual board members can track the board's progress and raise questions when the board seems to be diverting from its agreed priorities.

d. It *repays the trust* given by the congregation. A board that defines clear strategic priorities and keeps focusing upon their achievement normally will garner the respect and sustained trust of the congregation. As the board reports to the congregation through the year, it both articulates the priorities and notes progress made toward their achievement. When the congregation is encouraged to connect achievement of these priorities with achievement of the congregation's mission, then people are encouraged by the board's determination to advance the kingdom of God in that place.

e. It enables the board to *manage risk*. When a board understands what its primary work entails, then it can focus its attention upon managing risks related to those priorities. To spend a great deal of time and effort managing risk for a project that is not a strategic priority produces frustration and sometimes needless cost if something goes awry. If the board is going to embrace a risk, make sure the risk is proportional to the critical nature of the action for the congregation's mission. If the board should decide to approve something that is not a strategic priority and the project misfires with attendant problems, then the congregation is going to wonder about the wisdom of the board in even venturing to take on such a project when it was not within the orbit of its stated strategic priorities.

f. It enables the board to *celebrate gains*. One of the great privileges that a church board experiences is leading the congregation in praising God for significant advancement of the mission. Whether it is people saved and baptized, missionaries supported, facilities for ministry constructed and financed, or the development and hiring of additional ministry leaders, because the board has sustained focus upon strategic priorities the congregation can celebrate and give glory to God.

The church board chairperson's responsibilities touch on each of the six areas. As the board engages in defining and attending to its strategic priorities, the board chair's role also becomes more manageable and satisfying.

Case Study: The Case of the Unrecorded Minute —A Chairperson's Nightmare.[4]

About a year ago the church board had a rather vigorous discussion about hiring a part-time worship pastor. Up to that point in the congregation's history worship leaders were volunteers. The pastoral staff had presented the proposal, but only minimal details were in writing. The position description and qualifications seemed appropriate to the board members at that time. The board gave the lead pastor authority to oversee the recruiting process and to make the decision regarding the hiring, based upon the sketchy position description and qualifications approved by the board, which included the salary and benefits.

Jack, the board member who had made the motion to approve the proposal, had raised the issue of whether the position would be gender specific or not. The lead pastor indicated that according to current church employment policy it would not be gender specific. Jack, however, because he believed the position would involve some teaching of the congregation and because it carried the designation of "pastor," felt that it would be appropriate for the position to be filled by a male. Jack thought in making the original motion he had made his view quite clear. The motion as it appeared in the official minutes, however, did not reflect that perspective. At

---

4. Although the story in this case study may seem to resemble a real situation, the names, places, and actual circumstances do not describe any actual church, church board, pastor, or chairperson.

the following meeting when the board approved those minutes, no one said anything or sought to correct the minutes, not even Jack.

Several months later, the lead pastor announced to the board that he had hired a person for the position. The board members were quite excited, anticipating God's provision for a rather important role within the congregation. When he announced her name, Jack was stunned. Jack was a detail person and usually brought his file of past board minutes to every board meeting in case he needed to refer to prior board actions. He quickly brought out his thick file folder and began leafing through the minutes until he located the minute concerning this new position. To his dismay, he discovered that the minute said nothing about gender specificity. He then began to look through his copy of board policies and again discovered that no policy required gender specificity for any ministry staff position, except that of lead pastor. When he made the motion, he presumed the minutes would include some notation regarding his intent for this role to be gender specific. However, this aspect of the motion was not included in the official minutes.

When Jack asked to speak, the chairperson expected that he would join with other board members in congratulating the lead pastor on completing this project and hiring a well-qualified candidate. However, when Jack began to speak the chairperson knew immediately a more serious issue was in play, namely the accuracy of the board minutes and determining what decision the board in fact had made when it approved the motion. With some emotion, Jack explained to the board what he believed had happened and that the official motion had not adequately expressed his understanding of the motion. He thought he had made his intentions quite clear at the time. Bob, a close friend of Jack, spoke and affirmed that this was his understanding as well. However, two other board members objected because in their opinion the minute was clear and expressed what the board had decided. When the lead pastor indicated that he would not have voted for a motion that in his view violated board policy, the chairperson knew that the board was in a serious predicament.

The chairperson had worked hard to help the board understand that approved minutes, recording the board's decisions, were the official record that expressed the mind of the board. What a specific board member thought the board had decided was in fact irrelevant—the minutes, once approved and signed by the board chair or secretary, became the official record available for public perusal. When the chairperson spoke for the board, the minutes became his primary guide for discerning the board's direction. The chairperson quickly reviewed the minutes from that earlier meeting and discerned in fact that the official minute did not stipulate gender preference. However, the chairperson also remembered that Jack had raised this question because he found a brief notation about this in the personal notes he had taken during that meeting. Those notes were not official in any sense.

What leadership could the chairperson provide in such a situation? The lead pastor had already made the hire and he could not reverse it without significant repercussions. The chairperson also knew that Jack might tender his resignation as a board member over this issue. His friend Bob might feel constrained to do the same. The lead pastor felt that the person hired would do a good job and had no intention of reversing his decision, which he believed aligned with board policy and the motion as it appeared in the official minutes.

What advice would you give to this board chairperson?

1. Hindsight is always helpful. This case highlights the importance of the chairperson making sure that board members have in fact read the minutes and agreed that they truly represent the decision made by the board. Often the board treats this work in a perfunctory manner, especially when consent agendas are the norm. The board chairperson would be wise, when the board reaches that point in the agenda for approving minutes, to pause and very deliberately ask the board members whether they have read the minutes and are in agreement with them. It becomes very difficult to correct matters retrospectively.

2. Two conflicting dynamics affect the treatment of minutes within a church board. On the one hand, church board members like to operate with a certain informality and camaraderie. If the chairperson acts too officiously, they often bristle at the strictures being imposed. On the other hand, board operations are important legal activities that have to proceed with due diligence. This requires formality at times, regardless of what some board members would like. The chairperson has to find the right balance in these matters and help the board to attend to both equally well.

3. According to *Robert's Rules of Order* once an approved motion has been executed, partially or completely, then no motion to reconsider or rescind can be entertained, particularly if a contract has been entered into because of the motion. If your church board or congregation has adopted *Robert's Rules of Order*, then the motion as passed and implemented cannot be reconsidered or rescinded. Even if the motion could be reconsidered, probably too much time has passed for this action to legitimately occur. Even though an error may have happened or miscommunication has occurred, the board cannot change its motion at that point. All it can do, it would seem, is to reaffirm or change its

policy for future reference, provide explanation to the congregation about the error that the board made, and live with the consequences.

4. It is clear in this case that the board members were unfamiliar with the policy that guided the hiring of ministry staff. When the board is dealing with new decisions, the chairperson should ensure that the board is aware of any policy that applies to the decision and should have it reviewed by the entire board. This educates the board with respect to policy, reminds the board that it forms policy to guide itself, and enables the board to evaluate whether the recommendation is consistent with current policy. In light of the current policy, the board can change the policy, amend the draft recommendation so that it aligns with the policy, or reject the recommendation because it is inconsistent with the policy. This is also a good reminder that the board should review all policies consistently. A three year cycle is recommended and each new policy should include a date when it should be reviewed.

5. How should the chairperson help Jack and Bob come to terms with this situation? A friendly discussion about the relationship between a board member's personal views and the policies established by the board seems to be in order. A normal operating procedure for a board member is to work within board policies. The chairperson can suggest ways and means by which a board member can request a review of a specific board policy if he/she thinks the current policy is not in agreement with the congregation's statement of faith or has suggestions for its improvement.

6. Perhaps as well the chairperson should take note that some of the responsibility for the current situation does lie with him. As his personal notes indicate, he knew when Jack made the motion that he had certain understandings about gender and staff roles that were in conflict with board policy. Knowing this, he should have advised Jack in the board meeting that the board could not entertain his motion as presented (with the expectation that it restricted applicants to males) because it violated current board policy. If he wanted to make the motion as he intended, then he first needed to move for an amendment to the current board policy. If the board agreed with the amendment, then the board could consider his motion regarding this restriction for the hiring of the worship pastor. If the chairperson was not aware of the policy, then this raises the question whether there are other board policies of which that chairperson is ignorant. He should make a note to review all policies to make sure he is knowledgeable of the board's directions so that he can facilitate their decision-making appropriately.

Questions for Reflection

a. How would you evaluate the degree of collegiality that exists among the members of your church board? What action might you take as chairperson over the next six months to improve collegiality?

b. Does your board know, agree to and make decisions in light of well-defined strategic priorities? If the church board you chair had to make a critical decision about two equally good ministry options, would its strategic priorities enable it to come to consensus?

c. How relevant are the "fruits of the Spirit" mentioned by Paul in Galatians 5 or Paul's discussion about *agape* in 1 Corinthians 13 to board interactions?

Suggested Resources

a. Richard P. Chait, et al., *Governance as Leadership: Reframing the Work of Nonprofit Boards.*

b. Edgar Stoesz and Chester Raber, *Doing Good Better: How to be an Effective Board Member of a Nonprofit Organization.*

Chapter 8

Chairing an Ethnically Diverse Church Board

IN CANADA, PARTICULARLY IN urban settings, cultural diversity characterizes our society. Our churches usually reflect this reality. In fact, church growth in Canada occurs primarily among these new groups. As immigration patterns continue to bring hundreds of thousands of people to Canada from many different cultural groups, our multiculturalism becomes more pronounced. Evangelical churches reflect this diversity and need to find ways to invite these new Canadians into their leadership and governance processes. Both Jesus and Paul emphasize hospitality as a Christian virtue and practice that demonstrates God's love for every human being.

This cultural diversity is shaping the composition of church boards. Canadian church boards today may have members from three or four different ethnic or cultural backgrounds, as well as different age brackets, genders, economic levels, and educational experiences. This diversity is good and we celebrate it as one of the wonderful elements of God's family. We want to accept one another as equals in Christ, understand one another, and respect one another as board members. So far so good!

1. High Context . . . Low Context

We often fail to recognize that cultural diversity means that people in a diverse faith community have very different views about group interaction, appropriate kinds of communication, honor and shame, the nature of decision-making, the relationship between younger and older members, the exercise of authority, etc. Cultural realities shape how we all understand such issues and behave in response to them. James Plueddemann urges us to realize that the more we interact with each other, the more we need to understand each other's underlying cultural values.[1]

Each person in a team ministry needs to learn the language of respect that others use. Westerners may think they are being respectful when they engage honestly and directly with others, speaking the truth in love, only to discover that they have treated with considerable disrespect someone in the group who operates within a different frame of reference. Fostering cultural intelligence is a necessity today.

Consider, for example, the experience of a respected Christian leader who has recently (last five years) emigrated from mainland China and has been newly appointed to a church board. He is thirty-eight years old. For the first three board meetings, this new member contributes almost nothing to board discussions. He listens intently and seems attentive, but offers no comments. What is the chairperson, who was born and raised in Canada and for whom discussion and debate are normal in a team context, to make of this behavior? Is the person behaving in this way because he is shy or naturally reserved? Is this his first experience as a board member and his reticence results from uncertainty? Perhaps, but the other newly appointed, forty-five-year-old board member, who is a third generation Chinese-Canadian, born in Alberta, certainly is not shy about presenting his opinions.

As the chairperson begins to explore the dynamics of this situation, he discovers that Asian cultures tend to express respect and values differently than Western cultures. Chinese culture is a high-context culture. This means that a person will discern values and respect from the way people act, not from what they say. People give much more weight to nonverbal aspects of communication, i.e., the setting of the room, where members position themselves at the table, facial expressions, and body language. The majority of the information gets communicated through these nonverbal elements. Verbal communication tends to be more flowery in its expression. Western culture in contrast tends to be a low-context culture. In other words, almost all of the weight in communication is placed on the verbal communication, i.e., what is said explicitly. Plain, direct speech is the valued commodity. In highly stressful situations, people tend to revert to their cultural norm. We should not think that one way of communication is better or worse—they are just different.

The new board member's shyness is probably occurring because he is trying to get his bearings in this new leadership context. The room the board meets in is a basement of the house in which the church offices are situated. There is no apparent designated order in the seating arrangements. Other

---

1. Plueddemann, *Leading across Cultures*, 73.

board members dress very casually and there is plenty of informal joking and sharing. Interactions in discussions get very direct and are often rather confrontational as the board debates serious questions. The younger members do not seem to wait to get their direction from the older members. For someone used to the communication dynamics of a high-context culture, this ethos creates significant problems and confusion. It appears chaotic. He struggles to know how to read what is happening and so he is reluctant to participate lest he misunderstand what is happening.

What can a board chairperson do in this situation to help the new board member feel at ease and discern how to participate well? Perhaps the most important response is to find a way to help, but do so privately. Do not try to address this in a board meeting with everyone present. In fact, the chairperson should not do this personally. Rather try to find a bridge person, someone who has experience in both cultures. This person will find a way to connect with the new board member and express how much the chairperson respects and values this individual's involvement in the board. However, the representative will also indicate that the chairperson is concerned that the board may not benefit from the new member's important perspectives and ideas. The bridge person would gently explore whether everything is all right, whether a meeting with the board chairperson would be fruitful, etc. In all of this, the strong signal is that you want him to serve well as a board member and this can only occur if he is engaged in the discussions. In some cultures, indirect approaches show more respect and value than direct approaches.

The goal is not to induce the new board member to change. Rather the best outcome is that the both parties learn to respect and value the communication processes that each uses, rather than judging the other inappropriately. A second strategy would be for the chairperson in some of his introductory comments at a board meeting to acknowledge the cultural diversity, explain its implications for mutual understanding, and offer suggestions that will help the whole board to interact more effectively. Mutual respect and a willingness to learn from one another is an essential foundation for Christian hospitality.[2] Alternatively, some of these issues could be addressed in a board orientation for new members.

---

2. I am indebted to Dr. Mark Naylor, Coordinator of International Leadership Development at Northwest Baptist Seminary, Langley, British Columbia, for his assistance with this section.

2. Perceptions of Time and Organization

How do people embedded in divergent but equally appropriate cultural perspectives view and value time? The terms "polychronic" and "monochronic" identify two very different cultural understandings. High-context cultures tend to be polychronic and low-context cultures usually display monochronic characteristics. In a polychronic culture, interruptions essentially are nonexistent, because time is a limitless resource and people and relationships are more important than efficiency. To refuse to meet a person when you are present because of a prior scheduled event would express great rudeness. Other people in a polychronic context will understand when a leader stops what he is doing to attend to a visitor's situation, expecting that others present are competent to carry forward the discussion and arrive at a good decision. Stuff happens in the normal rhythm of life despite some prearranged schedule.

Conversely, a monochronic culture tends to view time as a commodity that people should not waste. Interruptions then become irritating because people are spending the scheduled time on something not immediately germane to the meeting. They place priority on efficiency. Distress emerges when the group cannot make the necessary decisions in the context of the meeting because of other circumstances, interruptions, or relationships.[3]

An example of how this works on the ground in a low-context, monochronic culture would be a board meeting in which the chair kept to the agenda and did not allow for diversions because it was important to make decisions in that meeting. The focus is to keep on task, working promptly and consistently. Conversely, in a high-context, polychronic culture, the chair of a board meeting would attend to interruptions and concerns both internal and external to the meeting, rather than completing the agenda. As emergencies intervene, the leader would put people ahead of task, assuming that they will complete the business at some time, but there is plenty of time. For example, if his cell phone rang, he would not hesitate to answer it because he knew that the meeting would continue as he responded to that interruption.

On the one hand, a chairperson who is enculturated in a high-context, polychronic way of living will give more attention to interruptions and relationships than in completing the agenda. On the other hand, a chairperson who is enculturated in a low-context, monochronic culture will struggle when the meeting does not follow the agenda and loses focus because other

---

3. It may be that intergenerational and gender diversity may also exhibit itself in different attitudes toward authority, respect for process, and use of social media, as well as how people perceive the relationship between leaders and followers.

things preempt the meeting's stated outcomes. Again, I would emphasize that these cultural perspectives are different, but one is not necessarily better than the other.

As a general principle, where the Bible leaves flexibility for various cultural norms to operate, then acknowledge that. However, it is probably wise to chair a board in accordance with the values of the local host culture. A chairperson needs to assess what that host culture's primary orientation is and help all board members discern how to work effectively as a team within those cultural assumptions.

In most churches whose attendees primarily are second- or third-generation Canadians, the cultural ethos will tend to be low-context and monochronic. However, as the membership of a church board may change and incorporate individuals whose cultural ethos is high-context and polychronic in character, then the chairperson should seek to find ways to respect and value aspects of that cultural perspective. For example, the chairperson might give space in the meeting for relationship building (i.e., times to share personal blessings and challenges, stop for prayer about particular issues, lead the meeting with attention to the agenda), but in a relaxed mode, not becoming agitated if the agenda is not completed at that meeting. Placing the most important items that need decision at the head of the agenda will ensure that the board makes the necessary decisions, but it will give time for other, unplanned discussions to occur in the meeting.

In a high-context, polychronic culture, the chairperson as leader understands that discussions within and without the board meeting are part of the decision-making process. He will know when the board needs to make specific decisions and moderate the discussions and manage the interruptions so that progress is made, but not in rude or disrespectful ways. In a low-context, monochronic culture, the chairperson enables the board to progress by careful attention to the agenda, the decision process, and existing policies.

If, as chairperson, you perceive that your board contains members from both kinds of enculturated perspectives, how can you facilitate the board's work without frustrating one or the other group of participants? The following might be some strategies to consider:

1. The chairperson needs to have a very good sense of the timeframe in which the board needs to make particular decisions. This will allow him in a specific meeting to guide the board's discussions in a relaxed, but intentional mode.

2. While the board meeting will normally be the context in which the board members make formal decisions, the chairperson can propose

to the board various contexts in which discussion leading to decision might occur. For example, at a social evening where the board members and spouses are meeting for the purpose of building relationships, the chairperson might engage the entire group generally in a discussion about an issue that the church is facing. The intent is not to reach a decision or to discuss highly confidential matters, but rather to let the discussion about this issue flow in a different rhythm and context. The board might enrich itself in its decision-making by hearing alternative viewpoints.

3. Develop a practice of introducing matters one or two meetings prior to the preferred deadline for a decision. Discussion can proceed within and without the board by the members, with plenty of time for diverse opinions and insights to be gathered. At the meetings, board members touch base, consolidating their thinking and noting new insights.

4. Engage the board members in some discussion about whether board members should answer cell phones during meetings. If the board grants permission to one another for this to occur, then board members need to agree as well that the board's discussions will go forward if a board member feels the need to answer his or her cell phone.

5. Engage the board members in some discussion about how they should respond to family priorities that from time to time conflict with board schedules. There will be different perspectives on this, but the board members should develop some common understanding, giving permission for board members to respond as they perceive their responsibilities, without other board members becoming judgmental.

In a sense, a chairperson's best response is to give considerable attention to developing agendas that allow the strengths of various perspectives to have play. The chairperson can help the board value this diversity and develop processes that enable it to work comfortably and effectively with this diversity.

3. *Power Distance and Board Leadership*

All cultures develop power structures. When you grow up in a specific culture, you learn how to navigate within its specific power structures. For the most part we acquire this knowledge naturally, like learning a language. However, we also tend to assume that all other cultures have the same understanding of power structures, but this is a big mistake.

James Plueddemann,[4] in his book *Leading Across Cultures*, devotes an entire chapter to something termed "power distance," i.e., "the extent to which the less powerful members of institutions and organizations within a country expect and accept that power is distributed unequally."[5] Some cultures possess *high-power-distance* values. In these contexts, large inequalities in power are the norm, with some people holding significant power and the majority having little power. Other cultures embrace *low-power-distance* values where equality defines power relationships and the culture strives to minimize the power status that various groups or people may possess.

How does power distance play out within an organization? If you live in a culture where high-power-distance is the dominant value, then people in that culture will expect leaders to possess more authority and status than followers. Often the leader assumes the right to make decisions unilaterally. Children will obey parents; employees will follow the boss's instructions; and students will accept what teachers communicate. In such a situation, when a leader seeks to consult and arrive at a decision based on consensus, it may communicate a lack of leadership ability. It is normal when such values are present for leaders to have special privileges and if these are not used, again questions arise about the person's leadership capacity.

If you have lived in a culture where low-power distance is normative, then you expect leaders to work collaboratively with teams and consult before making decisions. You expect to have a voice in the operations. A more democratic, consensual model of leadership and decision-making prevails. If a leader starts making unilateral decisions, people become agitated and upset and sometimes rebellion will occur in some form. In these contexts, good leaders are expected to break down barriers that divide. Privileges are a sign of corrupt leadership, not respected leadership.

Generally, North American- and Western European-influenced cultures tend toward low-power-distance values. Conversely, Asian, Eastern European, African, and Latin American cultures tend toward high-power-distance values. Of course, these are very broad generalizations. Variables affecting these generalizations include education, wealth, religion, occupation, and urban versus rural context. Plueddemann comments that in every country where high-power-distance tends to be normative, people tend to desire less power distance. After reviewing various biblical cases, he concludes that "Scripture seems to leave room for some flexibility regarding power distance in leadership style but not in leadership attitudes. The heart

---

4. Plueddemann, *Leading across Cultures*, 92–111.
5. Hofstede and Hofstede, *Culture and Organizations*, 46.

of every leader must be humble, seeking the good of others and suspicious of one's own motives."[6]

Challenges may arise when ministry teams are multicultural, with some members from cultures that value high-power-distance and some from cultures that value low-power-distance. If the members of the team do not understand this cultural phenomenon and determine to exercise great sensitivity and respect toward one another, the team will become dysfunctional.

When we set these dynamics in the context of a church board, practical processes such as decision-making may be affected. For example, individuals used to operating in a culture where high-power-distance values are the norm may not be comfortable with board discussion that seems to challenge the lead pastor's proposal for ministry strategy. Similarly the very thought of evaluating a leader when such values predominate will be distasteful. Further, discerning when a decision has occurred officially may also be confusing. Consensus decision-making may even feel disrespectful of the primary leader's prerogative.

Alternatively, those board members whose experience is limited to contexts where low-power-distance values dominate will bristle when a leader used to operating with high-power-distance values feels he has authority to make the final decision, despite what the board may say. Such board members will expect to evaluate the lead pastor and the more thoroughly this is done, the better.

Chairpersons facilitating culturally diverse boards will need to understand these dynamics. Careful delineation of which groups in the organization speak into which issues and which group has authority to make specific decisions may prevent considerable distress. Attention to the decision-making process will be necessary. Further, having some discussion among the board members to clarify their preferred means of working together will help the board members understand each other more fully. It may even be helpful, when the board achieves a decision only after considerable conflict and dissenting opinion, to review with the board what happened and help each person to understand why that decision seemed to be so difficult. Perhaps different understandings of power distance were responsible for some of the conflict.

We know that Scripture teaches us to respect one another and honor those to whom we entrust leadership. Scripture is also clear that we must mutually submit to each other, whether leaders or followers (Eph 5:21; 1 Pet 5:5–7). We are one in Christ and differences such as race, gender, and

---

6. Plueddemann, *Leading across Cultures*, 103.

socioeconomic status should not affect the way we value another believer in Christ (Gal 3:23–29). The concept of the priesthood of the believer is a fundamental New Testament principle. However, we also know that God has established order and commands us, as part of our subjection to Jesus as Lord, that we work respectfully with those whom the congregation has entrusted with spiritual/agency oversight. We must adapt the high-power-distance and low-power-distance values to work in conformity with biblical principles.

Case Study: Who's Boss? A Cultural/Theological Perspective.

In his second term as church board chairperson for the Evangelical Community Church, Jake was excited when the congregation selected John, a Korean immigrant residing in Canada, to serve as an elder and member of the church board. This was the first time Jake could remember a non-Caucasian serving in this capacity. Jake saw this as a significant indication that the congregation was responding positively to the multicultural reality of their community.

When Jake contacted John to set up a time for some basic orientation, John accepted this offer gladly. Two weeks later over breakfast, Jake had the opportunity to learn something of John's spiritual journey and his prior church involvement. He discovered that John had also served as an elder in his church in Korea. Jake knew that there would be some adjustments for John because the way church boards work in Canada probably was not the same as it is in Korean churches. In Korea, John was part of a Presbyterian church, but now he was serving in an cross-denominational Evangelical church.

Jake worked through the orientation materials in a methodical manner. John was listening intently and did not interrupt. Then Jake came to the part of his presentation where he talked about the relationship between the church board and lead pastor. He explained that every year the board, through its personnel committee, conducted a performance review of the lead pastor. When he heard this, John became quite agitated. He began to ask some questions. Could Jake clarify what the purpose of a performance review was? Who conducted it? What kinds of things did the board evaluate? Did the pastor like this process? What did the board do with the results of the evaluation? What did this process say about the relationship between the church board and the lead pastor?

Jake was pleased that finally John was asking questions. For him it indicated that John was tracking well and wanting to learn more about standard processes. He did not pick up the concerns that were behind John's questions. From John's experience in the Korean church, the pastor was the boss. No one had authority to evaluate him; rather he had the responsibility to evaluate everyone else in the congregation. To reverse this authority relationship and have the lead pastor accountable to the church board was a major paradigm shift for John.

Jake responded carefully to John's questions, emphasizing that the board intended the evaluation to help the lead pastor discern with the elders where to expend some effort in the coming year for his development as a lead pastor. The intent was not to judge or criticize in a harsh or destructive manner. John responded that God called pastors to their vocation and surely they were accountable to God, not a church board. Jake shared his view that responding to God's call vocationally was one thing, being accountable for exercising that calling in a local church was another. John said that he would have to think about this carefully. He was at this point uncomfortable with this process. When he agreed to let his name stand for elder, he did not realize that he would be part of an annual performance evaluation of the pastor.

Jake thanked John for sharing his concern and agreed to meet with him again in a few weeks to talk further about this matter. Meanwhile, he encouraged John to attend the first meeting of the new board and become accustomed to the church board's work.

When Jake left his meeting with John, he was not sure what to do. He thought that one thing could be helpful and that was to let the lead pastor know about John's concerns and have the lead pastor meet with John and explain how he viewed this process in relation to his vocation. Perhaps hearing from the lead pastor himself and seeing his comfort with the process would be enough to encourage John to stay involved.

Reflections

1. Jake's experience touches on some of the hidden dimensions of church board leadership when board members come from diverse cultural and theological traditions. Developing board coherence (i.e., unity without unanimity), is always challenging, but necessary. Learning where to allow for diversity and where to work for consensus is part of chairmanship.

2. John's struggle was not just cultural, but also theological. However, his Korean culture was influencing his theological understanding about

Christian leadership. Working in a Canadian context presented some challenges to John and required him to rethink some of his theological perspectives. This is a classic case of cross-cultural adjustment and contextualization.

3. Jake's patience will be an important factor in helping John work with the church board's policies. He may also need to encourage other board members to be understanding as John takes up this new role.

4. John's questions might provide an opportunity for the board members to discuss the policy regarding performance evaluations, affirm their theological understanding, and revise it as necessary.

Questions for Reflection

a. Although this chapter has focused upon ethnic diversity, we also realize that cultural diversity can be generated through generational differences, educational differences, gender diversity, or economic disparity. How can you as chairperson recognize these differences and enable them to contribute to a more effective board culture?

b. To what extent should a church board be representative of the cultural diversity within the congregation? Usually there is a lag between the cultural change and the composition of the board. What can you as chairperson do to create a more culturally representative board without upsetting historical practice?

Suggested Resources

a. James E. Plueddemann, *Leading across Cultures. Effective Ministry and Mission in the Global Church.*

Chapter 9

The Church Board Chairperson and Key Board Operational Issues: Internal Matters

IN YOUR WORK AS board chairperson, some key operational elements require your attention if you are to help the board accomplish its work and steward the trust placed in it by the congregation.

1. Board Member Orientation

One of the most important practices you can implement is an annual orientation for new church board members. Given how nominating committees operate in most congregational settings, as board chairperson, you may have little say in whom the committee recommends as nominees for the role of elder/deacon/board member. Similarly, the appointment of a lead pastor (or associate lead pastor) will introduce a new member to the board and some orientation will be helpful in his case as well. Do not assume that a new lead pastor will know or even agree with the way your church board operates or the policies and procedures developed to guide it. Orient him to the board as you would any other new board member, respecting, of course, his special role. This is a good first step in developing an effective working relationship with this leader.

Try to schedule this orientation prior to any new board member's first official board meeting. Set aside about two hours for this process. You could build it around a meal in order to enhance the occasion. If you have a vice-chairperson for the board, then include this person as well, because it will be a good training/mentoring opportunity. You might even assign the entire board orientation process to the vice-chairperson, but you should probably retain some role in it.

What are the key things you want to accomplish in the orientation? I would suggest three key goals:

a. You want to discern what prior board experience this person has had (within or without the church), whether this was positive, and what the person learned through this experience. This will help you gauge the degree of mentoring this person may need during the first year to enable him/her to learn how to make a good contribution to the board's work.

b. Describe essential elements of this church board's culture as a ministry team, stressing the spiritual foundations of all that the church board does together. Share the idea of worshipful work because this may be a new concept. Discuss the concept of entrusted stewardship and help the person understand what governance is within the setting of a church congregation—and what it is not. If the board has developed a description of its primary responsibilities, review this, as well as the code of board member conduct. Also, if there are parts of the church bylaws that define the work of the church board, particularly the nature of its authority, then review that as well, using some examples to show how this works in real terms. Include some discussion about the relationship between the board and the lead pastor.

c. The third area is the expectations that you as chairperson have of the board members. This would include the spiritual preparation of prayer and careful review of the business that the board members will be discussing at each meeting. Help the new member understand the importance of coming prepared, and his/her responsibility of due diligence. If the person brings expertise that is especially pertinent to the board's work (e.g., financial, legal, human resources, conflict resolution, etc.), encourage the individual to speak to the issues out of that expertise and thus assist the entire board in its work. After describing the board's standing committees, you might discuss where and how the new member might contribute to the board's work through participating in one of them. Make sure you cover the issues of conflict of interest, board confidentiality, board indemnification, and responsibility to advance the mission.

Provide documents for the new members to review (church bylaws, board responsibilities, code of conduct, all policies, latest year-end financial statement, any legal proceedings in which the congregation is engaged, annual ministry plan, statement of mission, vision and values, copies of minutes from the last six board meetings, etc.). Gathering this material the first time may be a bit of a challenge, but once you have it compiled, then you can enhance it for the next orientation.

After the first two regular board meetings, schedule coffee together in order to follow and see what questions or issues are emerging.

2. Code of Conduct

If your church board does not possess a code of conduct for employees and board members, then I would strongly urge you to make its development a priority in the next year. I have provided a sample in the appendix of resources. We tend to assume that members of a church board (and employees) automatically will conduct themselves appropriately and know the boundaries of behavior that board members should not violate. However, experience indicates that this is a misguided expectation. For many new church board members, this is their first experience as a board member and they do not know what the guidelines should be. A wise board will be explicit about these expectations, review them annually and expect all board members to sign the code of conduct either annually or upon reappointment, along with affirmation of support for the church's statement of faith.

Sometimes board members will balk at this, because they claim that the board or you as chairperson do not trust them to act appropriately. However, if the board as a whole establishes the code of conduct and adopts it as policy, then all board members without exception are bound to abide by it as the board may direct.

It would be wise to indicate in the code of conduct what occurs if a board member violates it. What actions might the board take and what process will the board follow? Stating this clearly should give some protection to the individual board member as well as the board itself. Appendices D and E provide a sample church board code of conduct and covenant.

3. The Board Agenda as a Reflection of the Annual Ministry Plan

A primary means by which a board chair exercises leadership within the board relates to the development of the meeting agendas. They keep the board on track, focused, worshipful, and accountable.

The first place to start is the development of an annual agenda. This is not as difficult a task at it might first appear. Sit down with the lead pastor and plot on a calendar the dates for the annual general meeting (AGM) and other key events in the congregational year—as well as the projected schedule of board meetings—that the board has to keep in mind in order to complete its responsibilities on time. For example, the board will have to ensure that a financial review or audit of the fiscal year is completed in time for the board to review it officially and present it to the AGM. Similarly, the budget for the next fiscal year will need to be developed, reviewed, and approved by the board for recommendation to the congregation at the AGM. The congregation will need to appoint a nominating committee several months prior to the AGM. The board will need to schedule the annual review of the lead pastor. What is a good time for the annual board retreat? If there are quarterly or semi-annual congregational meetings, relate these to church board meetings so that the board can process decisions and recommendations in advance of these congregational meetings.

Once you have noted these annual decisions, then identify at which meeting the board will have to consider specific issues so that the board is ready to make appropriate reports and recommendations. This also signals to the lead pastor when his board reports need to be prepared for circulation.

Your board can develop a greater degree of organization by creating a three-year board agenda and indicating when it will review specific policies or evaluate programs. It is a matter of scheduling and discipline. The more advanced planning you can do as board chair, the fewer surprises you will have to deal with and the more productive the board meetings will be. Scheduling like this enables the staff to integrate their work more effectively with that of the board.

In the case of the agenda for a specific meeting, as chairperson, you need to start preparations at least two weeks in advance. Remember the goal is to have the agenda, with necessary documentation, ready and circulated at least one week in advance of the meeting. With email access, this is quite doable. Two weeks prior to the board meeting you generate a proposed agenda. Circulate it to the lead pastor and the board secretary for their review and input. Scheduling your monthly meeting with the lead pastor two weeks before board meetings, you can use that occasion to discuss agenda items. If the board secretary normally formats the agenda and circulates it, then you, as chairperson, have to provide the secretary with the necessary information at least several days prior to the date for its circulation.

Once you have their feedback, then finalize the items and designate times in the meeting for each item so that you know that the discussion about one matter does not become so lengthy that the board cannot complete all of its business at the scheduled meeting. It is also helpful to place the name of the board member responsible for the item beside it in the agenda. When the board accepts the agenda, they also accept the time components built into the agenda. If the discussion regarding one item begins to go beyond the timeframe specified, then as chairperson you can ask the board whether they desire to amend the agenda or halt discussion and continue it at the next meeting. You might at that point determine whether the board needs additional information and how the board will receive it in time for the next discussion.

Put the items needing decision at the beginning of the agenda so that the board members are dealing with those when they have the most energy and attentiveness. Try to limit your meetings to a maximum of three hours.

Work carefully with the lead pastor so that items do not get parachuted into the meeting at the last minute. Sometimes unexpected things arise that the board has to deal with, but try to keep such diversions to a minimum.

Use processes such as discussion briefs and decision profiles to provide the board with the information they need to understand the issue, its implications, and possible directions they might consider. Appendix F provides examples of these two tools.

Incorporate the practice of the "consent agenda"[1] into each agenda so that you minimize time taken in a board meeting to deal with reports. However, always invite the lead pastor to give a verbal summation of his report, highlighting the ministry issues in the congregation that are generating excitement or raising concern. It may be that the board will want to lift one of these items and add it to the board's agenda.

---

1. A "consent agenda" is a part of the board's agenda that enables the board to indicate that it has reviewed and received minutes, financial reports, ministry reports, committee reports, etc. through one motion. Board members should review all of these materials before the meeting and come prepared to receive them with little discussion. If a board member does desire to discuss an issue raised in one of the reports, then this is noted and included in the board's agenda for that meeting. In the case of the lead pastor's report to the board, it is helpful to give this person several minutes to verbally share the highlights and make any other observations that might be pertinent and of interest. The lead pastor has the responsibility to bring to the board members' attention any issues that may be affecting his ability to lead or which are creating some risk to the congregation.

A Board Chair's Primary Tasks

Annual Tasks	Monthly Tasks	Intermittent Tasks
Prepare the board's report for the AGM	Prepare and circulate board agenda. This includes assigning board members to lead the board's worship session	Attend and be prepared to speak for the board at congregational meetings
Review and update annual agenda and schedule of the board	Ensure necessary discussion briefs and decision profiles are prepared and circulated	Represent the board and/or congregation at external functions, i.e., denominational conventions, civic functions, etc.
Update policy manuals	Meet regularly with lead pastor	Discerning potential board members
Orientation of new board members	Follow-up board assignments	Meet occasionally with ministry staff team
Maintain communication with board committee chairs to ensure that board business is proceeding well		Arrange board education opportunities
Board assessment processes		Planning some social functions for board members and spouses
Planning annual board retreat		
Lead pastor evaluation		
Appointment of board officers and committees		
Debrief retiring board members		

4. The Board Agenda as a Service of Worship

A church board, as I have argued previously, forms a ministry team that includes many of the primary spiritual leaders within the congregation. Its work is spiritual. Keeping this ethos constantly before the board members can be a challenge. Charles Olsen has offered some ideas that can help a chairperson sustain this board perspective.[2] The concept is simple, namely

---

2. Olsen, *Transforming Church Boards Into Communities*, 181–82, offers a sample

to use the rhythm of a worship service as the framework for shaping the board's agenda.

The agenda's structure flows along the following lines:

Normal Agenda Segments	Worship-Oriented Agenda
Call to order	Gathering to worship
Scripture reading & reflection	Hearing God's word
Prayer	Confession
Consent agenda (Reports)	Praising God for ministry advances—Celebrating the past
Key issues for decision—What does God want us to do?	Presenting our offering of service—The work of discernment & responding to God's word
Evaluation of the meeting, announcements, and adjournment	Thanksgiving and benediction

Your creativity can blossom, but if you struggle with this, why not have a conversation with the worship pastor/director and see what ideas he/she might have to help you develop a worship-oriented agenda.

5. *Focus on the Mission*

As strange as it may seem, focusing on the congregation's mission requires hard work and deep intentionality. So many things emerge within a congregation's life and the interactions within a board that distract the board members from concentrating on the main thing—advancing the mission. You might be surprised how much of a challenge it is, at least initially, for board members to bend their thinking in that direction. However, without this north star guiding their every meeting, the board is not keeping faith with the congregation that has appointed them.

Because the chairperson facilitates the board's collective work to fulfill its primary responsibilities, this person has to take responsibility for developing this capacity and passion among the board members. One way to do this is to print the mission and/or vision statement of the congregation as a header for every agenda. Additionally, when you have the opportunity to lead the board in its time of prayer and Bible study, focus your remarks upon the mission and vision and how the board exercises its most important

---

agenda built around the rhythms of worship. His first chapter, entitled "Simple Elegance: The Spirit of a Board as 'Worshipful Work,'" provides more direction.

ministry within the congregation as it tends to this mission. Make sure that every decision profile includes a section that shows how this decision will advance the mission and/or vision of the congregation. If the proposer cannot state this clearly, then why is the board dealing with this question? Encourage the Personnel Committee of the Board to develop protocols for staff evaluations based upon how their leadership in the past twelve months has advanced the mission. They should align the goals for their ministry with the key outcomes the board has discerned. As they achieve their goals, this should enable the congregation to celebrate missional gains. In its annual report to the congregation, the board should be able to articulate how its work during the past year has advanced the mission.

If the congregational mission and vision does not exist as a formally approved statement or the board has not reviewed or revised it in the past three to five years, then make this a priority in the board's agenda. When there is lack of clarity about the mission, vision, and outcomes, the board does not know how to discern its work or assess its performance.

Finally, as the board members perceive how their work together as a board truly is advancing the church's mission/vision, they become excited about their contributions and more committed to their responsibilities as board members.

6. Developing and Reviewing Policy

Policies are guidelines that the board develops to organize itself, define the authority of the lead pastor, describe the mission, vision, values, and ends of the congregation, and articulate effective practices that it will legally, ethically, and biblically adhere to. A church board develops and implements policies as a means to deal with its worry points. For example, if a church board has concerns about the scope of authority that their lead pastor should exercise, it develops a policy that states what the lead pastor cannot do (limitations), e.g., that the lead pastor cannot hire staff before the board has approved the budget for the position and the position description. Or, perhaps the board is concerned about the potential liability that short-term mission trips present to the congregation and so it develops a policy that defines how such trips are approved, the conditions for such approval, and the nature of fundraising within the congregation for such mission trips.

Policies usually apply to recurring situations and so a board develops guidelines that will reduce the decision time required by the board. Over time, board policies capture the wisdom of various generations of board members.

Some policies will deal with matters internal to the board (e.g., how the board appoints a chairperson, what kinds of operational assessment the board engages and how often, board ethics, conflicts of interest, etc.). Other policies will deal with staff matters (e.g., how annual salaries and benefits are determined, sabbatical policy, employee harassment, whistleblower protection, etc.), while others relate to congregational issues (e.g., the process used to approve people for membership, member misconduct and restoration, bylaws, etc.).

Once policies are developed, the chairperson should help the board create a two- to four-year cycle of review and revision. This serves several purposes. It reminds all the board members that such policies exist and this is important given the turnover of personnel in church boards. As the circumstances of the congregation change, policies also need to adapt because their provisions become obsolete. A formal review cycle reveals gaps that the board can address.

7. *Program Planning and Assessment*

Planning, implementing, assessing, and concluding programs form a series of significant board tasks done in close collaboration with the ministry staff. Through this process, a board defines vision and creates strategic initiatives to achieve that vision. More recently, governments and accrediting agencies have urged and even mandated nonprofits to pay more attention to program assessment. Programs are the means by which nonprofits deliver benefits to clients and if the board does not know whether the programs are achieving their designed objectives, it cannot discern whether they are fulfilling the agency's mission and using its resources appropriately. However, my experience with church boards is that program assessment is a relatively unknown and rarely practiced governance function. Boards assume that all current ministry activities must be good, whether they are achieving stated objectives or not. In addition, most church boards cannot name the specific programs that are operating in the church or explain how they align with the vision. Some programs are historic vestiges that have long since outlived their usefulness; some are private domains that the leadership tolerates because it does not want to upset key people in the congregation; others express an individual's initiative and passion, but are loosely aligned with the vision; and some have a very sharp focus and contribute significantly to the congregation's vision.

What is a program within the context of a church nonprofit agency? "A nonprofit program is a highly integrated set of resources and activities geared to provide a service or closely related set of services to clients."[3] A program will have inputs, processes, outputs, and outcomes. The inputs include all of the resources necessary to sustain the program, including personnel, facilities, finances, technology, etc. Every program has to be delivered in some fashion and the processes enable this to occur effectively and efficiently (e.g., children are discipled, youth develop a Christian worldview, homeless are fed, orphans in another country are cared for, etc.). Who is helped, how many affected, etc., would be the outputs (i.e., the people served), and outcomes define what change in fact is being achieved by the program (children grow up to be committed Christians, young adults define a Christian worldview and make life decisions accordingly, all homeless people in a one kilometer radius of the church receive a nutritious meal once a day, etc.). The outcomes function as a directional pointer for the program, keeping it on track and moving in the mandated direction. If the specified outcomes are not happening at all or not happening at a sufficient rate, then the program is ineffective.

Staff should be aligning every program with the congregation's mission, vision, and strategic plan. Programs that lie outside of these boundaries should be suspended or passed over to another agency, or else you need to redefine the mission and vision so that the program does align (but this may allow the tail to wag the dog!). If a Canadian Christian agency is supporting activities not defined in its mission, the Canadian Revenue Agency may determine that such activities are not charitable and withdraw tax-receipting privileges.

What should a program proposal include? Common elements would be outcomes, goals, strategies, and objectives. The outcomes, integrated with the mission and vision, have to be the first element because everything else follows. They should articulate the benefits to clients that the program will deliver. Specific goals define the results that the program should produce for the defined group. Write them in measurable, time-bound, specific, and realistic terms. The program strategies will include the means used to achieve the goals. Objectives describe staged milestones that will measure progress toward the goals. Although a program plan does not have to be perfect, it should give some thought to each of these elements so that the board and staff have a common understanding of the way the program will advance the mission. Taking time to do this well and insisting upon a good plan will alleviate future difficulties and create considerable clarity for all involved. A fundamental element in any plan will be the definition of key

---

3. Paragraph 1 under "What's a Nonpofit Program?" at http://managementhelp.org/programmanagement/nonprofit-programs.htm.

indicators of success: How will the board know that the program is successful within a set timeframe? Some would argue that every program needs a sunset clause, i.e., a date at which the program automatically ends unless there is deliberate decision to continue it. Sunset clauses can be a useful tool to require evaluation at set times and not allow programs to continue without assessment and new mandates.

With such a program assessment plan, the board has a means by which to assess the effectiveness of agency programs within a reasonable timeframe. The board will ask the program director to prepare such an assessment for the board within the first year or two of the program, with the board reserving the right to authorize its continuance based upon the results of the assessment.

As chairperson, you can encourage the board to develop and require a program planning template which various groups in the congregation can use to present to the board any plans for new programs. It would also be important for the board to identify the current programs being supported by the congregation and its resources, and who are the leaders responsible for these programs. Knowing what these are will help the board to discern the resources required to sustain these programs—an important element in the development of the annual strategic and financial plan.

Once this work is done, the board then should develop a program assessment template that program leaders can use to develop assessment reports for the board once every two or three years. The board can develop a cycle of these assessment reports that would enable it to track the development and effectiveness of all the congregation's programs within a defined period, thereby increasing accountability. Program assessment enables the board: 1) to know what impact the program is having upon the defined target group; 2) to discern ways to improve delivery of the service; 3) to verify that the program is doing what it was projected to do; 4) to discover stories of success that will encourage the congregation's support; 5) to discern possible duplication and overlap; and 6) to ensure that the board is allocating resources (personnel, facilities, finances) efficiently.

In designing a program assessment template, the board should consider:

a. What is the purpose for the assessment;

b. Who is the intended audience (in most cases this will be the board, but may include the entire congregation);

c. What data the board needs to make necessary decisions;

d. What means can be used to collect the information and from what audiences;

e. What resources may be required to complete an effective assessment;

f. When is the cycle of assessment: Every two years? Every three years?

I have provided more detail regarding program development and assessment because I think this is one of the weakest areas of church board governance, yet it holds promise of elevating the board's strategic leadership to new levels of effectiveness.

8. Managing Conflict Productively

Church board work by definition will involve conflict. R. Heifetz observes that

> music teaches us that dissonance is an integral part of harmony. Without conflict and tension, music lacks dynamism and movement.[4]

When the board is discussing ideas, some people will feel passionate about the issues. Often board members are choosing between two or more good ideas and vetting different values. Satan is trying to interfere. Congregations are complex entities and discerning the best way forward is not easy. The future is unknown. No wonder there is conflict within church boards. Add to this general cultural values and expectations about the value of personal opinions, differing perspectives on what is right, just, and fair, and theological and cultural diversity within congregations, and church board chairs know they are in for a bit of a ride. As chairperson, you can remind the board members periodically that the perspective of each member is valued, that good listening by all is expected, and that members are responsible to discern, name, and deal with conflicts of interest. You can review such matters in the orientation for new board members.

We do not have the space to outline processes for conflict resolution. Rather I will suggest some strategies that will help to manage conflict productively and when it does happen to an abnormal degree, what you as chairperson can do to help the board as a whole respond constructively and spiritually:

1. Strategies to manage conflict would include:

---

4. Heifetz, *Leadership Without Easy Answers*, 6. He also observes that "the exposure and orchestration of conflict—internal contradictions—within individuals and constituencies provide the leverage for mobilizing people to learn new ways" (22).

a. Develop your own spiritual and emotional intelligence so that when conflict does occur within the board, you, as chairperson, are not surprised, immobilized by its appearance, or prompted to respond inappropriately.

b. Cultivate the respect of each member for your leadership within the board. If each member trusts you and has confidence in your fairness, they are more willing to respond to proposed direction.

c. Develop and sustain unity around the mission, vision, and values of the congregation. The primary question in discerning a decision is this: Which option will advance the mission of the congregation in a way that is most congruent with its vision, values, and resources? Helping board members discern congruence of values in the preferred option is an important stage in moving from conflict to consensus.

d. Ensure that the process to achieving the decision is clear and that the right groups have appropriate voice at the right time.

e. Ensure that the board members have all of the information necessary to make a good decision.

f. Take the time to make a good decision. Rushed decisions usually become fertile ground for conflict. Rarely does a board have to make an important decision at its first discussion.

g. Prevent the discussion from becoming personal—focus the discussion on the issue at hand.

h. Encourage an attitude of indifference (i.e., controlling ego, releasing personal preferences, and seeking only what is good for God).

2. When conflict happens, the chairperson can:

a. Engage the board members in an exercise of discerning what is good about each of the possible directions and then ask for a time of prayer to discern which is the weightier good. One grid to use in this process is to have the board members define the congregational values that each option expresses. Presumably the more appropriate options would be those that are most congruent with the congregation's values, unless the values themselves need to be realigned.

b. Help the board to hold the discussion until it is ready to make a decision. In other words, the chairperson facilitates a context within the board where discussion proceeds safely until the board members work through respective personal adaptations that may need to occur in preparation for decision. This holding may extend over several meetings. Encouraging the board to exercise patience can be a significant direction from the chairperson, even as some board members may chafe at the slowness of the process.

c. Declare a brief recess in the midst of a particularly robust discussion for board members to decompress, pray, have coffee, talk informally, and then reconvene. Sometimes a solution will emerge or a way forward will be proposed.

d. Arrange after the meeting to have coffee with the person who seems to be struggling and seek to discern what his or her worry points are regarding the decision. Perhaps there is misunderstanding that you can clear away, or maybe that board member is discerning a risk that the other board members may not perceive, but should consider.

e. When conflict arises between the board and the lead pastor, the chairperson will need to manage this process with particular wisdom. The personal relationship between the lead pastor and the chairperson will be an important basis for seeking resolution.

The chairperson carries significant responsibility in helping the board manage conflict productively. The board appoints the chairperson to assist it in finding its voice, and this requires the development and exercise of some skill in conflict resolution.

9. Building Internal Board Relations

Board chairpersons often overlook how much internal church board relations contribute to the ability of the board to accomplish its work. Where mutual trust, respect, and "*koinonia*"[5] flourish, the Spirit's direction will also become evident. The spiritual leadership of the board within a congregation influences the spiritual ethos of the entire faith community.

It may be surprising to learn that church board members probably know very little about the spiritual journeys their peers have had, as well as their current challenges. The composition of most church boards tends to be weighted toward the male gender and sharing is not necessarily a valued male activity. Further, Christians have this perception that spiritual leaders

---

5. Commonly translated as "fellowship" in the New Testament. However, it can express the ideas of commonality or partnership.

have it all together and showing vulnerability tends to raise doubts about the suitability of the person to serve in spiritual leadership.

The chairperson then has a key role to play in developing internal board relations. First, the personal model he/she displays in this regard encourages other board members to follow this lead. How committed is the chairperson to developing good personal relationships with each of the board members? Do you show a spirit of hospitality toward and personal interest in other board members and their spouses (e.g., do you and your spouse host various board members and their spouses in your home throughout the year?)? Are you willing to share with the board members some of the spiritual and personal challenges you face and seek their prayers and encouragement?

Second, build into the meeting schedule space for board members to share stories and pray for one another. Enjoy moments of spontaneous humor. Celebrate stories of ministry success. If a board member becomes ill, encourage other board members to visit or show their support in some tangible way. When other serious challenges affect a board member, find ways for the board to encourage and assist. The board is a ministry team and journeying through times of significant challenge together deepens relationships.

Third, as I have indicated previously, within the annual board schedule build in one or two occasions when the entire board with their spouses can get together for a social evening, enjoying a meal together, sharing and praying together. Such events encourage spouses to be supportive of their husband or wife in their board work and provide an opportunity to say thank you to them for their help in this ministry.

Attention given to things such as the meeting room arrangements and refreshments can also enhance the relational ethos.

Internal relations can be the glue that enables the board members to work well through times of congregational crisis. They enable robust discussion to occur without individuals becoming offended, because they trust one another. Team dysfunction often occurs because team relations are dysfunctional. Patrick Lencioni places "absence of trust" as the "first dysfunction" which debilitates a team.

> Essentially, this stems from their unwillingness to be vulnerable within the group. Team members who are not genuinely open with one another about their mistakes and weaknesses make it impossible to build a foundation for trust.[6]

---

6. Lencioni, *Five Dysfunctions of a Team*, 188.

10. Risk Management as Ministry

The board of any nonprofit charitable agency constantly engages in risk assessment as it processes various decisions. Sometimes this occurs intuitively and sometimes boards build it deliberately into the decision-making process. Church boards have no immunity from such responsibility and the chairperson, in his or her service to the board, helps the board recognize, assess, and manage risk.

A church board deals with various kinds of risks—spiritual, legal, financial, congregational, and missional. Sometimes the board can manage certain kinds of risk through policy and holding a specific person accountable to ensure that they are applying the policy consistently and fairly (e.g., privacy of information, criminal record checks for all volunteers working with children, etc.). In such cases, the board still has to assure itself that the policy is being applied. Other kinds of risks relate to decision-making and discerning the implications of a particular decision on the health of the congregation or the achievement of the church's mission. Spiritual risks would be actions taken by the board regarding matters of theological conviction that may create tension between the congregation and public policy (e.g., stance regarding marriage).

Consider the following example of risk-taking. The church board finance committee brings forward a recommendation that the next fiscal year's expenditures should be increased 15 percent, even though the pattern of church growth, both in terms of number of people and amount of giving, has not changed in three years. The only rationale provided to support this recommendation is faith that God will supply. The primary cause for this major increase in expenditure is a ministry focus that one of the more influential board members on the budget committee has a particular interest in. During the discussion, no board member challenges the assumptions or identifies the risk such a budget increase might be to the church, if the congregation should also adopt this recommended budget.

The chairperson, however, has serious reservations about this recommendation, sensing that it has potential to exhaust the church's financial reserves and cause significant disruption in the church's ability to carry forward other segments of its vision. What is the responsibility of the chairperson in such an instance? In what way can the chairperson serve the board, exercise appropriate leadership to help the board understand the risk it will be embracing, and enable it to discern an alternative that carries less risk?

In this example, because this recommendation carries the weight of a significant board member, when the chairperson seeks to give leadership, there is risk that the board member may become antagonistic, that the board may become divided over the issue, that the chair may be accused of lacking faith, etc. The chairperson does not have an easy path to follow in such cases.

Risk management is a constant part of any board's life. So one of the strategies a chairperson might employ is to help the board identify, assess, and deal with risk. Some board members probably give little thought to this matter. However, the whole board has legal and spiritual responsibility to manage risk and the chairperson, as its servant, has to facilitate its ability to fulfill this responsibility. As chairperson, you need to be proactive and start with some education. Circulate a short article to the board about a board's responsibility in such matters and then present a case study from a situation your board had to deal with where risk was potentially significant. Make sure the example is at least a year or two old so that it does not reignite latent emotions.

Second, as chairperson, you might find out what policies the board has developed to manage risk. Suggest, if necessary, that the board begin to review them, bring them up to date, and make sure they are being implemented. This means some sort of reporting mechanism will need to be developed. In some cases, this can be built into the lead pastor's normal reports to the board.

Third, you might suggest that the board review annually its liability insurance to ensure that board members, employees, and volunteers have appropriate protection from specific risks.

Fourth, you might explore with your board how it would guide the congregation in dealing with matters of member discipline. Unfortunate as these situations might be, church boards often encounter surprises because they never developed an appropriate process to oversee such cases. Being proactive in introducing such discussions enables the chairperson to help the board avoid foolish mistakes that might harm the congregation and the specific parties involved. This is risk management.

Fifth, you can encourage the board's personnel committee to review the church's employment policies and ensure that the church complies with current labor laws.

Sixth, urge the board to put in place processes that enable it to manage financial risk effectively, i.e., a required annual financial review or audit, quarterly financial reports that identify areas of potential risk, etc.

A church board's responsibility is not to manage risk on a day-to-day basis, but to oversee risk management and make sure that appropriate policies, accountability, and reporting are in place and working. It seems that for church boards, employee issues, member discipline actions, facility usage, and financial management present the greatest areas of risk. Privacy rights, harassment protection, safety issues, and possible criminal behavior of employees or volunteers (e.g., child molestation) require boards to insist that appropriate policies are in place and that paid and volunteer staff implement them conscientiously and consistently. To write and approve policy but fail to implement or require accountability from the primary employees (i.e., ministry staff) is a formula for disaster. All such policies must be consistent with current legal requirements.

Other kinds of risks, not of the legal variety, also challenge a church board. These relate to matters of spiritual health, mission fulfillment, and member care. When a church board is making decisions, it must continually ask itself these questions: 1) will this decision truly advance the mission; 2) will it build unity within the congregation; 3) will it add value and bring help to those the church is seeking to serve; 4) will it damage the reputation of the church in the community; and 5) will it enable the church to be a good employer? The chairperson reminds the board members to ask such questions and not to avoid the hard questions, no matter how heavily supported the proposal might be by some board members or others in the church.

In helping the board manage risk, the chairperson applies both spiritual and emotional intelligence, while exercising a strong sense of responsibility to his or her role as servant of the board. Sometimes it requires considerable boldness to stop proceedings and ask the tough question. The chairperson must be thinking about the implications of all church board actions and the risks inherent in each one. This requires forward thinking, a sense of the current congregation's ethos, and good preparation for each meeting, as well as considerable prayer for God's wisdom and protection.

The initial period of worship that should begin every church board meeting becomes an important opportunity to help the board members recalibrate their minds and hearts to the church's mission so that their deliberations and decisions truly occur with the best interests of the church in full view.

Case Study: Tradition—The Game of Who Remembers and Who Cares?[7]

Ron had served on the board of First Baptist Church for twenty years. Even though he was sixty-seven years old, he still enjoyed the stimulus that the board meetings provided. He loved his church. At this point, the seven

---

7. Although the story in this case study may seem to resemble a real situation, the names, places, and actual circumstances do not describe any actual church, church board, pastor, or chairperson.

other members of the church board were relative newcomers, none serving for more than five years. They all kidded Ron and called him the "old man of the board." He did not mind.

Changes were happening in the church. In the last five years, new growth was occurring because a large housing development was emerging near the church and the township was forecasting up to ten thousand new people would be moving into that area in the next few years. Of course, growth brings change. Ron was excited about this. He had known the lean years of slow growth and even decline and the hardships it brought to the congregation.

The annual board retreat was happening in the next few days and the agenda held promise of vigorous and visionary discussion. Ron was praying that God would guide the new board chairperson to lead the meetings well. He anticipated that his wisdom would help from time to time to keep things in good alignment. One of the proposals was to add a second morning service to cope with the congregational growth.

Twelve years previously, the church had experienced a similar growth spurt. Ron remembered that the board recommended that the church provide a second service. The congregation agreed, but instead of generating more momentum and growth, the opposite occurred. Attendance began dropping and discontent with the congregation swelled. Finally, the board decided to return to the single service format. The crisis passed. As a result of that experience, the board of that day passed a new policy. If God were to bless the church with similar growth in the future, then the board was committed to planting a new congregation rather than starting a second service. Ron remembered that policy motion. He assumed others would know it as well and this agenda raised a bit of concern for him.

It was late Saturday morning and the church board retreat was progressing well. The chairperson felt everybody was working well together and it looked like it would only take about thirty minutes to process the next agenda item—the proposal to initiate a second service. The lead pastor, who had just completed his seventh year of ministry with the church, introduced the proposal, explained why a second service seemed to be the wisest course to follow, and offered solid plans to deal with the certain logistical issues. Several other board members spoke in favor and within ten minutes the board had moved and seconded the recommendation. Ron was not sure what to do. Did a policy motion passed by this church board twelve years ago have any relevance? Should he just ignore this? Ron felt he had a duty to raise the issue and so he spoke up.

The other board members could hardly believe what they were hearing. No one had ever heard of this policy motion before. The board secretary was not even sure whether minutes of those board meetings still survived! The only evidence available at the board retreat was Ron's memory. Soon the rationalizations began. Some thought that a board policy motion made so many years ago was not binding on the present board. Others questioned whether in fact such a policy motion existed and wanted to press ahead. The lead pastor wondered aloud whether Ron was just being obstructionist because he did not agree with a second service.

The retreat host announced that lunch was ready. So the chairperson called a recess and asked the pastor to offer a prayer of thanks for the meal. The chairperson was not at all sure what he was going to suggest as a direction when the board convened after lunch.

What guidance do you think the chairperson might provide to the board at this point?

1. Given that the content of the current motion did not require immediate implementation, the chairperson could recommend that the board table the motion until the secretary and chairperson had opportunity to do some research. They would seek to locate the board minutes from the board meeting twelve years ago and discern whether in fact the board had made such a policy motion. However, because this would be a board policy, the present board would have the authority to change the policy, should they so choose. Now if the board knew that a significant number of people in the congregation would remember this prior situation, then they would be wise to communicate with the congregation their decision and the rationale for the decision at the next congregational meeting to make sure all understood the proposed direction. This would be information for the congregation, not a matter of seeking their approval.

2. This case study indicates why it is important that boards preserve their records, particularly the board minutes. These documents represent the decisions of the board and are the only official voice of the board. It is wise practice for the secretary to gather policy motions together so that the board and its leaders have ready access to previous policy decisions. Excel or other computer programs make this process fairly simple. It is just a matter of discipline to ensure that the secretary does this consistently. Perhaps this situation served as a wakeup call to the chairperson to make sure that the board's records were in good order.

3. How do church board chairpersons (and lead pastors) inform and educate themselves as to actions of the board taken prior to their term as board leader (or lead pastor)? Often a chairperson will be someone

who has served several terms as a board member and will usually remember recent board actions. However, the only way to develop good understanding is to read prior board minutes. It does not take that long. This will also give the chairperson a good idea of what board records exist in the church. If the chairperson discovers deficiencies in the records, then the board can take action to remedy the situation. The chairperson should sign officially adopted board minutes and the secretary should deposit them in a secure place, along with other official board records. Again, given computerization, the board secretary can easily create an electronic file or dropbox where board members can access such records.

Questions for Reflection

a. Are there conflicts within the church board on which you serve? Which of the strategies proposed in this chapter might be useful in leading to some resolution?

b. Diverse cultures deal with conflict differently. Sometimes saving face is more important than reaching a good decision. What are the cultural factors influencing conflict resolution in your church board?

c. Has your board ever assessed a ministry program in your church? What would it take to implement such an assessment process and what benefits would accrue?

Suggested Resources

a. *Exceptional Board Practices. The SOURCE in ACTION.*

b. Edgar Stoesz and Chester Raber, *Doing Good Better: How to be an Effective Church Board Member of a Nonprofit Organization.*

Chapter 10

The Church Board Chairperson and Key Board Operational Issues: External Relations

1. *Congregational Communications—Leadership of the Annual General Meeting (AGM)*

WHO SPEAKS FOR A church board? The board chairperson is the voice of the board. When a chairperson carries out this role well, he or she serves the interests of the church board and the congregation. In cases where the chairperson does not execute this responsibility appropriately, needless suspicion and mistrust arise, leading to significant internal difficulties.

Once a church board has reached a decision by stating and approving a formal motion, the chairperson is empowered to communicate that decision to the appropriate parties as expressing the mind of the board. Other board members may, as appropriate, refer to such decisions in conversation (unless the board has determined that the decision should be confidential for some reason), but should not as a rule seek to speak officially for the board in such matters, unless the board has so authorized. In this limited way, the chairperson represents the board to the congregation and other public groups. However, if the board has not formulated its thinking in a formal motion, the chairperson has no way of knowing what the mind of the board may be on any particular issue, even though the board may have discussed the matter. Without a formal motion, the board has not expressed itself.

The concepts of confidentiality and transparency often create confusion around this principle. Confidentiality refers to the agreement among the board members that all matters discussed within the context of a board meeting remain the business of the board and its members and no one else, until such time as the board expressly decides otherwise. Without such commitment, board members become reluctant to speak candidly to matters on the board's agenda. What board members express during a formal board meeting stays there. The board's code of conduct protects board members and congregational members from being maligned or misrepresented during a board meeting, because that code will define board members' interactions and require that members speak truthfully, respectfully, and with integrity. One of the ways to protect confidentiality is not to name the mover and seconder of motions in board minutes. It is irrelevant who makes a motion, if the board decides to accept it. Once the board adopts the motion, the motion becomes the board's motion. In fact, the proposer of the motion may not favor the motion, but makes the motion in order to bring the board to a point of decision.

Transparency refers to the manner in which the board conducts its business. Approved minutes (unless in camera) are available to the congregation as they may request, agendas are public documents, and board decisions are communicated clearly and in a timely fashion. The board adheres to bylaws and its own policies that guide its operations and decision-making processes—the congregation knows this. It uses policy to identify conflicts of interest and records in its minutes the appropriate action to deal with them. This demonstrates that the board is functioning with deep integrity. The board, through the chairperson, reports openly and honestly to the members at church business meetings, especially at the annual general meeting.

Confidentiality defines how the board works internally, and transparency describes how the board demonstrates to the congregation and others that it is operating with integrity and following all appropriate policies. The board chairperson has significant responsibility to ensure that both confidentiality and transparency are working well for the board and its members.

We should consider two other terms that often are misunderstood. The board may decide that part or all of a meeting will be held *in camera*, i.e., without any nonboard members present. Some nonprofit board consultants argue that an *in camera* session should be scheduled at every board meeting to allow board members to ask questions about sensitive matters. Others suggest that *in camera* sessions will only be necessary when the board is working with sensitive personnel or other matters and requires opportunity for candid discussion and decision-making about a matter that may have legal or other serious implications. The board minutes will record that the board has moved into an *in camera* session. The secretary keeps separate minutes of such sessions in a secure place. The results of such discussions and decisions remain confidential to the board until such time as the board may determine otherwise.

The other term is "executive session." It is helpful for the board at each meeting or every second meeting to have a few minutes where employees are not present to raise issues that may concern board members. These are not fishing expeditions or occasions for gossip. If the board decides that such short sessions would be useful, the chair has a responsibility to communicate decisions made by the board in such a session to the lead pastor in a timely and accurate fashion. An executive session enables board members to ask questions and voice concerns and see whether others among the board members are similarly unclear. Sometimes our Christian politeness makes a church board member hesitate to ask a tough, but significant question in the presence of the lead pastor. In an executive session, that issue can be voiced and then shared with the lead pastor by the chairperson without the board person feeling that he or she will be misunderstood or fearing that an important relationship will be damaged.

In the public domain, sometimes the chairperson will be required to speak in court or in civic contexts as official representative of the congregation and its board. In a nonprofit agency, the board normally appoints the chief employee and/or the board chairperson as the primary communicators for themselves and the congregation. It is important that such communications come through one or two approved people, with board members and congregational members advised to refer questions from external people (reporters, etc.) to these appointed representatives for comments about specific issues or circumstances.

Finally, the chairperson is the board's voice to the lead pastor and all of the other paid staff. When the board desires to communicate officially with the lead pastor or the entire staff, the board chairperson will be the one through whom the board communicates its message. If the issue is minor and affects staff generally, then the board will probably delegate this responsibility to the lead pastor. However, when dealing with major issues, it is advisable for the board chairperson to do this face to face with the staff. This allows the lead pastor to participate in constructive ways in the conversation.

One of the most important contexts where the chairperson gives voice to the board occurs in the annual general meeting (AGM) of the congregation. The church board chairperson oversees preparations for the AGM. As board chairperson, you may or may not chair the AGM, but you must ensure that it is planned well and the members of the local church receive reports that demonstrate the accountability of the board in relation to the church's mission, vision, and values. Such reports will affirm that the congregation meets all legal requirements that your external jurisdiction may have for the governance of nonprofit charities. Of course, scheduling an AGM is not optional for most churches because they are legally registered charities and must by law, at least in Canada, hold an AGM and conduct specific business at that meeting as defined in the bylaws.

What is the key purpose of an AGM? This meeting of the congregational members provides the primary annual occasion for the church board to demonstrate how it has advanced that local church's mission and managed the trust the members have placed in the board with excellence and integrity. It is the board's accountability session with the congregation who has elected them. While various people may report about several different aspects of the church's ministries, including the lead pastor, they do so on behalf of the church board. I realize that most church AGMs are not planned or presented from this perspective, but legally—and also, I would argue, spiritually—this is what should be occurring. This assumes that the lead pastor is responsible to the church board for his leadership and through the board to the congregation. Of course, the lead pastor will be sharing stories of God's work and his perceptions of where the congregation needs to give particular attention, but he should be doing this as part of the church board's presentation to the church—because he is a member of the board. You will probably need to have a conversation with the lead pastor about this to develop good understanding in this matter and ensure that he realizes the board is not seeking to usurp his role or limit his voice.

Since this is the nature of the AGM, the church board and its chairperson need to be involved with the lead pastor in planning the agenda, overseeing the presentations and reports, and making arrangements for the meeting. A first step would be for the chairperson to discuss with the board members their understanding of the purpose of an AGM, and help them appreciate its importance and potential for good. An outcome of this conversation would be a clear statement of the two or three key outcomes that the board desires the AGM to achieve. The second step would be for the chair and the lead pastor to develop a proposal for an effective, vision-focused AGM that delivers the accountability required while also being future-oriented. Once the board has reviewed this proposal and achieved consensus about it, then the chair and lead pastor should be empowered to implement it.

At least four key things normally happen at the AGM:

1. The board, through its chairperson, provides an accurate, honest, transparent account of the state of the mission that the last twelve months of ministry have generated. The church board members are accountable to the congregation that has appointed them and entrusted them to provide spiritual and governance leadership on their

behalf for the mission of the church. The AGM provides the most significant opportunity for the church board to report how they have fulfilled this responsibility, indicating both the positive and, as necessary, the negative.

The AGM is an accountability session. The church board chairperson reports on behalf of the board to the congregation. Normally the church board will also invite the lead pastor to present a report focusing more on the ministry aspect of the congregation's development. It is quite possible that the chair and lead pastor will decide to present a joint report, with each emphasizing different aspects of the board's work. Because this report does represent the church board's governance, it is important that the board members have opportunity to review the report prior to its circulation so that they support its contents.

The report should be available in printed format (as well as in electronic format) to members of the congregation in advance of the AGM. It is a public document and so the board should write it with that in view, i.e., that all in the congregation and those outside the congregation (government officials) will have access to it. It is helpful to put this report close to the beginning of the meeting because everything else in the agenda will build upon this report.

Normally linked to this report will be the treasurer's report regarding the state of the congregation's finances. Consider including a paragraph or two that explains what the different figures and categories mean, i.e., what are the two or three key indicators that reveal the true financial state of the congregation. Putting this in print will take a lot of the mystery out of the process and educate the congregation in these matters. Remember that the financial document is just another way to express the missional focuses and priorities of the congregation.

The board should make every effort to provide a financial statement prepared by a credible external agency. Preferably the people involved should not have direct connection with the church and have financial expertise and can make some expert pronouncement regarding the report's validity. Though dollars might be scarce, scrimping on this part of the report may prove to be a serious mistake. People generally link financial credibility with other kinds of credibility. You should ensure that the report affirms that the board has completed in a timely way all required financial reporting to the government for purposes of retaining charity status. Also, the board's report should indicate how many members/partners are formally part of the society, and which members the board has removed or who have voluntarily resigned. It is important to keep the membership current because this number will affect things such as quorum requirements.

2. Elect key officers and church board members. The members of the congregation normally appoint the Nominating Committee and so it reports directly to them. While the church board oversees its work and one or two board members may be part of it, it does not report to the church board but operates at arm's length. It will need some time in the agenda to present its report regarding recommendations for new board members,[1] plus any other official positions that the church bylaws require the congregation to elect directly. The committee's report should be included in the materials sent to all members two weeks prior to the AGM. If the bylaws allow for nominations from the floor, then the chairperson should manage the logistics for this (i.e., ballots, pencils, etc.). The chair of the meeting will need to appoint scrutineers to secure the ballots and count the votes on behalf of the congregation. Once the scrutineers have counted the ballots and reported the results, there should be a motion to destroy the ballots. When the chair of the meeting announces the results, this presents a good opportunity to publicly thank those who have served and contributed their time and expertise to the congregation's mission, as well as to pray for the new board members and officers.

3. Review and approve changes to foundational documents (i.e., bylaws, church policies, etc.). It is always a challenge to keep core documents up to date. However, working with unrevised and inaccurate bylaws and policies creates confusion, inhibits the ability of new and current board members to carry out their responsibilities, and can lead to a manipulation of processes because no one knows what the appropriate processes are. Preparing for the AGM provides an annual opportunity for the church board to review these matters and develop any recommendations for change. Every five years there should be a major review of these documents—institutions change more quickly than we realize.

4. Review and approve key plans for the coming year, explaining how these plans fit the vision and will advance the mission. Consider integrating a report regarding mission-directed plans for the coming year along with the presentation of the proposed budget. If you lay before people a set of numbers devoid of context, then it will be confusing and for most an exercise in frustration because they will not understand

---

1. The Nominating Committee's report may also include a recommendation for the appointment of the board chair. This will be necessary if the congregation is required in the bylaws to appoint someone to this office.

the rationale behind the numbers. However, if you lead with a summary of four or five key ministry initiatives that the church board (and the ministry staff) believes the vision requires for the coming year and tie these then to the proposed budget, the budget becomes a planning tool, a way to express anticipated, missional gains. When people link numbers to mission and vision, they become motivated.

Give yourself enough time to enable the church board to prepare well for the AGM. It would be wise to introduce some discussion about the AGM into the board's agenda at least two months prior to its date. Remember that you need to have materials out to the congregation, at least in the Canadian context, about two weeks prior to the actual meeting. So if your church board meets monthly, this allows six weeks for preparations to be made. This also enables you to work with the lead pastor to draft the board's report and seek the board's input prior to the AGM.

If possible, provide some children's care so that parents of younger families can attend. Encourage people to see this as an opportunity to celebrate, praise God, and pray together for his continued guidance and help in this mission. While the members have to do some business at the AGM, it is all related to mission fulfillment. You can emphasize this spiritual framework by asking the worship coordinator to introduce the meeting with praise and prayers of thanksgiving.

Finally, you might consider asking the board to appoint someone, other than the board chairperson, to chair the AGM. If you as board chairperson are giving reports and perhaps making motions, it will be awkward to do that and simultaneously chair the AGM.

2. *Working with the Other Major Ministry Team—The Paid and Volunteer Staff Leadership*

The three major decision-making groups within an Evangelical congregation would be the congregation, the pastoral ministry team, and the board ministry team. The decisions allotted to each will vary from denomination to denomination and church to church, and the congregation's bylaws normally will identify their respective jurisdictions. The board needs to manage well their interrelationship and interdependence if the health of the congregation is to flourish.

In my view, the primary responsibility for ensuring that these relationships are working well lies with the church board. The congregation gives to this spiritual leadership group in the church the mandate to guard and advance its mission. Designing and maintaining a good, productive relationship with the pastoral ministry team is a crucial element in achieving this congregational mandate. When the relationship between the church board and the ministry staff becomes dysfunctional, the congregation's health and welfare suffers. In congregationally led churches, the church board has the responsibility to support and assist the lead pastor to accomplish his role. The lead pastor in turn has the responsibility to work closely and collaboratively with the church board, helping it accomplish its mandate. It is not a question of one dominating the other, but rather both should respect the role that the congregation has entrusted to each, as well as their respective lines of accountability.

Much of the leadership exercised by a church board chairperson involves helping the board manage its relationship with the pastoral ministry team well. In order to do this productively, a board chairperson has to have a good working relationship with the lead pastor. We have already discussed many of the dynamics that contribute to a healthy relationship in chapter 4.

A second component is managing the communication between these two primary ministry teams. How does the church board receive proposals from the pastoral ministry team? How does the pastoral ministry team discern the concerns and learn about the decisions made by the church board? While we might conceive of a situation where too much communication is occurring, in most cases these groups suffer from a lack of clear and consistent communication. For example, does the pastoral ministry team receive copies of church board minutes? After all, these are not secret documents, but should be accessible to any congregational member. If there are confidential matters that board members are discussing, these can be handled through an *in camera* session. Similarly, does the lead pastor include in his reports to the board information about the key things that the pastoral ministry team is discussing? Do the two ministry teams ever meet together to discuss the congregational mission, to pray together, to celebrate God's provision? If you let these two ministry teams operate as independent silos, at some point things will break down. The lead pastor and the church board chair are responsible to ensure that this two-way communication process is working well.

Third, has the board clearly defined the roles of these two ministry leadership teams, and do the members of both ministry teams understand these respective mandates? As chairperson, you guard the mandate of the church board, particularly as you work with the lead pastor to develop the agendas for board meetings. Two of the questions you will need to be asking continually are: Why is this item on the board's agenda? Is it within the board's mandate? In smaller congregations where the church board will be a working board, the agenda will have to include both policy issues as well as management issues, but they can and should be distinguished in the agenda. In larger congregations where the pastoral ministry staff is more developed, the board's agenda should focus primarily on policy issues, protecting resources, managing risk, strategic planning, and evaluation. Exceptions will occur. Maintaining the discipline of the agenda is an important step in managing the relationship between the board ministry team and the pastoral ministry team. The church board governs and the ministry team manages.

Fourth, you know that some decisions will require more careful attention. Matters dealing with resource allocation, performance evaluations of personnel, salaries and benefits compensation, strategic direction—all of these possess potential to create harmful divisions and crippling misunderstandings. Some boards have operational traditions about some of these matters that generate constant turmoil. For example, how much expenditure can the lead pastor authorize without seeking direct board approval? Does your board have a policy about this that gives the board comfort and authorizes the lead pastor to act responsibly, without constant reference to the board? If the funds are already in the budget and authorized, the lead pastor should have authority to spend it. If it requires some transfer of funds between budget items, then set a reasonable limit and still require a balanced budget. If it is an expenditure for something not in the budget, then that probably will require a church board decision and perhaps ultimately a congregational decision to change the approved budget if the amount is significant.

Fifth, use discussion briefs and decision profiles as the preferred means by which the pastoral ministry team communicates its issues to the board. Some will resist this requirement, but in the end, it prevents considerable misunderstanding, enables the decision to be made more quickly and with greater confidence, and develops respect between church board members and pastoral staff. It is a discipline well worth cultivating.

3. Evaluation and Accountability

For most church boards, the spiritual ethos of the congregation, personal friendships among the members and pastoral staff, and the feeling that the "fruit of the Spirit" does not include assessment, all conspire to make evaluation and accountability some of the most challenging aspects of a church board chairperson's leadership. Yet, if a church board avoids this responsibility, it has little hope of discerning whether by its work it is advancing the mission. Three entities benefit from consistent (i.e., annual) assessment—the board, the lead pastor, and key ministry programs in the congregation.

The keys to healthy and beneficial assessment include 1) a well-defined process that is fair; 2) consistent application of the assessment process; and 3) appropriate use of the results to celebrate and commend, as well as to discern and implement helpful change. If your process is haphazard and not documented, then the group, individuals, or programs involved will become suspicious of the motives and usefulness of the evaluation. Be very clear about who does the evaluation, who sees the results, and what the board will do with the results. In the case of staff, it is the lead pastor or executive pastor who should oversee employee evaluations. Connect every evaluation to the congregation's mission. How is this group, person, or program working to advance that mission? Has the board or lead pastor defined this linkage clearly? The people responsible should have some statement that defines how the twelve-month goals defining their work or program aligns with the congregation's mission. Evaluation should focus on progress made toward achieving those goals.

Communicate the results in person, allow for the individual(s) being assessed to respond and offer corrections, and have the person or group sign off on the final report. This indicates they have read it, have had opportunity to interact with it, and, while they may not agree with everything it says, have respected the process. Place a copy of the performance review in their personal file, or if it is a program review, in the office congregational files. In the case of the church board evaluation, the board should include its key findings in the board minutes for future reference.

Using the results is equally important. A good assessment requires a significant investment of prayer, time, and thoughtful reflection, so failure to use the results (either by the board, the lead pastor, or the employee) is poor stewardship of resources. Further, it is rather discouraging for an employee to spend time and effort preparing a good self-evaluation only to have it disregarded. Next time the request comes, it will be hard to motivate the employee to take the process seriously. Sometimes employees for whatever reason fail to give attention to the results of the evaluation. One way to ensure that the results are used would be to require the next annual ministry plan developed for that position to include responses to specific recommendations, e.g., plans for professional development, reworking of parts of the program, development and implementation of new processes to correct weak areas, etc. When people see that the board takes assessment seriously, that it is an important spiritual exercise, and that it is personally and vocationally beneficial, they generally will respond positively to it. The more normal such processes become, the less intimidating or threatening they will be. If a board or lead pastor initiates an assessment only with a view to staff dismissal, then it will not go well. It may be prudent to link the expenditure of budgeted professional development funds for ministry staff directly to areas for professional growth identified in the performance evaluation.

As chairperson, you can encourage the board to implement an annual cycle of board assessment. Such activity builds into the board members a desire to improve their work together for the good of the church. You can schedule such assessments during board meetings. Alternatively, an in-depth formal survey done electronically every few years would generate more significant results. Appendix G contains an example. Whatever direction you choose, try to relate the assessment to any written statement the board has developed which defines their key responsibilities. An assessment should give some indication, at least from the view of board members, about how well they are fulfilling their responsibilities. The results of such assessments should give some direction for the board's development in the following year. Building an assessment process into the schedule of the annual church board retreat generally works well.

4. *Caring for the Employees*

Managing a church board's relationship with the congregation's employees well needs to be high on the list of a chairperson's priorities. From various vantage points, the ministry staff represents the most significant investment and resource that the congregation possesses. Apart from facility costs, staff salaries normally form the largest segment of the church budget and good stewardship requires careful oversight of it.

We easily forget that church employees get demoralized and upset, like any other employees, when they perceive the church to be treating them unfairly or the board to be disregarding their proposals for ministry advancement. Unhappy ministry staff usually results at some point in unsettled congregants. People talk.

Five aspects of employee care require the chairperson's ongoing interest.

> a. *Hiring and releasing staff.* Churches are always hiring and releasing staff. The turnover rate can be quite dizzying at times. In larger churches, significant staff turnover occurs every year. It is important then for a church board to oversee this aspect of congregational life well. It often has a public dimension and people evaluate the way the board handles such matters.
>
> What aspects of this can the board handle by good policy? One issue that boards wrestle with constantly is who has authority to do the hiring and releasing and whether the congregation needs

to give its assent in every case. Work with the board members to develop a grid that indicates who has authority to hire and release people for which positions. Does the lead pastor have authority to hire the worship director without consulting the board? Does the congregation need to approve the hiring and appointment of a worship leader? One method of categorization is to require all pastoral positions to be appointed by the congregation; all director positions to be appointed by the board; and all assistant staff positions to be appointed by the lead pastor. Of course, this does not address how to give appropriate groups voice in the process.

If this categorization is an appropriate way to oversee the hiring process, then perhaps also the same groups have the authority to release the employee. However, remember that releasing a person is always more difficult than hiring. If the congregation has to approve the release of all pastoral staff, then the board will need to bring such recommendations to the congregation with great care.

In any case, the board must retain the authority to approve all new positions and the position descriptions and should require the lead pastor to inform it of any major changes in position responsibilities for all employees. New positions usually require budget adjustments and this normally means a congregational decision is necessary before the board authorizes the lead pastor to advertise and fill the position.

A word of caution might be appropriate here. If the board authorizes the lead pastor both to hire and release some categories of employees, then make sure the board has defined for the lead pastor through the employment policy the process that has to be followed, particularly when releasing employees. Although the board may delegate this to the lead pastor, it cannot absolve itself of its overall responsibility in such matters.

b. *Employment policies.* When a church board has only one or two employees, the board members can deal with most employment issues as they arise. However, boards need to be thinking forward and so even though there is only the lead pastor and part-time secretary, it is time to begin putting in place employment policies relating to vacation, overtime, compensation for mileage, sick leave, benefits, professional development, jury duty, computer/internet usage, etc. In most cases, you can borrow materials already developed by other larger churches in your denomination and then adjust them to your particular circumstances. Keep the documentation primarily in digital format so that it can be easily updated and edited.

All employees, as a condition of employment, should be required to sign a code of conduct, a statement that says they support the mission of the church, and a statement that says they have read the employment policies and are in agreement with them. It is wise to include such information in the position description as conditions of employment. It should go without saying that every employee should have an up-to-date position description and a letter of appointment that details the terms of employment, the nature of accountability (including salary and benefits), and whether or not the position is a term position or a permanent position. It is always wise to stipulate a three- or six-month initial probation period with evaluation, at which time a decision will be made as to whether to continue the employment or not. Make sure these policies mandate annual performance evaluations. Also, be clear about which positions require the person to be a member of the congregation.

c. *Compensation.* Although it is impossible in small churches to keep the salary of the lead pastor confidential because that salary is the one that shows in the budget approved by the congregation, the church board and not the congregation should establish the compensation. The principle of fairness is very important in discerning the compensation level. One of the best ways to establish this is to contact your regional denominational office and get their advice. They will have a very good sense of what lead pastors in churches similar to yours are receiving as compensation.

To prevent this subject from becoming an annual debate within the board try to help the board define several basic principles that will guide their determination of annual compensation adjustments. For example, the board can develop an annual salary grid increment that it applies to compensation for each year of employment. Decide how the annual salary should recognize cost-of-living increases that happen in society generally. Also, give some consideration to initiative taken to improve vocational competence, i.e., additional degree earned, etc.

d. *Professional development.* Remember that the pastoral staff forms a key resource essential to the health of the congregation. Investing in their development makes good sense, because it should in most cases result in improved service and better performance within the congregation. It is important then to build into the annual budget some amount to support employee development. For example, if the lead pastor desires to attend a conference or take a course that he believes will help him develop a better competence in a critical area of pastoral leadership and if it is out of town and lasts for several days, the costs will easily exceed a thousand dollars, including transportation, accommodation, registration fees, meals, etc. So be realistic. Putting two hundred dollars in the budget for pastoral development, while it might be a small step forward, will not get the job done. If board members fear that the money will not be used wisely, then build in some process whereby the lead pastor develops a proposal that defines clearly the benefits to the congregation and its mission, for the board to review and approve.

e. Cultivating new church board members. One of the more challenging aspects of a chairperson's leadership is recruiting new board members. While the chairperson does not carry this responsibility alone, he/she has to be concerned about this question. The board's ability to accomplish its work depends to a significant degree on discerning qualified and competent board members. Also, the confidence of the congregation in the board's leadership hinges upon the quality of the spiritual leadership within the board.

In most churches that possess a congregational polity, the nominating committee manages this process on behalf of the congregation. Some think that for the church board or the chairperson to suggest names to the nominating committee is manipulative and somehow subverts the intended process. Indeed, the board and chairperson can abuse the system, but this should not be the case. The perspective rather is that the chairperson and the board know what qualities, gifts, experience, and spiritual maturity are required for a person to function well as a board member. Being proactive and talking informally as chairperson with one or two people that you consider good candidates in order to encourage their consideration of serving in this way represents, in my view, good, forward thinking. Making suggestions to the nominating committee is still within the prerogative of the chairperson who is a member of the congregation. The renewing of the board based on the best leadership available requires a chairperson's attention.

Case Study: Who's in Charge?
Negotiating the Sudden Inspiration.[2]

As chairperson, you thought the church board meeting was going quite well. The basic items on the agenda received good interaction and the board made reasonable decisions. There were two items left. One was a discussion about the agenda for the AGM that would occur in four weeks. The other was an item that Tom, the board vice-chairperson, requested for the agenda at the beginning of the meeting. He had called it "new ministry opportunity." You were curious as to what Tom had in mind, but you had worked together for a number of years on the board and so you did not really give it a second thought.

So after the board had settled matters related to the AGM's agenda, you turned to Tom and gave him the floor. About two minutes into his presentation you realized that Tom was about to present to the board for immediate decision a major issue. Tom was friends with the owner of a Christian preschool that offered it services in rented quarters two blocks from the church. However, the owner of that facility wanted to evict the Christian preschool. The preschool owner contacted Tom and pressed him to bring to the church board a plan for the Christian preschool to rent part of the church facility. Time was of the essence because the preschool operation had to vacate in less than ten days by the time the church board met. Tom urged the board members to approve his motion to rent part of the church facility to the preschool operation.

One of Tom's more persuasive arguments was that the income from the Christian preschool would provide much needed funding for upgrades to the building facility. They needed to replace the roof and this would cost almost $75,000. The congregation already was 15 percent behind in its giving toward the budget and had no reserves. Tom stated that "this was God's provision" for their need. It would be a good ministry and help the congregation connect with the community. According to Tom, very little change to the facility would be needed to allow this to go forward and he was willing to donate time to get the changes done.

You raised several questions about liability, whether or not this ministry was in alignment with the mission and vision, and what implications this would have for other ministry uses of the facility. However, Tom seemed to have an answer to every objection and when he called for the question, the board supported his motion six to three. Throughout most of

---

2. Although the story in this case study may seem to resemble a real situation, the names, places, and actual circumstances do not describe any actual church, church board, pastor, or chairperson.

the discussion, the lead pastor said very little, but in the end did vote to support the motion. The board authorized Tom to confirm the arrangements with the Christian preschool.

As the meeting concluded, the various board members gathered around Tom and thanked him for his proactive proposal. They seemed encouraged that the congregation might finally receive some financial help toward the facility repairs. You were not so sure.

Two days later Tom emailed you a note that he had finalized the arrangements with the Christian preschool supervisor and had a signed, written understanding.

That Saturday you were browsing through the local paper when your eye caught the words "preschool being sued. . . " As you read through the first paragraph you realized that the article was about the Christian preschool that now had a written agreement to use your church facilities. Two of its teachers were being accused of child abuse.

What options did this chairperson have in handling this situation?

1. One issue this case study raises concerns the addition of items to the agenda. On the one hand, it is important for board members to know they have the privilege of shaping the agenda. On the other hand, board members also need to add items in a responsible manner. Just because a board member wants to add an item to the agenda should not determine how the board decides to handle the item. These are two separate items. The board members should feel no obligation to act upon an item just because another board member has asked that board to add it to the agenda. Similarly, the chairperson should exercise appropriate leadership on behalf of the board and ensure that the board is following normal operational procedures. In this case, the chairperson would appropriately recommend to the board that it ensure it has all of the necessary information in hand before it arrives at a decision, lest it incur unwise risk. If time was of the essence, then the board could agree to meet in a week to review and ratify a proposed agreement.

2. A second issue relates to policy that guides the manner in which the church board will enter into a formal, legal relationship with another agency. Such a policy, for example, might stipulate that all such agreements receive a legal review, be limited in term, and define the basis upon which the agreement becomes void. It probably should also require the church treasurer to evaluate the proposal and assure the board that the projected financial projections do indeed represent reality. The agreement should also stipulate what employee within the church is responsible to give oversight to this arrangement. Will

this responsibility fall under the lead pastor's position description, the facility manager's, or the board chairperson's? As churches grow, the potential for these types of interagency relationships will become more frequent. This is a matter of risk management that the board has to exercise judiciously.

3. Tom seemed to make some general arguments that establishing this relationship would contribute in some ways to the advancement of the congregation's mission. However, did he make the case that this was a strategic move? Church boards receive many different proposals for ministries and many different opportunities to engage in various enterprises, but in every case the board members must determine whether any of these truly are strategic for mission advancement. Often these proposals include some good things, but they are not strategic for advancing the mission of this congregation. The board should now be focused on the two or three key things in the current situation that are strategic for advancing the mission intentionally and consistently. Tom's proposal probably did not meet this criterion.

4. As chairperson, you should never allow someone in the congregation, not even the lead pastor or another board member, to sign an agreement on behalf of the board without the board first seeing, reviewing, and officially approving it. The board cannot shift its liability in such matters to the person who signed the contract. The board is responsible for all legal agreements made by the agency it is leading.

5. What can you do as board chairperson to limit the potential damage to the church that might arise because of these impending legal issues with the preschool? I think one of the first things I would do is talk to the preschool CEO and determine as clearly as possible what the situation is. Then I would call an emergency board meeting to inform the board members and seek their counsel. One of the things I would recommend is that the board seek legal advice regarding the suspension or annulment of the agreement. If the press hear that this preschool is about to occupy your facility, undoubtedly an enterprising reporter will be seeking comment. Ensure that the board, staff, and church members do not to talk to the media, but refer such requests for comment to the board chair or the lead pastor. Limit the number of voices speaking to the media about this.

Questions for Reflection

a. In what ways and how frequently are you, as chairperson, communicating with the congregation about the work and decisions of the church board? What might you do to improve communications and build greater trust?

b. Does your church board ever use *in camera* sessions? For what purpose? How do you communicate the results with the lead pastor?

c. Review your preparations for the last AGM. What might you do differently in planning for the next one to enhance the accountability of the church board?

Suggested Resources

a. Hugo Heclo, *On Thinking Institutionally.*

Chapter 11

Church Board Chairpersons, Legal Issues, and Finances

I AM NEITHER A lawyer nor an accountant, so please do not construe the contents of this chapter to be, in any way, legal or financial advice. For that kind of specific advice, you must consult with a lawyer or a certified accountant. In this chapter I consider some of the principles that church board chairpersons can use to help their boards and themselves avoid harmful mistakes that have potential to destroy the life of a congregation. Both legal and financial issues have potential to initiate external interventions in which the board and you as chairperson would undoubtedly be involved.

As followers of Jesus, we are taught to trust other believers and we do not want to operate with an attitude of suspicion. However, the congregation owns its resources and assets, and the board and its chairperson are accountable to the congregation for the protection and responsible use of all its resources and assets. There is a trust in the word "trustee" that requires constant vigilance.

In the last five years, I am aware of church boards that have made poor decisions resulting in wrongful dismissal lawsuits, Canada Revenue Agency audits, bankruptcy, and loss of property assets. These things do happen, but church boards can avoid serious mistakes by exercising common sense, due diligence, and following good process. For example, if someone is trying to influence you as board chairperson to persuade the board to invest some congregational funds with promises of unusual returns—run the other way! It is too good to be true. If an employee seriously has contravened the code of conduct and dismissal becomes necessary, do it properly and as graciously as possible. Make sure the facts clearly demonstrate that the infraction has occurred. Document things as much as possible. Respect privacy of information guidelines. Be generous, even though you may be upset and saddened at the turn of events. The reputation of the congregation and its witness in the community is more important than inappropriate acts of retribution.

Legal Issues

Employee and member relations provide the most fertile ground for legal problems. For example, most congregations have bylaws that say something about removing people from membership in the society. However, when you read them closely, you will discover that any description of clear process is absent. Someone, and usually it is the church board, has to figure how to get from point A (i.e., the action that the member allegedly has committed) to point B (i.e., the actual motion to dismiss from membership, in a way that preserves the dignity of the individual under discussion and preserves the congregation's safety and reputation). Things can get messy very quickly.

The first thing I would suggest is that you figure out your process. The more of this you can define in policy before the board faces these issues, the better the board will be able to provide good leadership to the congregation when such events happen. Use a case study to challenge the board to think through good process for dismissing people from membership. Spend part of a board meeting discussing various scenarios and responses that the board might develop. Try to define with some clarity what actions will constitute grounds for recommending removal from membership. What biblical principles and values should inform this process? Are there any external legal issues that must be considered, i.e., human rights principles, etc.? What stages of restoration could the board engage before dismissal became necessary? Who takes the lead in these various stages? When does the church board officially get involved? Does the congregation have to vote on a motion to dismiss an individual from membership or is this something the board has authority to do? What reporting does the board give to the congregation when the board makes such a decision? If the congregation has to vote on such a recommendation, what information would be shared and under what circumstances? Once the board has defined a process, at least in draft form, discuss it with the congregation, and if possible, have them approve it. When informing prospective members, make sure the pastors or board members involved cover this part of member care. A prospective member's signature on the application for membership indicates their knowledge of and agreement with these standards and processes.

While the board cannot prepare for every eventuality, it can prepare for those events which most commonly occur within congregations and for which good process is essential.

Secondly, follow your process as closely as possible. If the matter becomes litigious, then it is my understanding that the questions will be: Did the board have a process? Is the process reasonable and fair? Was the membership aware of the principles and process? Did the individual concerned know the principles and process? Did the board follow the process? If a case of employee dismissal becomes contested the authorities will want to know the answers to specific questions. What process for dismissal does the employer define in the employment manual, and did the person or body authorized to make the decision follow the process carefully? In the case where employees do not seem to be productive and the church dismisses them, were the employees told about the problem? Did the supervisors outline actions to help the employees become productive, with clear measurements that would demonstrate acceptable levels of productivity? Did the supervisors establish a timeframe within which productivity had to improve before they would initiate further action? Have the supervisors explained to the employees these steps in advance? Did they document this in writing?

Sometimes financial exigency arises within a congregation because of an external crisis or some other "black swan"[1] event. The congregation does not have the resources to meet its current obligations. One response is to reduce costs by reducing the number of employees. Such events are unfortunate experiences for a congregation and the board's approach will either generate confidence in the board or erode the very fabric of that faith community. Again, process becomes critical. In these instances, there are regional labor laws that require compliance. Meeting the legal requirements will often fall short of ethical expectations held by people in the congregation. Effective boardmanship balances the financial constraints facing the congregation with fairness toward the employee(s) so that the board preserves the Christian reputation of the congregation. The legal requirement, for instance, may require an employer to provide two weeks of severance pay for every year of employment or notice equivalent to that amount of time. If the employee has worked for the congregation for ten years, this may obligate the church to pay twenty weeks of severance or give twenty weeks of notice, or some negotiated compromise. If the board acts fairly and even generously, it may not mitigate all of the hurt and pain, but it will go a long ways toward ameliorating some of it. As well, it gives the board a chance to lead the congregation forward.

Once the pain and difficulty have passed (perhaps six months later), you should then do a third thing—give the board members an opportunity to reflect upon the experience. What wisdom have they gained? What changes would they suggest to the process? What would they have done differently and why? In light of this discussion, revise the process and capture what the board members have learned. If the situation allows, you may even

---

1. Nassim, *Black Swan*. See chapter 12 for a discussion of "black swan events."

want to ask the released employees what the board might have done to make the process work better from their perspective.

Another action the board can take is to develop a relationship with local legal counsel so that they can access their advice as needed. The board can use this legal counsel to review bylaw changes or vet significant contracts (e.g., property transactions). The board should establish such a relationship through a formal motion. If a member of the congregation is an accredited lawyer whose area of expertise matches the needs of the congregation, there is nothing preventing the board from using that person as legal counsel. However, if the person becomes a board member, then it would be wise to secure different legal counsel to avoid potential conflict of interest. Within the Canadian context, the Canadian Council of Christian Charities provides excellent advice and resources relating to matters of taxation exemptions, employee relations, and use of funds. Although your particular congregation may not be a member, your denomination may be and can enable you to access those resources.

In the matter of contracts, clear policy can assist here. First, consider what contracts the administration can engage on behalf of the congregation. One guideline will be financial, i.e., contracts whose value is below a set figure. There might also be a requirement to get competitive bids before accepting a contract. For example, most church boards require the administration to purchase certain kinds of insurance annually to reduce risk to the congregation. The board may require by policy that every two years staff must seek several competing bids in order to demonstrate that the cost is competitive. Second, if the board has to approve a contract, then make sure there is a motion in the minutes authorizing this. As chairperson, you can only sign a contract on behalf of the board with appropriate authorization. It is also wise to include in the motion some of the key details regarding the contract's contents.

Another important matter is securing liability insurance for the board members, officers, and employees. Your congregation probably already has this in place. If not, then this should be one of the first actions as chairperson that you help the board to take. Without this in place, the board is jeopardizing the financial integrity of board members, employees, and congregational members. With activities such as short-term mission trips and youth retreats, and with safety issues in the facility, transportation issues, and risks associated with pastoral counseling, a board is extremely unwise not to invest in this kind of insurance. It is too late after the event.

Let me comment on two specific issues. First, congregations view ministry among children and under-age youth as an important part of their mission. The laws regarding child abuse have changed substantially in the last decade and requirements for agencies providing services to children have become much more stringent. Today criminal record checks for all staff and volunteers working with children are a common requirement before an agency permits them to work with any children. You cannot afford to allow any exceptions. If an incident occurs and your congregational leaders have not only required this but also implemented it consistently, it will help you avoid major problems. In the case of employees, you should build into the hiring process the requirement that a prospective employee provide a criminal record check before any hiring decision is complete.

The second worry point will be the danger of harassment within the staff. This is not limited to sexual harassment, but includes physical and emotional harassment as well. Supervisors are in positions of power and abusing that power to coerce staff to do certain things is harassment. The employment manual should have a section that defines harassment, warns all employees that the board does not tolerate it, and describes appropriate, safe procedures employees can follow if harassment occurs on the job. In many cases, the board will not have to write such policy from scratch, but can locate well-expressed and well-designed harassment policies that other congregations have developed and implemented. Most policies require that a harassment officer be appointed to whom employees can take their concerns. The board should require by policy that the harassment officer will present an annual report to the board that documents compliance with the policy and, if the officer has received complaints, assurance that the officer has dealt with them according to approved procedures.

Finances

As chairperson, you should be able to read and analyze a financial statement and determine what it says about the financial health of the congregation.[2] There are two aspects to this. One is the performance of the annual budget, the other is the year-over-year financial stability of the agency.

In the case of the annual budget and its progression, your treasurer should be reporting not only how things are going month-by-month, or quarter-by-quarter, but showing two ratios. One is the percentage of the twelve-month budget projection spent in each line. This allows you to see at a glance which elements in the budget projection are over budget or under budget. Allow for the fact that some large expenditures only occur at specific times in the year, e.g., insurance premiums. A way to overcome this problem is to have the treasurer prorate such annual expenditures on

---

2. *Guide to Financial Statements.*

a monthly basis. This can prevent unpleasant surprises. The second ratio is a year-to-date comparison with the previous one—or better, two—years. This information helps you to gauge whether the current budget projection and statement are out-of-balance or behaving normally. These same ratios should be applied to the income side of the ledger as well. You need to be tracking both expenses and income.

When you review the financial statements, you want to perceive where the financial risks may be. It would be good to ask the treasurer to attach to the quarterly financial report a brief one-page statement that identifies areas to celebrate and areas of potential risk for the information of the board. Are the bills being paid on time, i.e., are the liabilities expanding or contracting? Is the lead pastor or treasurer ensuring that employees receive salaries and benefits regularly? Is income keeping pace with expenditures?

At the end of the fiscal year, the financial report should indicate whether the financial health of the agency has improved or decreased over the past twelve months and what key factors contributed to this change. If the financial situation has worsened, what adjustments is the board recommending to the congregation? A series of cumulative deficits will sap the ability of the congregation to fulfill its mission. If the board has to dip into reserves to balance the budget several years in a row, then this is a signal that the congregation is encountering serious financial risk. The sooner the board can take action to alleviate the deficit situation, the better it will be for the congregation.[3]

Another important tool to manage financial risk is a three-year budget projection. Once you have prepared your annual budget projection, have the treasurer plug in some numbers, e.g., 3 percent annual increase in expenses across the board, impact of projected new employee salaries, projected facility maintenance costs, etc. This kind of projection helps the board to gauge what new income will be required to resource the growing ministry activities of the congregation. If expenses begin to outstrip projected income, then the board has time to consider strategies to deal with this risk. Also, do the same on the income side of the ledger. Does the congregation have the growth potential to manage progressive budget increases?

A contentious issue is whether a congregational budget should include contingency—after all, this is a faith-based agency and God will provide. However, it is prudent for the board to establish a contingency fund

---

3. This is, in effect, one aspect of risk management. In seeking solutions, the board may form an ad hoc committee to examine the situation and bring forward recommendations that the board might consider in order to deal with the deficit. This committee, though chaired by a member of the board, could certainly include members from the congregation who are not part of the board but have appropriate expertise.

equivalent to two or three months of operating expenses. In other words, if income suddenly fell drastically, how much time does the board have to plan and implement a response? These are tough dollars to segregate, but the board can contribute to such a fund during financially robust times or when the congregation receives unexpected funds. The board can recommend that the congregation place part or all of year-end surpluses in the contingency fund. Whether this fund can also double as a replacement reserve for the facility will be a discussion the board will have to have.

The board has a responsibility to ensure that the church is conducting its internal financial matters with absolute integrity. It is rare that embezzlement or fraud occurs within a church office, but it can happen. More importantly, donors want to know that the board is managing the funds they are giving scrupulously. Recently the Canada Revenue Agency has also been giving more attention to the way in which charities are managing and spending their funds.

Some simple procedures should be in place to avoid any problems and protect the staff and volunteers who manage the funds from false allegations. First, always ensure that at least two people, approved by the congregation, board, or head teller are involved in counting and depositing all offerings. Second, one staff person should track the reception of funds and another staff member should make the deposit of those funds. Third, the treasurer should affirm that every expense has necessary documentation and approval. Fourth, two signatures of approved signing officers must be on every check issued by the agency. Fifth, one employee should be in charge of the petty cash fund and responsible for its accounting on a monthly basis. Sixth, employees should provide receipts to support all requests for reimbursement of costs. Seventh, once a budget line has been spent, additional expenditures will require special authorization.

The board may also want to state clearly whom it holds accountable for managing the budget. Is it the lead pastor, the executive pastor, the treasurer, or some other administrator? Defining this will help to adjudicate conflicts regarding budget expenditures.

It is the board's responsibility to maintain the agency's financial integrity. Normally it manages this responsibility through a standing committee (often named the finance and audit committee). A board member with financial expertise should chair the committee and be assisted by the church treasurer and one or two others from the congregation. It is this committee that recommends to the board the firm or person who will do the annual audit or financial review. They meet with the auditor/financial reviewer to receive the report and review any recommendations for improving financial management. The committee then recommends the auditor/financial reviewer's report to the board and any action that the board should take in response to the recommendations given in the report. Once the board approves the report, it authorizes the treasurer or financial officer to sign it on behalf of the board. The board presents this report to the Annual General Meeting as part of its accountability to the congregation.

Lack of discipline in financial matters will undermine the board's credibility. If the board is not giving due attention to these matters, then as chairperson you have a responsibility to draw it to their attention and urge, indeed to require, greater compliance. An initial step might be to educate the board about some of these responsibilities so they have clarity. Perhaps your denominational office would be able to recommend someone who could brief your board on these matters.

Overseeing the investment of church funds is an important part of the portfolio of responsibilities given to the board's finance and audit committee. What congregation has investments? Many do because people have donated estate income, or the congregation has built up surplus funds over the years, or the congregation is accumulating funds for a major project and the board decides to invest the funds for the short term. I would suspect that most churches have some funds invested. As part of the quarterly financial statements, the treasurer should be reporting to the board how the investment portfolio has been performing.

A key part of the finance and audit committee's work will be the development of an Investment of Funds Policy that can guide the board in its decisions regarding such investments. These are common policies and so the committee would be able to locate samples and, with some revision, present a recommendation to the board. Essentially the policy will define what kind of investment instruments the finance and audit committee can use. Part of the regular reporting from this committee to the board will be a description of all investments and their type so that the board members can discern whether or not the stipulations of the Investment of Funds Policy are being met.

Spiritual leaders have different views as to whether or not congregations should borrow funds externally or internally. If your congregation agrees that some debt for some reasons will be appropriate, then it is vital that the board make sure that it is managing the debt in full compliance with its terms. If it is a mortgage, then the monthly or quarterly statements should show whether or not the payments are being made fully and on time. In the case of internal borrowing, it is imperative that the lenders be treated respectfully and all agreements in terms of interest and repayment be honored scrupulously.

Who approves the fund appeals made to the congregation over and above support for the budget? Today when many other charities are appealing for funds, including missions groups, and members within the congregation are requesting financial help to pursue specific ministries, it is difficult to arbitrate among them all. Policy once more can come to your rescue as board chairperson. First, you have to help the board discern and set some boundaries. In terms of priorities, you desire your congregation to support the ministries expressed in the annual budget. You will want to encourage people in the congregation to engage in ministries, whether they be short-term mission projects or other worthy ministry ventures. However, in this case, it is important to have these requests made formally to the congregation's missions committee and then empower them to bring forward a recommendation to the board for specific cases. If you are part of a network of churches, then your congregation will also have some interest in supporting those collective ministries, i.e., camps, church planting, Bible colleges, seminaries, refugee houses, homes for abused women, etc. Finally, some members within the congregation will have special interest in external charities and here the board will need to exercise wisdom in knowing which ones to endorse. Remember that your charity can only issue tax receipts for funds collected in support of projects it officially endorses. Further, it has to be careful, given the close family relationships in a congregation, that those giving do not direct their gifts specifically to support family members. CRA does not permit charities to issue tax receipts in such cases.

In Canada, the courts have identified four general categories of charitable purposes. If a charity engages in one of these four categories, the Canada Revenue Agency will recognize it as a registered charity. The four categories are:

- the relief of poverty;
- the advancement of education;
- the advancement of religion; or
- other purposes beneficial to the community in a way the law regards as charitable.[4]

Most congregations would fall under the category of "advancement of religion." This means that the church board has to ensure that the activities of the charity for which it provides governance are advancing religious purposes. The annual T3010 report that all Canadian charities must

---

4. https://www.canada.ca/en/revenue-agency/services/charities-giving/charities/policies-guidance/guidance-019-draft-purposes-charitable-registration.html#toc1.

submit requires the board to affirm that the charity is operating within these guidelines. The board should know when the treasurer or finance officer has submitted the annual T3010 report to the CRA. Failure to submit this annual report will result in action from CRA, including fines and, if such failure persists, withdrawal of charitable status. Government bodies in your jurisdiction may have different regulations and requirements.

For a church board chair to keep up to date on these issues represents a considerable challenge. Here is where one or two board members might agree to assist, particularly those that have accounting competence or are engaged in business operations. They might also agree to keep abreast of developments that affect charities in particular by checking the CRA website occasionally, etc. Subscribing to the Canadian Council of Christian Charities newsletter would also be a good source of advice. If the board works with an accounting firm to do the annual audit or financial review, that company should also be able to provide some service in this regard.

Case Study: Downloading to the Next Generation[5]

When the audit committee reported to the church board that there was a surplus of $15,000 in the prior year's financial operation, the board members felt immensely grateful to God for his wonderful provision. Nothing like this had happened in recent experience and it indicated that spiritual health was returning to the church family. The board chairperson knew that the board would have to formulate a recommendation for the use of these funds to the annual general meeting that was six weeks away.

The chairperson wondered at the irony of this situation. On the one hand, God's gracious provision was evident. On the other hand, he knew from previous discussions in the board meetings that reaching consensus on what to do with these funds would prove difficult. Two members of the board believed that it was not right for the church to have financial reserves. In their view, if God gave the funds, the congregation should expend them as soon as possible on ministry activities. Further, if in the future a financial crisis arose, God would at that point provide the resources through the faithful response of his people. Their theology seemed sound and they cited many precedents to support their position.

Conversely, several members of the board were business owners and they knew the importance of building some reserves to carry a business

---

5. Although the story in this case study may seem to resemble a real situation, the names, places, and actual circumstances do not describe any actual church, church board, pastor, or chairperson.

through "rainy day" periods. They firmly believed in God's ability to provide, but also believed that God required them to exercise wise stewardship of the resources once provided. They too could provide theological warrant and precedent for their perspective.

At this point in its history, the congregation had no financial reserves. If a financial emergency occurred, then the board would have to lay off some ministry staff in order to sustain the congregation. As well, a recent building renovation had left a debt of $300,000 which would take their congregation of 150 people another four to six years to repay. They were managing now, but they had already partially used a line of credit from the bank to support operations in the past six months. If some serious repair became necessary, there were no funds to pay for it.

The chairperson himself believed that it would be prudent for the board to give leadership in developing a contingency fund equal to two of three months of the church's normal operational budget. The current budget was $25,000 per month, and so this principle, if acted upon, would require a contingency fund in the range of $50,000 to $75,000. In addition, even though they had recently renovated the church building, there were no funds being set aside to pay for replacing equipment or carpets, repainting, or other things necessary to maintain the facility properly. The current generation was using the facility, but not paying for its maintenance. In essence, they were downloading these costs to the next generation. He thought good stewardship required the board to lead the congregation in setting aside $5,000 a year to cover such replacement and facility renewal costs. He had shared with the board his concerns previously and suggested that the board establish a combined contingency and replacement fund over a three- to four-year period. However, significant voices in the board had not responded very positively to his suggestions. Maybe this unexpected $15,000 surplus could form the initial basis for such a fund.

The board would debate this question again, in order to formulate a recommendation to the congregation. He was not sure, as chairperson, how hard he should push his proposals, even though he knew it was the prudent thing to do. Five years ago, when the church was enjoying some surplus the practice had developed of giving the surplus away, or, as some called it, tithing to some external ministry.

What leadership was the chairperson going to provide to the board members about this?

Possible Responses

1. As chairperson, he could present his viewpoint during the board's discussion and see what the response would be. He could emphasize again the need for this current generation to exercise appropriate stewardship for its use of the facility. It might be positive or negative, but whatever the board decided, at least he had tried, even if they rejected the idea.

2. Another tactic might be to introduce the concepts again and encourage the board to recommend that 50 percent of the surplus be used to initiate such a fund and that the rest be used in accord with previous patterns. This would get the fund established with $7,500 as seed money. It would be a good start and could build consensus between the two views.

3. Another direction the chairperson could take would be to talk with the leader of the board audit committee and seek his advice. For example, did the auditor support the establishment of a contingency fund and would this lead the auditor to alter his report, upgrading his estimate of the financial health of the congregation? Further, he might have a side conversation with the lead pastor suggesting the consequences to his ministry leadership should cutbacks to staff become necessary because the church had no resources to weather a financial crisis. This might encourage his support of a modest investment in a contingency fund. In other words, some quiet work in the background might enable some board members to see the prudence of such a direction in a new light and be willing to give it support. Board education is a continuing exercise. He might even ask the chairperson of the audit committee to lead the charge on this issue.

Questions for Reflection

a. Does your church board appoint by formal motion the auditors or the financial review firm? Does your board review the management letter from the auditor or financial reviewer?

b. Does your board receive regular reports (at least quarterly) regarding the performance of any investments?

c. Is there an employment manual that collects all of the policies related to staff issues? Does every employee have an up-to-date position description? Has every staff employee signed their agreement with the employment manual, including the congregation's statement of faith and the board-approved code of conduct?

Suggested Resources

a. Dick L. Kranendonk, *Serving as a Board Member? Protecting Yourself From Legal Liability While Serving Charities.*

b. John Pellowe, *Serving as a Board Member: Practical Guidance for Directors of Christian Ministries.*

Chapter 12

Chairing in the Midst of "Black Swan" Events

THE RESIGNATION OF A lead pastor, moral failure of a significant church member, financial mismanagement or fraud, an accident in which people associated with the church are injured or killed, facility failure, a church split—the possibilities for hard news within a congregational setting surely present a daunting array. And they do happen, at points when you as chairperson least expect.

Nicholas Taleb wrote a book in 2007 entitled *The Black Swan*.[1] No, this is not about environmental issues! As a metaphor, "black swan" appears as early as the poetry of the ancient Roman poet, Juvenal. Apparently it was a popular expression in sixteenth-century London to describe something impossible, because the presumption was that swans were white. Then in 1697, a Dutch explorer, Willem de Vlamingh, discovered living black swans on the Swan River in Australia. The expression "black swan event" denoted then "a perceived impossibility that later may be found to exist."

In the *New York Times*,[2] Taleb characterized "black swan events" in the following terms:

1. outliers—outside the realm of regular expectations because nothing in the past can convincingly point to its possibility;
2. carrying extreme impact;
3. after the fact we concoct explanations for their occurrence, making them explainable and predictable.

The financial crisis in 2008–2009 is characterized as a "black swan event" precisely because it took so many people by surprise. Some may have been predicting some financial crisis was coming, but few seem to have paid

1. Taleb, *Black Swan*.
2. Taleb, "Black Swan."

attention. When it occurred it had an immense impact precisely because, for many, it was quite unexpected. After the event, various explanations were being given for its occurrence. Organizationally business leaders are wondering how to anticipate and deal with such unexpected realities. Can leaders develop organizational resiliency so that when unexpected, serious threats arise, the organization will survive or continue without significant impairment? Taleb also observes that a black swan event to one entity may not be one for another. What is a black swan event for the chicken is a normal occurrence for the cook.

Church board chairpersons encounter black swan events in the life of a congregation from time to time. For example, recently a church was hosting a youth musical event. The crowd was loud and energetic. Partway through the event, the floor of the church facility collapsed, injuring several. The church board chairperson could not have predicted this would happen. That board spent two years working through the consequences of that unexpected accident. Other examples might be the moral failure of a trusted and esteemed senior ministry leader and its impact upon a congregation and their board. In smaller centers, it could be the unexpected decision by the major employer in town to shut the mill or the mine, leaving the church congregation wondering how it will survive into the future.

Recently, I had to come to terms with a situation where one of our key church partners (members) declared their intention to shift to another congregation. It was hard to hear this news and to process it properly, seeking to learn what God might be saying to our board, ministry team, and congregation through this event. As I reflected upon this experience, I concluded that the following were important things I learned as a church board chairperson:

1. *The element of surprise is difficult spiritually.* Hard news usually catches us in unguarded moments. The surprise factor in this often can be overwhelming initially. You start to question your own leadership or second-guess decisions recently made by the board. Sometimes the news causes you to wonder whether you have a clear grasp of what the true state of the congregation is. Surprise leads to doubt, but often equally to a desire to find someone or something to blame for this. "Whose fault was it?" becomes a common question or maybe it is the unanswerable "why?" question. Perhaps what might be most surprising to us in such moments will be the questions we have of God, particularly the "why" questions, which can be most difficult to manage. The emotional and spiritual impact of this processing takes a toll that should not be underestimated, and it takes some time to recover your

equilibrium. Periods of prayer, careful reflection on God's calling, and self-examination of your heart become important activities as you personally seek to make sense of what has happened and gain control of your emotions.

2. *It is all about relationships.* Often the hard news will involve someone you know and respect. Not only do you have to contend with the difficult news, but you also have to figure out how to relate to that person in light of what has happened or is supposed to have happened. The issues of guilt or innocence often become complex to sort out. People look for someone to blame, but the person or persons who are at the center of the controversy are friends, members of the church, people you have served with, people you trust! As board chairperson, you have to balance both the relationships you may have with those involved and the good of the whole congregation—not an easy balancing act to accomplish in the midst of a spiritual storm.

3. *The chairperson has to work hard to help others in the board and among the church leadership to make sense of this hard news.* As the hard news becomes more widely known, others within the church leadership group will experience their own spiritual and emotional responses. At the same time as you are wrestling with your own personal challenges, board members will expect you to help them process this situation individually and collectively. The same questions you contend with personally will probably become the same questions the board will have to wrestle with as it seeks to make sense of what has happened. This becomes an exercise in crisis management, with all of the attendant challenges.

    It will be important to allow space for the board members to express their perspectives within the context of the board as an initial step to help healing begin, and as a way for the board to come to terms with what may have happened. You, as chairperson, will need to facilitate that discussion in a context of prayer and careful reflection. Helping the board to discern an appropriate response for the health of the congregation that is in line with the congregation's values will be the primary goal. Above all, it will be important that the board have good, reliable information, and as clear a picture as possible about what is happening so that wise and appropriate decisions are made. Sense-making is a key aspect of leadership. Humility will probably be an important part of this response.

4. *The chairperson has an important role to play in ensuring that the board has followed appropriate processes in responding to the hard news.* I think

one of the key roles that a board chairperson has in facilitating a board's work in a time of crisis involves the careful attention to policy, process, and values. Not only must the board discern the right thing to do, but it must also determine to do it the right way. This is the primary way the chairperson can help the board to limit potential liability, maintain credibility, lay a good foundation for healing to begin, and demonstrate Christian integrity. It may be costly to do so, but in the end, you have to ensure that the board leads in doing what is right for all concerned. Sometimes these processes will apply to the internal operations of the board (e.g., a conflict of interest issue), and sometimes to the congregational process (e.g., resignation of a pastoral leader).

One of the significant elements in these matters is for the board to make sure all of its members are working from the same page. If the board becomes divided in a time of crisis, then no unified action will be possible within the congregation. While it may take some time for the board members to sort things through in order to discern consensus, it has to be a priority for a chairperson. At such times, it is particularly important for the board to speak with one voice. The chairperson articulates the board's voice. If the chairperson also serves as moderator of congregational meetings, this dual role will add even more weight to the chairperson's message on behalf of the board.

5. *Use crises as educational opportunities for the board.* Of course, it is probably not wise to pursue the educational aspect as the crisis is happening. Once it seems that the board has begun to move beyond the crisis, the experience may serve as a wonderful opportunity to help the board develop its capacity to govern. For example, the board members may have discerned that a current policy proved to be inadequate and needed substantial revision to be of service. Or, the board may have discovered that its mechanisms for ensuring adherence to policy were insufficient. Or, perhaps the board found that its liability insurance was barely adequate to deal with the matter. Whatever the crisis was, it always gives the chairperson an opportunity to help the board reflect and learn. Sometimes it provides a teachable moment in which to use a consultant to help the board formulate new vision, new policy, and new processes.

6. *It will take extra time.* Working through a crisis will always take longer than you anticipate. Recovery may also require more energy (e.g., additional board meetings) and expenditure of resources than you initially discern. As chairperson, your priority is for the reputation of God and the health and vitality of the congregation. The initial

diligence you take to ensure that things are handled well, even though the expenditure of time or resources may seem inordinate, will usually be rewarded in the months following the crisis. Other matters may have to be set aside until the crisis passes because you will have to give it your undivided attention.

Congregations are fragile entities with trust and mutual commitment being critical glue that sustains the community. A crisis has the potential to dissolve this glue, resulting in fragmentation. Retaining trust and nurturing commitment will require meetings with key leaders in the congregation and additional consultations with the board and the ministry staff. Sometimes extraordinary congregational meetings will be necessary and you will have to plan each one well to ensure a good outcome.

7. *Your personal example is incredibly important.* How you act personally in response to the crisis will affect the ability of the board and the congregation to weather it well. Your example of wisdom, prayerful reflection, and commitment to fairness and due process has the potential to become a stabilizing influence. Remember that you chair the board—the group of mature spiritual leaders in whom the congregation has entrusted its good governance. If the board does not demonstrate spiritual intelligence in the response to this crisis, how can it expect the congregation to handle it well? Spiritual self-control and kindness will be important "fruits of the Spirit" that you will need to demonstrate.

It is my experience that every two to three years a church board chairperson will encounter a black swan event that challenges the very ability of the board to cope and taxes a chairperson's personal leadership ability to the max. What can a church board chairperson do to help a board prepare itself for such unanticipated, unpredicted, paradigm-changing events?

First, a board that has learned how to work well together and to trust one another in the good times has greater capacity to weather a black swan event. Often when such events occur, finger-pointing becomes the name of the game as individuals under considerable pressure seek someone or something to blame. However, if the board has developed deep trust in one another, then praying through such events becomes the norm and confidence in the integrity of other board members will be strong. The hard work you, as chairperson, do, meeting by meeting to develop board trust and mutual integrity, will pay dividends when such things occur.

Second, learn the stories of how the board and the congregation have responded previously to black swan events. What victories can the board celebrate and use to build confidence that God will provide the board with the necessary wisdom when another such event happens? If the board handled a previous event poorly, with harsh results, then the board can even use this as a learning experience to discern how to do it better next time.

Third, keep insisting that the board must develop good policies and processes and educate itself so that it knows how to make good decisions, adopt useful processes, and work together to solve difficult issues. What can the board discern from changes in the external environment that might require the board to lead the congregation through some drastic change? Perhaps in one session this year have the board do some brainstorming about potential threats to the congregation's current vision. Use one of these threats as a case study and do some scenario planning, evaluating to what degree the board and the congregation would be prepared to deal with such an event in a Christian manner. If leadership changes are on the horizon, plan well for the succession. The more advanced preparation you can make as chairperson, the less of a threat the surprise will be because you can pray and plan your way through it.

Four, be discerning in all that you do. If your board is hiring new leadership, make sure the board follows the known procedures so that you learn what you need to know about the candidate before the hiring process is completed. Your chances of changing the person in any fundamental sense after employment begins are nil. If you are dealing with financial risks, exercise the greatest prudence possible. Never let private interests drive a board's decisions. Try to keep things simple because complexity often carries within it the seeds of its own destruction. As the board approves new ministry plans, try to consider ways to build in some redundancy of systems (i.e., institutional and operational resiliency), so that if one part fails, the whole plan does not implode.

The last thing I will suggest, though other strategies are certainly possible and helpful, is to make sure that the church documents define the board's areas of responsibility clearly. When a church board enters into a season of crisis, it is not the time to sort out jurisdictional issues. Emotions are running too strongly for good decisions to be made about such matters in those contexts. As chairperson, you should review these documents and assure yourself that you understand what the lines of authority are, what authority the board has to act, and where the congregation must be brought into the picture. Test your understanding with the rest of the board members and the lead pastor. If you discover significant lack of clarity among the board or in the perspective of the lead pastor about these matters, this should then become a major issue to resolve in the near future and before the next black swan event happens.

Black swan events often are highly public matters, known in the external community. The actions of the church board and the congregation in these circumstances become opportunities to incarnate the gospel and its values. Getting it right becomes an evangelistic necessity.

Perhaps in the context of the New Testament the response of non-Jews to the gospel became for the early church a black swan event (Acts 10). Did anyone (apart from Jesus) predict that this would happen? When it did occur, was anyone really prepared to accept the implications of the gospel regarding gentile and Jewish relations in the Messiah's assembly? No one knows what the next black swan event will be in your experience as a church board chairperson, but you can be certain that it will come. Prepare now so that you are not left with broken eggs, but can in fact create a new omelet.

Crises come and crises pass. They are opportunities to grow our faith, to discern God's faithfulness, and to improve the life and ministry of the congregation. As chairperson, you will find yourself in the midst of spiritual struggles that are beyond your ability to resolve, and so you will need to walk with strong faith in and dependence upon the Holy Spirit. Sometimes relational healing will not happen. Sometimes damage is severe and irreparable. In such situations, your confidence in God's care and ability to bring good out of something that is debilitating may be the means God will use to start the journey into a better future.

One of the black swan events that, as chairperson, you know one day will come, relates to pastoral change. Few events in the life of a church board chairperson are quite as breathtaking as the words of your lead pastor, "I want you to be the first to know that I am giving serious consideration to a pastoral position in another congregation." When you receive the actual letter of resignation, life truly changes, both for the short and long term. Although each church group has different processes they follow when such major leadership transitions occur in a local church, for the board chairperson some of the challenges seem to be common. Some of these challenges affect a chairperson personally and others affect the role of church board chairperson during such transitions.

1. *Personal challenges.* No matter how hard you try, even if you have a reasonably good relationship with the lead pastor, you are going to experience some negative feelings. While you want the best for your ministry colleague and know that for him to follow God's will is the most important thing, you are going to feel let down, perhaps even angry and betrayed. There is a sense of grief and loss. So working through these feelings and working with your lead pastor to help him finish well will need certain attention and some grace.

CHAIRING IN THE MIDST OF "BLACK SWAN" EVENTS

Such transitions rarely happen at convenient times, and so your schedule over the next few months, perhaps even as long as a year, will suddenly be filled with more matters requiring your attention than normally is the case. You will need to be careful that you do not become frustrated or overwhelmed by the increased demands. It might be helpful to see what aspects of your current responsibilities in the church, over and above your chairing, you might hand over to others for the time being. In other words, try to create space to cope well.

Let your spouse know that you will be carrying some additional responsibilities and seek their help and understanding during this period. It may be that you will face some criticisms about your leadership as things move forward and when this happens, it is hard for your spouse to hear these things and not be upset. Of course, you too will need special spiritual resources so that you are able to respond well to all of the various changes and difficulties that will occur.

2. *Challenges as Church Board Chairperson.*

   a. *Ending the employment relationship well*

   The church board has the responsibility to ensure that the employment relationship with the lead pastor ends well. Because emotions may be somewhat roiled in this period, the board members need to make decisions based upon principles, both biblical and legal. Be fair in all financial matters, and do not be afraid to err on the side of generosity. If the church has entered into specific agreements with the lead pastor (often these will relate to housing), then make sure that all details related to their resolution are handled appropriately. This may require legal advice or other technical expertise. If the church has supplied the pastor with a computer to support his work, then review the agreement related to that and follow the stipulations that will permit him to purchase it, should he so desire. As well, the board should arrange some congregational gathering in which people can express appreciation for the pastor and his wife for their leadership. Above all, do what is morally right with respect to severance. This is not a time to scrimp financially.

   b. *Getting Advice*

   Take the time necessary to review your congregation's policies regarding pastoral transitions and appointments. Understand the processes. If you need clarity, then seek advice from a denominational resource person, a prior board chairperson, or someone else in whom you have confidence. Most denominational offices will have good resources to assist you in such situations.

c. *Preparing the Church Board*

It is wise to alert the board members to the lead pastor's decision as soon as possible. Probably you should call for a special meeting of the board within the week. At this meeting, you should share the letter of resignation. Your primary goals for this meeting will include: letting the board members process the news among themselves, settling all financial and employment issues, reviewing church policies regarding how to proceed in the period of transition, what process is set out for seeking a replacement, and how to oversee the ministry of the congregation during this interim period. If the lead pastor was your primary employee, then more responsibility for day-to-day management will fall to the church board and its chairperson. If your church has an associate pastor, then you might consider asking that person to serve as interim lead pastor. However, if that person sees himself as a potential candidate for the role of lead pastor, it may not be advisable to appoint that person as interim lead pastor.

The board will want to ensure that they support the pulpit ministry well, maintain a good level of pastoral care within the congregation, and manage decisions regarding the administration of the congregation (i.e., supervision of other employees or volunteer ministry leaders, financial oversight, etc.).

If no one currently employed by the congregation is able to serve as interim lead pastor, then the church board will need to seek external help or make some other arrangement. The board should also determine what to communicate to the congregation and how this will be done. You may also ask the board to arrange for an exit interview so that you can gather from the outgoing pastor any insights that might be helpful for the board going forward.

It would be advisable at the next meeting to review such things as the lead pastor's position description, policies regarding moving expenses, salary expectations, housing issues, the congregation's vision, and the kind of pastoral leadership required in the coming decade to enable the congregation to flourish. If the bylaws require the appointment of a search committee, then the board should also discuss this committee's mandate, process, and composition, so that they can work with the congregation to implement the process as soon as possible. Consider as well what costs might be entailed in this process, i.e., costs of advertising for candidates, costs for interviewing, costs for interim leadership, costs for moving new hires, etc. While the congregation may save some money on salary during an interim period, it is wise to keep the salary budget in place to cover costs associated with the transition.

d. *Communicating with the Congregation*

If there is one thing a board chairperson needs to oversee well, it is communication with the congregation during this period. Although the church board will not have all of the answers to every question, some ongoing formal communication from the board to the congregants will be necessary to assure them that the ministries of the church will continue, good leadership is in place, and that such transitions, while difficult, are normal in the life of a church. It would probably be wise for the church board to schedule a congregational meeting shortly after the lead pastor has completed all of his responsibilities in order to review with them the process the church will follow to discern their next lead pastor, indicate how the board is arranging interim leadership, and answer questions that they may have. While you and other board members may have been through this kind of experience before, for some believers in your church, this will be their first pastoral transition.

e. *Dealing with Unintended Consequences*

Undoubtedly, in this transition, issues and questions will arise that are new. Some people may decide this is a time for them to leave as well and volunteer leadership resources may dwindle. Hopes will rise and fall as promising candidates decide not to respond to the congregation's invitation. Finances may dwindle. Other staff may decide that it is an appropriate time to make an employment change or become less responsive to supervision. Be wary of making large-scale adjustments to vision or programs during a transition period, unless they are deemed absolutely necessary. As chairperson, you may discover one or two board members become more strident or more fractious in discussions as they seek to cope with the uncertainty and pressure. The more you can demonstrate faith in God's timing and provision, clear understanding of process, and consistency in following policy, the more you will help the board to make good decisions and retain the confidence of the congregation in their leadership.

Finally, be careful about assuming that your authority has changed. You are still only the chairperson of the church board, unless and until that board decides otherwise and may empower you to expand the scope of your leadership.

Case Study: The Drama of Dismissal[3]

When his cell phone rang about 10 p.m. Wednesday night, Jack, the church board chairperson, had no inkling what it portended. The person calling identified herself as the administrative assistant to the lead pastor and proceeded to share a story that Jack could scarcely believe. She claimed she had witnessed the lead pastor rather passionately embracing and kissing one of the younger female members of the congregation. Jack knew the lead pastor, married with three children, was working under considerable pressure and his family situation was somewhat strained, but he never imagined such factors might push their pastor to do anything grossly immoral. As the conversation ended, Jack thanked her for her call and assured her that she had done the right thing in sharing this matter. He also asked her to prepare a short account of what she had told him, sign it, and date it. He would pick up a copy sometime tomorrow.

Jack was not sure what his next step should be. It was late and so he committed the pastor and this serious situation in prayer to God, asking for wisdom.

The next day Jack phoned his regional denominational director and shared what he had learned, asking for advice. He knew that whatever transpired he needed to protect the reputation of the congregation, the reputation of the lead pastor, and the reputation of the church member involved, as much as possible. However, he also needed to help the board follow a fair but rigorous process in dealing with the situation. Fortunately, the church board chairperson had a standing personnel committee. He asked the chair of that committee, Paul, to meet him for breakfast the following day. Meanwhile he got a copy of the administrative assistant's account.

Over breakfast Jack shared the written statement with Paul. Once Paul had absorbed the shock, they began to explore what process the board should follow to ascertain the truth (as best they could) and then act upon it fairly and in line with their newly approved code of conduct. Fortunately, the board had required all employees to sign, in writing, their agreement to

---

3. Although the story in this case study may seem to resemble a real situation, the names, places, and actual circumstances do not describe any actual church, church board, pastor, or chairperson.

the code. They decided that they would meet with the female congregational member and discern her part in this matter. Then they would meet with the lead pastor and ascertain his response to the accusation. These meetings had to proceed quickly. If these meetings confirmed the essential truth of the story, then within twenty-four hours they would call for an emergency executive session of the board.

They were not quite sure in the meantime how to manage things in the office. It would certainly be awkward, if not intimidating, for the administrative assistant to continue in her work under the supervision of the lead pastor.

A few days later at the emergency board meeting, Jack and Paul shared with the board how things had unfolded and the results of their conversations with the female congregational member and the lead pastor—initial denials from both parties had eventually changed to admissions of an inappropriate relationship when they revealed the testimony of the staff person. They had confirmed the written statement by the administrative assistant in its essential details. The board invited the lead pastor into the meeting and a very strained and emotional interchange occurred. In the end the lead pastor confirmed that he had acted immorally. The lead pastor was extremely remorseful and asked that the board initiate some process of restoration.

When the lead pastor left the board meeting, Jack gathered the board members into a time of prayer. He then reviewed with them elements from the code of conduct and the employee manual that might be pertinent to help the board respond appropriately. Now the board had to decide what action to follow, what to communicate to the congregation, and how to protect the whistleblower while securing the reputation of the congregation.

What would you advise this board to do? Do you agree with the steps that Jack as chairperson, took? Does your board have the structures and policies that Jack was able to use in order to help his board navigate such a difficult situation?

Some Observations

1. The emotions that emerge when such tragic events occur cannot be underestimated. People are angry, terribly saddened, and feel betrayed. Those directly involved live in a relational windstorm. This violation of trust damages office relationships. Those in leadership have to recognize the reality of these emotions, but not let such emotions govern decisions or processes.

2. Jack's appeal to denominational leaders was an important action. It is hard to admit to others the moral failure of a trusted friend, but the interests of the congregation superseded personal concerns at this point. The denominational leader was able to affirm Jack, provide some good advice, and assure him of his help at any time should he need it. He also urged Jack to make sure that all decisions taken were fully compliant with pertinent labor laws.

3. Crises reveal the value of policy—as well as its limitations. This board had some operational processes it could call upon to help it process this situation. When boards lack these policy tools, their ability to provide spiritual leadership for the congregation is greatly compromised. Of particular importance was the code of conduct that all staff and board members signed annually.

4. The protection of the staff person who blew the whistle is also an important consideration. Few church boards have any policy regarding whistleblowers, or guidelines to help them live through such a situation and continue their employment with the congregation. In many cases, others will attack their integrity as a means of justifying their own actions.

5. Be wary of making any promise for reinstatement in the immediate moment. With such a serious moral lapse, dismissal is a necessary step. This leaves all options open to the board and assures the congregation that the board is taking the lapse seriously. This also gives full freedom to the employee in terms of his future. The board, in the future, has the option to consider the possibility of reinstatement, but on the board's terms and once the offender has demonstrated serious and effective remedial efforts. In a multistaff context, one of the associate pastors can carry the preaching for two weeks until the board has time to formulate some longer-term plan. The denominational leadership should be able to assist in arranging some interim pastoral leadership—perhaps for three months.

6. Be generous to some degree because the actions of the individual will probably have serious impact upon his family. The dismissal should be immediate, but with one month's salary minimally to help the family in this time of readjustment. One idea is to limit the continuing salary to the minimal period for considering reinstatement, i.e., three months.

7. The more difficult decision will deal with possible reinstatement. The board should work out what steps must be completed before it will consider reinstatement. The denominational family may also have

policy in such cases. Try to build your board policy with as much compatibility with the denominational policy as possible. Reinstatement is a possibility, not a right. Put a timeline in place by which the board will make a decision so that if reinstatement does not occur, the congregation can get on with the selection of a new lead pastor within a reasonable timeframe.

Questions for Reflection

a. When was the last time the board you chair experienced a black swan event? What did the board do well? What could they have done better? Why?

b. Making sense of unforeseen situations is always a challenge. Who are some counselors you might refer to in order to help you, as chairperson, make sense of a crisis? Why is sense-making so important in such circumstances?

c. Stress often causes individuals to act out of character. What spiritual resources can you be developing to enable you to lead consistently, faithfully, and fearlessly when a crisis comes?

Suggested Resources

a. Mindy R. Wertheimer, *The Board Chair Handbook*.

Chapter 13

Keeping it Fresh

How long do you have and how far can you go?

THE QUESTION SOUNDS RATHER apocalyptic in tone, but is not meant to be. Rather, it is a sober recognition that the time any person has to contribute as chairperson to the development of a board is necessarily limited. I am not sure how long a person on average serves as a church board chairperson, but based on informal surveys I have done, the average time is three to six years. Also, the specific term for a church board chairperson is probably one or two years at most, with the possibility of several reappointments. However, some churches will stipulate in their bylaws that a person can only serve a limited number of terms before rotating off the board. However you look at it, the time a church board chairperson has to advance the work of that board is limited. One of the key questions that savvy board chairpersons ask themselves is this: What are the primary things I should seek to achieve during my term as chairperson in order to improve the governance capacity of this board, and what is the best way to work with the board to attain these goals in the time available?

Church board chairpersons often do not approach their role with this mindset because they consider the chairperson's function to be a kind of referee or facilitator for a committee. I have argued in this book that the significant role of a church board in the life of a congregation requires the chairperson to regard this role with much greater seriousness. In your role as chairperson, you can become the coach of the board by:

a. *Considering the categories.*

As board chairperson, you know that the board deals with diverse issues. Some have to do with the board's own operations, some with congregational operations, and some relate to fiduciary responsibilities. Previously I described these as redemptive, strategic, and fiduciary competencies. It might be helpful to take each category and ask yourself this question: What do I believe the board needs to accomplish in each area in the current year, the next three years, and the next five years. Now obviously you are not in control of these possible outcomes, but you do exercise considerable influence. For example, if one of the categories is board operations, then perhaps your goals might include developing an annual agenda, planning and holding an annual board retreat, ensuring that board minutes are properly filed and protected, and implementing the use of discussion and decision briefs. Or, perhaps there is no official statement that defines the role of a church board member and the responsibilities that such a person fulfills, and you think it would be a valuable thing for the board to debate, formulate, and then follow.

b. *Considering the missional priorities of the congregation.*

As you look forward two or three years, what do you regard as the most pressing issues that the congregation faces? Are these on the church board's radar? In your conversations with the lead pastor, what do you discern his ministry priorities might be, and how can you work with him and the church board to address these? For example, if you know that the congregation has plans to build new facilities or add to the current ones, must the board implement them in the next three years for the health and growth of the congregation? Will you make it a priority, as chairperson, to help the church board recognize and respond to this need?

c. *Considering the preparation of the church board.*

This is a question of the role of a church board and the degree to which it currently has the capacity to fulfill its responsibilities effectively. And secondly, what proposals might you bring forward for the board members that would improve their effectiveness as a ministry team? For example, do the board members have clarity as to their responsibilities? Is there a code of conduct for board members? Does the board ever evaluate its effectiveness given its responsibilities? Is there a conscious awareness within the board as to the process for making decisions and about what matters it should be making decisions about? What about managing conflicts of interest? Does the board need to develop and implement an expense policy for staff? What improvements should the board consider in the annual general meeting? What are the two or three critical issues about which the board must educate itself in order to accomplish its work well within the next twelve months? After you have served the church board for two terms, what improvements in the board's capacity to govern will have occurred under your leadership? Presumably you want to leave the board in a better position than when you began. Recruiting key leaders to the board might also be a critical contribution to the board's development.

d. *Considering the mindset of the lead pastor.*

Undoubtedly, the lead pastor will have ideas and opinions about ways to help the church board do its work well. However, here again, with considerable sensitivity, you may need to help the lead pastor develop over time a deeper appreciation for the role of the board in the life of the church. If the board desires to implement a process of annual pastoral evaluation, then you probably will need to spend considerable time with the lead pastor assuring him of the positive benefits this will produce for him, as well as making sure there are safeguards in the process to protect the pastor from inappropriate actions on the part of the board. Developing a spirit of true collaboration between the pastoral staff ministry team and the church board ministry team should be a high priority for you and the lead pastor.

e. *Considering your personal investment in these goals.*

Using your time, talents, and treasure to advance the work of a church board signals an important personal investment for you as its chairperson. Given what you have to invest in the role to accomplish it well, you will desire before God to be a good steward of your resources, as well as the resources of the other board members and the congregation. What legacy do you want to leave once you have completed your ministry as church board chairperson? What do you have to learn in order to fulfill this role well? How will the mission of the church advance because you have attended to this role with diligence, creativity, and discipline?

It is my experience that when a church board chairperson takes this role seriously and seeks to help the board deepen its capacity for governance, that the other board members will bless you. Their past experience as board members may not have been very positive or personally satisfying. Perhaps they struggle to see their work together as ministry and truly advancing the mission of the congregation. When you help the board intensify their personal and collective commitment, you enable each board member to serve the Lord Jesus with greater passion and excellence. Generally, a side benefit of a church board that is working hard to improve its capacity will be less division within the church. The congregation will sense that the church board is taking its ministry role seriously, is exercising good leadership, and shepherding the congregation with care.

What Can You Do to Sustain the Pace?

The Bible places a premium on patient endurance in obeying the will of God. Jesus sets the standard when, according to Luke 9:51, "Jesus resolutely set out for Jerusalem," knowing what lay before him, but determined to be an obedient son anyway. In a moment of considerable candor, Paul shares that "we do not lose heart . . . For our light and momentary troubles are achieving us an eternal glory that far outweighs them all" (2 Cor 4:16–17). In that context, he explains how he understands the ministry in which God has placed him. His goal is simple—to please the Lord Jesus Christ (2 Cor 5:9).

Serving as chairperson can be tough, with significant pressure and stress. You can become the lightning rod for the anger and distress that people in the congregation are feeling, even though you personally may not be responsible for the specific issue. Yet, they consider you to be responsible and expect you to do something about it. Maintaining Christian grace and displaying appreciation for all will be a significant test. Seasons of tremendous celebration and joy provide important compensation as you see God working powerfully in the lives of people. It is all part of the territory that board chairpersons traverse during their term of leadership.

If your service as chairperson probably will only last from three to six years—not a long time—it is important to sustain the pace effectively. What can you do to grow and flourish as a church board ministry team leader in the midst of these very diverse experiences, concurrently being the cheerleader and coach for the board and encouraging the lead pastor in his leadership?

    a. *Keep learning.* You can build your capacity to serve as chairperson by educating yourself about nonprofit board work, locating good print resources, attending workshops, accessing materials online, talking with experienced board leaders, etc. The more you know and understand about the role and the work of church boards, the more comfortable you will feel because you grasp the dimensions and potential. We all struggle with feelings of inadequacy as leaders, but we can address those feelings by becoming more knowledgeable about the role, the ministry team dynamics, the work of the church, the role of the lead pastor, etc. When you lose your passion to learn more about the role and to keep developing your understanding about it, perhaps it is time to consider stepping aside.

b. *Seek a mentor.* One of the best encouragements you can have in your leadership role is a mentor, coach, or prayer partner. Each will contribute something different, and which will be most helpful is a decision you will need to make, but at least seek a prayer partner, someone who will meet with you consistently and commit to praying for you. This could be another spiritual leader in the congregation, but probably not currently a member of the board. You want to connect with someone who will keep confidences. This relationship will help you remain spiritually accountable.

c. *Keep your focus.* The most critical work of a church board is advancing the mission of the congregation. This is a primary task of spiritual leadership. Your focus, as board chairperson, is to help the board collectively achieve this Great Commission goal. Many things will land at the board's table that will distract the board from this focus, and your responsibility, as chairperson, is to help the board discern what has priority and what does not. Sometimes the lead pastor generates the distraction and you will have to exercise all of your spiritual wisdom to help him understand his untoward influence. At other times, a board member is advocating for a special interest that, while good in itself, is not in alignment with the mission and vision of the congregation. If you keep your focus, you will enable the board to maintain its focus.

d. *Keep short accounts.* Some will say things about you as chairperson, both in the board and within the congregation, that might be hurtful or abrasive. Learn how to deal with these things quickly, lest a spirit of anger, contention, and divisiveness grow within you. Talk with the person who has said those things and try to understand what lies behind them. If the criticism is justified, learn from it and be thankful. If the person has misunderstood, offer explanation and ask for forgiveness for communicating poorly. If the issue is more complex, then seek the help of another elder in pursuing restoration. Above all, do not let it fester. This is particularly important in your relationship with the pastoral staff. You are a spiritual leader in the congregation and have a responsibility to model the fruit of the Spirit.

e. *Celebrate the wins.* Even when the days seem darkest, God is still working in you, the board, and the congregation. Discern God's actions and celebrate his energetic work within you and your colleagues. This is a matter of faith and a demonstration of the gospel. At every church board meeting, identify how God is working among the congregation and celebrate it as part of your worshipful work.

f. *Grieve the failures, learn, and move on.* You will not accomplish every goal. People will fail you. Implementation will not occur despite board motions. People in the congregation will come and go. Pastoral leaders will come and go. Take time to grieve these things, but then move forward. God has not finished his work yet. Learn from these events and become a stronger, more effective leader through them. Paul experienced failure, but he kept his eyes on Jesus, his Lord, and the One he was serving ultimately.

g. *Listen to the board, listen to the congregation, listen to the Holy Spirit.* The key leader often is the last to learn about an issue that is emerging within the congregation. As board chairperson, you cannot afford to let this happen. Find out who the unofficial leaders are within the congregation and develop a relationship with them so that you can keep abreast of the matters about which the congregation has concern. When you discover what they are, be preemptive. Talk with the lead pastor about them; consult the board; discern whether it is a critical issue or something that is insignificant. In your reports to the congregation, address the concern and what is being done to alleviate it.

    God employs a plurality of elders or spiritually mature people to lead his church. The same Spirit is guiding each of them. As chairperson, you do not know which of the board members the Spirit will use to express his wisdom and direction. If the majority of the board members are expressing a similar perspective, listen carefully. Even though you may not agree, perhaps it is the Spirit's voice that is finding expression.

h. *Keep the relationship with the lead pastor strong.* I have addressed this issue numerous times already. Suffice it to say, maintaining your pace will depend in large measure on your ability to develop a solid, respectful, working relationship with the lead pastor. You do not have to become friends, but you do need to find good ways to work respectfully together. If this relationship breaks down, then you may need to reconsider your leadership in the board. The health of the congregation is more important than your leadership of the board.

A simple mechanism to gather feedback about your effectiveness as board chairperson would be to ask for an annual evaluation from the board members. Your request signals how seriously you take your responsibilities and your desire to learn to lead even more effectively. The process does not need to be complex. It is best done by another board member (or two), in your absence, with results shared afterwards. If you have a board chairperson position description, then this should form the basis for the evaluation. An evaluation should be completed several months before the chairperson's term ends so that the individual discerns how the board is responding to his/her leadership. Appendix C provides a sample evaluation form.

Your personal belief in and commitment to the mission, values, and vision of the congregation, as well as your conviction that Jesus wants you to serve as board chairperson for this time in the congregation's life, are the two critical factors that will keep the board chairperson's role fresh, invigorating, and satisfying for you.

Case Study: Where, Oh Where, Is the Next Board Chairperson?[1]

Brian celebrated his sixty-seventh birthday a week ago. This also coincided with the tenth anniversary of his service as chairperson of the Sixth Baptist Church. Brian enjoyed his role as board chairperson and felt that his gifts and experience enabled him to contribute significantly to effective board leadership. Board members continued to be affirming of his leadership.

For the past year or two, Brian knew that his time of service with the board was drawing to a conclusion. It was time for younger leadership to step into the role of board chairperson. Several times he had raised the issue with his lead pastor and they had agreed generally that transition should occur sometime in the next year or two. He had also voiced his intention to complete his role as chairperson with several other board members. However, he knew that if something was going to happen in an effective and orderly manner, with a good result for the board and the church, succession planning was necessary. He had discussed this with the current vice-chairperson, but he indicated that he did not feel that he should step up to the chairperson's role.

---

1. Although the story in this case study may seem to resemble a real situation, the names, places, and actual circumstances do not describe any actual church, church board, pastor, or chairperson.]

Brian had never been in this situation before and so he was unsure how to proceed. According to the congregation's bylaws, the board selected its own chairperson from among the elders appointed by the congregation. Several years previously, the board had adopted a description of the roles and responsibilities for the chairperson and this probably needed to be updated. Brian was uncomfortable with the idea that he should give the nod to some candidate. Rather, the board as a whole needed to discuss this and come to some decision regarding succession. Brian's primary concern was that the board begin implementing this transition at least six months before he completed his term so that he could coach the new chairperson and orient him to this role. He wanted the board to appreciate how important the role of chairperson would be to their continued effectiveness.

If you were in Brian's shoes, what recommendations would you make to the board regarding leadership succession?

Observations

1. The issue of succession in the role of chairperson seldom receives the attention it deserves within church boards. However, if this role is as critical to the effective operation of a church board as many contend, then it requires careful and prayerful attention. Time and energy devoted to selecting a qualified and perhaps experienced candidate should, all things being equal, pay significant dividends. It also communicates to the congregation that the board is taking its work seriously.

2. The process used in the case study may not work in your particular situation. However, your church board would do well to consider some search-and-selection process that results in the appointment of a qualified candidate. The board generally will follow the lead of the current chairperson if a recommendation of a succession process is proposed. You can shape the board's expectations in this regard and educate them in the importance of good leadership for their effective work together.

Questions for Reflection

a. Have you ever asked the members of your church board to evaluate your leadership as chairperson? What did you learn? What did you change in your leadership as a result?

b. What goals have you set for yourself as chairperson? In the next twelve months, what are the two most significant things you can do to enhance the capacity of your church board? How will you accomplish these goals?

Suggested Resources

a. John Carver, *Carver Guide No. 4. The Chairperson's Role as the Servant Leader to the Board.*

Chapter 14

Finishing Well

AT SOME POINT, YOUR role as chairperson of the church board will come to an end. In the experience of some chairpersons, the transition occurs with little fanfare. Perhaps the personal situation of the chairperson changes and he/she no longer considers this ministry role to be a priority in his/her Christian service. Sometimes health issues or alterations in employment require this adjustment. Often the chairperson knows three to six months in advance that this will be the final term and signals this to the board and lead pastor. However, sometimes a chairperson's term ends suddenly and unexpectedly. Perhaps the internal dynamics of the congregation initiate this change or the relationship with the lead pastor breaks down. Regardless of the cause, the time a person serves as board chairperson will be limited.

This means one thing—you have to start the work of finishing well when you begin. In fact finishing well should be a key goal for a chairperson when he/she accepts the role.

When is it time to finish?

Transitions in leadership are always tricky things to discern and negotiate. Both the individual and the ministry agency experience vulnerability at these times. The more a board chairperson can prepare for it in advance, the better for that person and for the board. Planning for appropriate succession is a key responsibility for the chairperson.

Timing depends upon several factors. First, there are personal life transitions that signal that the time has come. I have already enumerated some factors, but essentially you assess changes to your personal capacity to sustain the spiritual commitment required for this leadership position. Sometimes people just get tired and desire to engage new ministry challenges. Leadership is a burden and sometimes it just gets too heavy. Second, there are internal board factors that suggest a cycle in the board's development is concluding and it is time for fresh perspective to facilitate the board's move to the next level of strategic leadership. Experienced, well-gifted, younger individuals now serve as board members and you need to move out of the role and let some of them step up to that ministry opportunity. You may continue as a board member and serve as a mentor to the new chairperson. Third, the internal dynamics of congregational life may suggest it is time for change. Perhaps you have chaired the board as the church has gone through an incredibly difficult pastoral transition and for the sake of the board's credibility, fresh leadership of the board needs to be matched with fresh pastoral leadership. Or, maybe the congregation has just completed an exciting but exhausting building program and you feel that a new board chairperson is required to lead the board into the future.

Remember that no one is indispensable and that the health of the congregation is more important than your desire to serve as board chairperson. Studies tend to show that leaders who hang on too long can do incredible damage to their own legacy as well as to the health of a ministry agency. Being chairperson of the board is not a right, but a service.

What Preparations Will Enable a Board Chairperson to Finish Well?

Leadership service as a board chairperson depends upon many different relationships. Concluding this role necessarily affects each of those relationships in diverse ways. As much as possible, a chairperson's goal should be to finish with those relationships intact and harmonious. However, those relationships in many cases will no longer be the same. For example, your relationship with the lead pastor will change. In many situations, this altered relationship may be the most challenging to negotiate for you personally. You will not have the ear of the church leadership and losing this privileged role can be tough to accept. The relational dynamics will alter and preparing yourself for this reality is important.

If this transition also coincides with a completion of your role as a board member, then your role in the congregation will undergo a double shift. This can be tricky sometimes. If your personal identity becomes too closely associated with the role of chairperson or board member, then perhaps there will be some fear felt as you wonder how you will be valued afterward.

Some congregational members will expect you to be a champion of the status quo. As the church board may bring forward recommendations that generate some controversy, perhaps even changing directions that the board had set when you were chairperson, you will have to resist the temptation to become the spokesperson for those that might oppose. Be present, but be supportive of the board as they provide strategic leadership for the congregation. It may feel flattering when people ask your opinion and desire you to advocate for their perspective in opposition to the board's recommendation, but the health of Christ's body supersedes everything. Whether you experience guilt or anger, fear or grief as the transition proceeds, remember that God can help you deal with these emotional responses.

As chairperson, you have access to many documents and are privy to many confidential conversations that have transpired within the context of the board or discussions with the lead pastor. When you transition from this role, what should you do with those documents (e.g., board minutes, discussion briefs, reports, etc.)? I would suggest you return them to the church office. Given that much church board business transpires electronically today through email, you should delete such files from your computer. If someone in conversation begins to probe into the details of a board discussion or pastoral actions, your standard response should be that these things are confidential matters and refer them to the new board chairperson or the pastor for comment. Integrity remains a critical issue in these matters.

When your term as chairperson is nearing completion, you should review the various matters that the board currently is discussing and discern which of these can be completed before your term ends. For example, if the board has engaged in a lengthy discussion extending over several meetings about a specific recommendation, try to move the board to decision during your term. In other words, make a serious attempt to clean up the board's agenda as much as possible so that the new chairperson can concentrate upon new issues. This can be important if a controversial issue has been occupying the board's attention for several months.

In a relay race, the hand-off of the baton often is critical to success. As you prepare to do this, ask yourself what the previous chairperson could have done to make your assumption of this role more effective and simpler? Are board documents (i.e., policies, board orientation materials, code of conduct, position description of the chairperson, etc.) in good shape and easily accessible? Are board processes (i.e., process for evaluation of the lead pastor, for review of liability insurance, for financial reviews, for annual agenda development, etc.) working well? Are current board committees and task forces functioning well, with good leadership and clear mandates documented? Are there any issues in terms of employee relations that need sorting?

During your terms as board chairperson, you will have accumulated considerable wisdom. How can you distill this and share it with the new chairperson so that this leader starts at a point that is far in advance of where you had to begin? I think there is value in putting such thoughts in written form and sharing them over coffee or lunch with the new chairperson, perhaps with the lead pastor present. Even if you discern only two or three key ideas or pieces of wisdom, this is still valuable. The goal in this is to capture and preserve the progress made by the board in its governance leadership during your term. In this action, you are advancing the mission of the congregation. As well, you are putting in place an effective example for the next chairperson to follow.

What will be your final comments to the board? It is helpful for the board members if you, as chairperson, review with them the wins you have celebrated and the hard lessons learned together. Further, indicate what you regard as the key challenges and opportunities that the board will be considering in the next twelve to eighteen months. You are not setting their agenda, but rather stimulating their collective thinking as they look forward. Above all, remind them that their work is ministry—all of it. Be thankful.

Is There a Successor at Hand?

This is a delicate question. On the one hand, board members may be reluctant to deal with the anticipated change and to propose a new chairperson too far in advance of your projected completion date. On the other hand, board members may go back to default mode and just appoint whoever is willing. However, as chairperson, your responsibility is to help the board advance its own understanding and governance effectiveness and this will include assisting the board to provide wisely for its leadership.

If the board is responsible to appoint its own chairperson, then the person will already be a board member. The individual should have served at least one term with the board and have had opportunity to discern the board dynamics and demonstrate leadership competence. If the congregation appoints the board chairperson at the AGM, then it is more difficult to ensure they make a good selection. In this case, it will be important for the current chairperson to meet with the nominating committee and explain the qualifications and skills that a chairperson should bring to the task—and perhaps even offer two or three suggested names for the committee to consider.

If you have three to four months in which to prepare for the transition, draft a discussion brief about this issue and make some recommendations that will help the board plan for its leadership succession well. In proposing these things, you are not manipulating or predetermining the outcome, but rather enabling them to put good policy and procedures in place. What might these recommendations suggest?

1. The current chairperson should signal to the board at least four months before the end of the current term whether he/she is willing to

continue as chairperson for another term. Usually church boards meet monthly and so this should give the board three or four meetings in which to negotiate these matters. If the chairperson is willing to serve for another term, then ask the board to discuss and decide the matter at least two meetings before the term officially ends.

2. If the chairperson indicates that he/she is unable to continue for whatever reason, then the board needs to initiate a process to discern its next chairperson. Some ways in which this could proceed include:

   a. Ask the board to form an ad hoc committee of two board members to make a recommendation at the next meeting. This allows board members to deliberate carefully outside of the board meeting with various people.

   b. If the current vice-chair is open to accepting the role of chairperson, then the board may ask him/her to consider and confirm this at the next meeting.

3. If the board can complete the process several months in advance of the transition, this gives you opportunity to meet with the new chairperson once or twice and orient this person to the role. The mentoring you provide through this can be critical to the board's continued development.

The items you discuss in an orientation process with the new chairperson will depend partially upon the experience of the candidate, the situation of the congregation and the state of the board's development. If the person has considerable board experience, then you might focus more upon the current issues and the vision for board development. If the person has little board experience or has not served in such a leadership capacity previously, then perhaps you might place more emphasis upon preparing the candidate for such leadership responsibilities. In this case, the mentoring may extend several months into the new chairperson's term, as he or she may desire.

Looking Beyond—The Challenges of Staying Connected

If your term as chairperson concludes simultaneously with your board responsibilities, then you may experience a growing loss of connection with the congregation in the following months unless you discern a new ministry opportunity into which you can pour your energies. Sometimes it is a new ministry opportunity that is motivating a chairperson to conclude his/her responsibilities. Your connectedness with the congregation will minimize a sense of dislocation. However, if you complete your term as chairperson and there is no immediate prospect for new ministry opportunity, then data suggests that you will be at risk of losing interest in the congregation's mission.

A helpful way to avoid this potential problem is to begin discussion about this with the lead pastor several months in advance of the transition. Seek his advice and prayerful support.

If the final months of your term have involved heavy, difficult issues in the board's ministry, then a few months of rest and recovery may be the best advice. Sometimes healing is required. However, your transition is not dropping out or being put out to pasture, but rather discerning new, fresh opportunities to serve the Lord Jesus.

Some experts advise that an exit interview would be a helpful part of the process. Meeting with several members of the board to reflect upon your experience as chairperson, and to seek their counsel as to future ministry involvement could assist you to discern God's direction.

Over several years of intense ministry together as a team, considerable camaraderie usually develops among board members. If this becomes your fortunate experience, then you will miss it, but be thankful to God for the opportunity you have had to serve together in the great kingdom enterprise of Jesus Christ.

Questions for Reflection

a. Take a few minutes and evaluate what you think would be a good timeline for completing your service as board chairperson. What factors lead you to define this timeline?

b. Whether your point of transition is near or distant, consider what ministry role you would like to have as you continue to serve in the congregation. What would you have to begin doing now in order to prepare well for such a transition?

Suggested Resources

a. Mindy R. Wertheimer, *The Board Chair Handbook*.

Appendix A

Sample Church Board Chairperson Role Description

(You can adapt this sample position description to fit the particular bylaws and annual cycle of your local church. It does not pretend to be complete in every respect.)

Position Description for the Church Board Chairperson

General Guidelines

1. The board chairperson is appointed annually from and by the board at its July meeting, with the appointment taking effect at the end of that meeting in time for the new fiscal year that begins September first. The chairperson is nominated from and by the board members and appointment to the position requires a 75 percent majority vote of board members voting. If more than one candidate is nominated, then a paper ballot is required.

2. The term of the board chairperson is twelve months. It is prudent for the board to select a new chairperson every four to five years. This fosters the development of new leadership and prevents any sense of entitlement from emerging. However, it is also prudent to have considerable continuity so that the board learns to work well together.

3. The chairperson can resign, in writing, to the lead pastor and/or vice-chairperson of the board. The board can at any time decide by majority vote to replace the chairperson and appoint a new chairperson.

4. At the July meeting of the board, all other board positions will be filled, including vice-chairperson, secretary, and personnel committee.

Position Description for the Board Chairperson

1. The chairperson is responsible to ensure that the board of (church name) operates in accord with the board's guiding principles, the mission and values of (church name), and the legal requirements for non-profit charitable societies, and that it accomplishes its responsibilities as defined in the bylaws of (church name).

2. The chairperson is directly accountable to the board for the fulfillment of this position's responsibilities. As a member of (church name) the chairperson also is responsive to the spiritual counsel of the lead pastor.

3. The chairperson will be committed to the board's success in fulfilling its responsibilities with excellence so that (church name) will be spiritually healthy and institutionally robust. He/she will promote outstanding board development and governance practices. He/she will celebrate the hard work and sacrificial service of individual board members and the entire ministry team.

4. The chairperson will understand and be passionate about the mission, values, and vision of (church name), encouraging all board members to demonstrate the same disposition. He/she will uphold the spiritual, ethical, and legal principles that define (church name) as part of Christ's body in (place name).

Primary Duties

1. In regards to the board:
    a. ensure that board has appropriate governance guidelines, these guidelines are being followed, and they are being reviewed biennially;
    b. chair all meetings of board;
    c. ensure that board meeting agendas are developed and circulated at least one full week before a board meeting and that other reports necessary for decision-making at board meetings are circulated in advance so that board members can come informed to the meetings;
    d. promote meaningful dialogue at board meetings and give every board member an opportunity to contribute;

e. ensure that accurate minutes are kept of all meetings and these documents are kept secure;
   f. cooperate with the board in mentoring a successor.
2. In regards to board members:
   a. ensure that every board member understands and carries out the roles and responsibilities of board service;
   b. be the contact person for the board members on board issues;
   c. oversee an annual board evaluation process;
   d. assist the lead pastor in developing the board members (individually and as a team) with respect to leadership capacity and spiritual walk.
3. In regards to board committees:
   a. ensure that the board appoints necessary committees and taskforces to fulfill its responsibilities in a timely way;
   b. ensure ongoing communication by committees and task forces with the board;
   c. serve as *ex officio* member of all board committees.
4. In regards to the lead pastor:
   a. cultivate a mutually respectful, trustful, and humble relationship with the lead pastor;
   b. communicate decisions made by the board in regards to the lead pastor's role, contract, welfare, and evaluation process.
5. In regards to the (church name):
   a. cultivate good relationships with members and other stakeholders;
   b. serve as one of (church name)'s community ambassadors and advocate for its vision;
   c. speak at the membership meetings and church functions on behalf of the board and prepare documents as necessary.
6. Partner with the lead pastor and other board members:
   a. to oversee the spiritual life of (church name);
   b. to oversee fiscal affairs and organizational assets;
   c. to participate in strategic planning and program evaluation;
   d. to ensure legal and ethical compliance of all board work;

e. to organize the Annual General Meeting of (church name);

f. to practice fiscal transparency and ensure that all board work is done in an open, nonsecretive manner;

g. to ensure that the board is exercising appropriate risk management on behalf of (church name);

h. to ensure that appropriate directors' liability insurance is in place and up to date.

Appendix B

Sample Church Board Role Description

The board of (church name) is formed from individuals elected by the membership as pastors or elders (perhaps in some cases deacons). The chairperson of the board assists board members to fulfill their responsibilities, in consultation with the lead pastor. The essential role of the board within (church name) includes the following:

i. Ensuring that the (church name) mission is being implemented passionately and persistently through a congregationally approved vision (1 Thess 5:12);

ii. Taking responsibility for the spiritual health and pastoral care of the congregation, ensuring that all aspects of (church name)'s vision for ministry are being carried forward effectively (1 Tim 3:5: "taking care of the church of God"; Heb 13:17) and protecting the church from doctrinal error (Acts 20:28–31);

iii. Ensuring that evangelism remains central to our vision and that through prayer, training, strategic planning, teaching, and preaching, we remain faithful to the Great Commission as a church;

iv. Ensuring that relevant biblical teaching is occurring throughout the congregation (Acts 6:4; 1Tim 5:17);

v. Praying for all aspects of the church's ministry and its people (Acts 6:4);

vi. Processing all matters of member discipline and restoration (1 Thess 5:13–15);

vii. Recommending policies to the members or creating policies within the areas assigned to the board by the congregation which are consistent with the constitution, bylaws, and values, so that (church name) functions in a biblically consistent, ethical, fiscally responsible, and legal manner (1 Tim 3:5);

viii. Caring for and nurturing all employees (1 Tim 5:17–18).

All pastors are part of the board, but only the lead pastor is a voting member on the board (this provision will have to comply with the congregation's bylaws). The board normally meets every month (except in the summer months). It is responsible for the spiritual leadership of the congregation, the casting of vision, strategic planning, financial oversight, employee welfare, and the establishment of policies that will nurture the welfare of the congregation.

Appendix C

Sample Church Board Chairperson Evaluation Instrument

(The wording of the questions and which questions to include would change depending upon the role description that your church board has developed for the chairperson.)

On a scale of 1 to 5, please indicate your assessment of the chairperson's service on behalf of the church board:

1 — Do Not Know

2 — No

3 — More No Than Yes

4 — More Yes Than No

5 — Yes

1. The chairperson ensures that the church board follows its operational policies.
2. The chairperson helps the board to develop its annual schedule of meetings, including an annual retreat.
3. The chairperson provides clear, well-developed board meeting agendas.
4. The board agendas are circulated at least a week in advance of meetings.
5. The chairperson facilitates open and robust, but respectful, dialogue among the board members.
6. The chairperson is able to help the board achieve spiritually discerned decisions.
7. The chairperson ensures that each board member's voice is heard.

8. The chairperson ensures that minutes of board meetings are accurate and circulated in advance of meetings.
9. The chairperson helps the board determine areas for board development and plans for such educational opportunities in the annual agenda.
10. The chairperson ensures that new board members receive an orientation to the role of a church board member.
11. The chairperson assists the board to organize itself at the first meeting of each annual cycle, appointing officers and establishing necessary committees.
12. The chairperson effectively communicates board decisions to the congregation and employees.
13. The chairperson effectively represents the board in congregational meetings.
14. The chairperson ensures that the legal and financial responsibilities of the board are attended to in a timely fashion.
15. The chairperson ensures that the board has time for worship and spiritual development.
16. The chairperson works effectively with the board and the lead pastor to organize the annual general meeting.
17. The chairperson ensures that the board has a voice in the development of the vision and strategic plans that will enable the congregation to fulfill its mission.
18. The chairperson assists the board in the appropriate exercise of risk management.
19. The chairperson treats all members of the board with respect.

Appendix D

Sample Church Board Covenant

Church Board Covenant — Guiding Principles for Board Members

(A covenant expresses expectations for interaction among board members as they function together.)

As spiritual leaders in our congregation, we must demonstrate by example godly Christian relationships, attitudes, and behavior. As members of the church board, we commit ourselves to:

1. pray daily for members of the church board, the pastoral team, and the ministry of our church;
2. speak respectfully about each other in all contexts;
3. address and resolve conflicts quickly and biblically;
4. extend forgiveness when offended and carry no grudges;
5. care for other board members when they are in difficulty;
6. come to board meetings prepared, informed, and in prayerful dependence upon the Holy Spirit for wisdom;
7. support the board once the board has taken a decision. If unable to do so, then be willing to resign;
8. be honest in all board dealings and discussions, voluntarily identify potential conflicts of interest, and never pursue a personal agenda;
9. hold all board discussions in complete confidence;
10. agree that the board chairperson speaks for the board;
11. hold one another accountable for this covenant, and agree to resign if significant and/or consistent violations of its provisions occur.

Appendix E

Sample Church Board Code of Ethical Conduct

(A church board should establish a Code of Ethical Conduct that applies to board members and employees without distinction.)

Church Board Code of Ethical Conduct

It is the policy of the (church name) board that board members uphold the highest standards of ethical, professional, Christian behavior. To that end, board members shall dedicate themselves to carrying out the mission of (church name) and shall:

1. hold paramount the safety, health, and welfare of the congregation and public in all of its actions;

2. act in such a manner as to uphold and enhance personal honor, integrity, and the reputation of (church name), and not engage in unethical practices—business or otherwise;

3. treat with respect, fairness, and consideration all persons, regardless of race, religion, gender, sexual orientation, maternity, marital or family status, disability, age, or national origin;

4. engage in carrying out (church name)'s mission as competently as possible;

5. collaborate with and support one another, staff, and volunteers in carrying out the mission of (church name);

6. recognize that the chief function of (church name) at all times is to serve the best interests of its beneficiaries;

7. accept as a personal duty the responsibility to keep up to date on emerging issues and to conduct themselves with professional competence, fairness, impartiality, efficiency, and effectiveness;

8. respect the structure and responsibilities of the board, provide it with facts and advice as a basis for making policy decisions, and uphold and implement policies adopted by the board;

9. conduct organizational and operational duties with positive leadership exemplified by open communication, creativity, fortitude, dedication, and compassion;

10. respect the board chairperson's role to speak on behalf of the board;

11. exercise their collective discretionary authority in ways that do not violate institutional bylaws or applicable laws and ordinances;

12. serve with respect, concern, courtesy, and responsiveness in carrying out (church name)'s mission, not misrepresenting (church name) in any negotiations, dealings, or contracts;

13. demonstrate the highest standards of personal integrity, truthfulness, honesty, and fortitude in all activities in order to inspire confidence and trust in such activities;

14. avoid any interest or activity that is in conflict with the conduct of their board duties;

15. respect and protect privileged information to which they have access in the course of their board duties;

16. strive for personal excellence and demonstrate spiritual maturity in all board operations, discussions and activities;

17. in the event of serious misconduct (e.g., sexual misconduct, criminal behavior, promoting false teaching, fraudulent actions, acting divisively, harmful addictive behavior, etc.) resign as a board member.

Appendix F

Sample Discussion Brief and Decision Profile Templates[1]

Discussion Brief

Template

Issue: (A concise statement reflecting the subject or issue facing the board)

Mission Statement

(If the church has a mission statement, the relevant phrase from the statement that provides meaning for the discussion could be placed here.)

Central Question: (Phrasing the question in such a way to focus thought and direct discussion using the standard how, what, why, when, where and by whom format.)

Questions to Get You Thinking:

(A list of relevant statements that would serve to guide the board toward a healthy discussion that would include questions that need to be answered and issues that need to be addressed.)

Relevant Study Resources:

(A concise list of resources either made available to the board with the discussion brief, or recommended to the board for further study. Typically, this would include reading material, experiences, and recommendations for further action.)

Study Group:

(The names of the person or group assigned to prepare and guide the discussion. This allows for clarity in assignment.)

---

1. Dr. Lyle Schrag developed these templates and I use them with his permission.

Further Notes

1. The discussion brief should be prepared either by a person or by a committee appointed for the task by the board, and assigned to conduct the preliminary research on the issue in order to guide the discussion in a careful and prayerful fashion.

2. Since this is a discussion brief, care should be taken to avoid presenting leading questions or specific recommendations. While it is always helpful, even biblical, to assign people who care about an issue to conduct the preliminary research, it is important for them to present a guide that is objective and allows for honest discussion.

Decision Profile

Template

Decision Required:

(A concise statement reflects what the decision is and how it relates to the board's mandate.)

Strategic Relevance of Issue:

(A concise statement that explains why the decision is on the agenda.)

Background:

(A list of brief summary statements recording the steps taken from the initial stage where the issue was identified, the essential factors were recognized, the research was gathered, and the impacts were weighed. Since it is a briefing sheet, it is helpful to keep the list simple, direct, and bulleted in a logical fashion. Each point can be described in greater detail during the meeting, but having the points printed will help keep the discussion oriented toward the specific focus.)

Alternatives Considered:

(A list of two to three actions that the study committee considered, stated in such a way that they would serve as a motion for the board's action. Subheading may include both the positive and negative consequences of such an action, but such points should be simple and concise. Typically, alternatives are presented without impact statements in order to focus the energy on the primary recommendation. It is probably best for the study group to keep such a list to themselves for reference should questions arise. Since these are alternatives, their status of endorsement for the board should be identified as Plan B, Option Two, or Rejected.)

Recommendation:

(A definitive statement of recommendation that would serve as a motion for the board's action. As with the alternatives, subheadings that address positive and negative impacts may be listed. Experience suggests, however, that the study group should keep these separate in order to present a clean recommendation.)

Appendix G

Samples of Church Board Assessment Instruments

Sample 1:

Annual Church Board Self-Assessment

Responses would be:

1 Yes
2 Qualified Yes
3 Qualified No
4 No
5 Do Not Know

1. Church Board Focus
   a. The board understands that its primary responsibility is to advance the congregational mission.
   b. The board understands that its responsibilities include financial responsibility (particularly preservation of financial resources), annual accounting, and overall financial control.
   c. The board ensures that communication of the congregation's mission, values, and vision occurs regularly and in an attractive, up-to-date format.
   d. The board oversees the external relationships that the congregation has engaged (e.g., denominational linkages, community organizations, etc.).
   e. The board reviews its policies for risk management annually to ensure the safety of all those served by the organization and the security of all resources.

2. Relation to the Lead Pastor
   a. The board has a policy that describes the process for selecting and appointing a lead pastor.
   b. The board has an up-to-date position description that guides the lead pastor in his responsibilities and clearly outlines his authority and accountability.
   c. The board delegates to the lead pastor full responsibility for all duties except those reserved for the board.
   d. The board reviews with the lead pastor an annual performance plan and monitors and evaluates his implementation of this plan annually.
   e. The board has a succession plan for the position of lead pastor and other key leadership positions.
   f. The board recognizes the importance of the lead pastor's physical, mental, spiritual, and social health, and commissions the personnel committee to address these matters specifically and sensitively with the lead pastor.
3. Mission, Policies, Goals, and Plans
   a. The mission, values, and vision of the congregation are clearly defined and approved by the board.
   b. The board consistently focuses its attention and time on ends matters (i.e. mission fulfillment, goal achievement, and values), and is future oriented, rather than being preoccupied with internal operations and procedures.
   c. The board holds itself responsible for the strategic and long-term plans for the congregation and gives time each year to review, evaluate, and update those plans.
   d. The board approves an annual operations plan each year.
   e. General operating policies, personnel policies, and position descriptions are in writing, easily accessible, and regularly updated.
   f. The organization meets all laws, regulations, and licensing standards above and beyond the bare minimum required, including quality and safety.
4. Monitors Financial Structure and Activity
   a. The board approves all changes in financial policy.

APPENDIX G: SAMPLES OF CHURCH BOARD ASSESSMENT INSTRUMENTS   231

    b. The board approves and recommends to the congregation an income and expense budget in line with policy.

    c. The board receives and reviews a three-year financial projection.

    d. The board approves and monitors all long- and short-term borrowing.

    e. Insurance coverage for board, staff, facilities, programs, etc., is reviewed annually.

    f. The board authorizes an annual independent financial review or audit and reviews the report with the reviewer or auditor.

    g. The board oversees all fundraising activities.

    h. The board establishes financial procedures which are completely and consistently followed, including billing, accounts management, accounting, taxes, etc.

5. Reviews and Evaluates Administrative Leadership

    a. The board approves the operational/organizational relationships, expressed in an organizational chart, and the appropriate lines of accountability.

    b. The board reviews and approves compensation for all staff.

    c. The board approves company benefit plans, pensions, or exceptions to plans as applicable.

    d. The board, through the personnel committee, ensures that annual performance evaluations are completed for every paid staff person.

    e. At least quarterly, the board receives and monitors financial, statistical, and operations reports. Such reports identify areas of financial risk.

6. Board Operations

    a. The board operates within the congregation's bylaws and board members are familiar with these guidelines.

    b. The roles and responsibilities of board members are clearly defined.

    c. The role and responsibility of the board chairperson are clearly defined.

    d. The role and responsibility of the board secretary are clearly defined.

    e. The board creates appropriate committees and the mandates for respective board committees and task forces are clearly defined.

    f. Board members understand and model appropriate ethical conduct.

    g. New board members have received orientation in all aspects of the board's work.

    h. Training for board work is part of the board's annual agenda.

    i. A procedure for annual assessment of the board's work collectively is in place.

    j. Board members understand the concept of conflict of interest and operate with integrity in all such matters.

    k. Board members understand that their work is spiritual work, and that all of their activities are devoted to the care of the congregation.

    l. Board members participate in discussions with respectful openness and honesty.

    m. The board continues to earn the trust of the congregation.

7. Board Meetings

    a. All members actively participate in each meeting of the board and the committees to which they are appointed.

    b. The board has an effective procedure for decision-making, which it follows. All appropriate persons are involved in the process.

    c. Board meetings are effective, i.e., they advance the mission of the congregation.

    d. The board has executive and *in camera* sessions (without staff present).

    e. The board receives regular reports from the lead pastor.

    f. Agenda and other board materials, including study documents, are available for members in sufficient time for review in advance of board meetings.

    g. Board members know how to add items to the board agenda and are free to do so.

    h. Board and committee minutes are circulated to members within ten days of each meeting.

APPENDIX G: SAMPLES OF CHURCH BOARD ASSESSMENT INSTRUMENTS 233

    i. There is a clear separation of board functions and responsibilities from management functions and responsibilities.

    j. Major proposals are thoroughly processed before they are presented and are available in written form.

    k. Dedicated time for worship and prayer occurs in every meeting.

Sample 2:

Board Performance Evaluation

Score each comment from 1 (NO, very poorly) to 10 (YES, very well)

1. The board, as a whole, has a good understanding of its governance philosophy, including its role and its overall responsibilities._____
2. The board knows the organization's mission statement and major goals. _____
3. The board considers strategic issues that may affect the organization. _____
4. The board knows the operation structure (officers, committees, and staff) of the organization. _____
5. The board has worked with staff to review and approve the strategic plan. _____
6. The board deals primarily with policy related issues. _____
7. The board avoids micromanaging the organization. _____
8. The board monitors the staff's progress in implementing the strategic plan. _____
9. The board approves the annual financial budget of the organization. _____
10. The board receives regular reports on the financial performance of the organization. _____
11. The board receives understandable reports on financial performance. _____
12. The board receives regular reports on the program performance of the organization. _____
13. The board receives understandable reports on the program performance. _____

14. The board's agenda is circulated before meetings in adequate time for review. _____
15. Board members come to the board meetings prepared, having read precirculated materials. _____
16. The board meetings are orderly. _____
17. Board discussions focus on the debate of issues and policies. _____
18. Board discussions are conducted in a nonthreatening environment. _____
19. Interactions at board meetings are courteous and professional. _____
20. Individuals' comments at board meetings are treated as confidential. _____
21. The chairperson ensures ample time is provided at meetings for all interested parties to be heard. _____
22. The chairperson ensures no single individual or group dominates the discussions at board meetings. _____
23. The chairperson ensures that board work is appropriately distributed among the board members. _____
24. The board objectively assesses the work and recommendations of its committees and task forces. _____
25. When a board decision is made, the entire board supports its successful implementation. _____
26. The diversity of the members and/or stakeholders is represented on the board. _____
27. The board regularly monitors the performance of the CEO/lead pastor by monitoring the achievement of the organization's goals. _____
28. The board regularly monitors the performance of the CEO/lead pastor by utilizing a documented evaluation process. _____
29. The board monitors the ongoing effectiveness of policies in a regular manner. _____
30. The board effectively represents the organization to the community. _____
31. The board effectively represents the organization to its members and/or stakeholders. _____
32. The board undertakes training on a regular basis. _____

Please add your personal comments to the following questions:

- In what areas did the board make its greatest contribution to the mission, and in retrospect, were they the highest priorities that needed attention? (Please provide your rationale.)
- What areas are the most pressing for the board to focus upon in the coming year? (Please explain and suggest ways and means to achieve.)
- What other initiatives, not contemplated in the long-term plans, should the board consider?

Bibliography

Addington, T. J. *High Impact Church Boards*. Oakdale, MN: Sandbox Resources, 2006.
Basinger, Rebekah. "The Board Chair-CEO Relationship Is Like a Pair of Chopsticks." https://rbbasinger.wordpress.com/2011/07/11/the-board-chair-ceo-relationship-is-like-a-pair-of-chopsticks/.
Biery, Richard M. *About Governance, and Why Does Policy Governance®Work ?* https://www.dbaseler.org/wp-content/uploads/2014/08/01-About-Governance-and-Why-PG-Works.pdf.
———. *What is Biblical About Policy Governance®?* http://www.dbaseler.org/wp-content/uploads/2009/10/05-What-is-Biblical-About-Policy-Governance.pdf.
The Board Chair and President Relationship. Branford, CT: BWB Solutions, n.d. http://bwbsolutions.com/wp-content/uploads/Board_Chair.pdf.
The Board Chair Question and Answer Guide. Chicago: Brody, Weiser, Burns, 2002.
Campbell, R. Alastair. *The Elders: Seniority within Earliest Christianity*. London: T. & T. Clark, 2004.
Carver, John. *Boards that Make a Difference: A New Design for Leadership in Nonprofit and Public Organizations*. 2nd ed. San Francisco: Jossey-Bass, 1997.
———. *Carver Guide No. 4: The Chairperson's Role as the Servant Leader to the Board*. San Francisco: Jossey-Bass, 1997.
Carver, John, and Miriam Carver. *Reinventing Your Board: A Step-by-Step Guide to Implementing Policy Governance*. San Francisco: Jossey-Bass, 2006.
Chait, Richard P., et al. *Governance as Leadership: Reframing the Work of Nonprofit Boards*. Washington, DC: Boardsource, 2005.
Dorsey, Eugene. *The Role of the Board Chairperson*. Washington, DC: National Center for Nonprofit Boards, 1994.
Exceptional Board Practices: The SOURCE in ACTION. Washington, DC: Boardsource, 2008.
A Guide to Financial Statements of Not-For-Profit Organizations. Toronto: The Canadian Institute of Chartered Accountants, 2012.
Heclo, Hugo. *On Thinking Institutionally*. Boulder, CO: Paradigm, 2008.
Heifetz, Ronald. *Leadership Without Easy Answers*. Cambridge, MA: Harvard University Press, 1994.
Hirsch, Alan, and Michael Frost. *The Shaping of Things to Come: Innovation and Mission for the 21st Century Church*. Peabody, MA: Hendrickson, 2003.
Hofstede, Geert, and Gert Jan Hofstede. *Culture and Organizations: Software of the Mind*. 2nd ed. New York: McGraw Hill, 2005.

Holland, Thomas P., and David C. Hester. *Building Effective Boards for Religious Organizations: A Handbook for Trustees, Presidents, and Church Leaders*. San Francisco: Jossey-Bass, 2000.

Hopkins, Bruce. *Legal Responsibilities of Nonprofit Boards*. Governance Series Volume 2. Washington, DC: Boardsource, 2009, sec. ed.

Hotchkiss, Dan. *Governance and Ministry: Rethinking Board Leadership*. Durham, NC: Alban Institute, 2009.

Hubbard, David. "Starting at the Top: What to Remember if You Find Yourself Appointed Chairman of the Board." In *Church Board Member Orientation Guide*. edited by Building Church Leaders, , s.l.: Building Church Leaders, 2007.

Hybels, Bill. *Courageous Leadership*. Grand Rapids: Zondervan, 2002.

Kranendonk, Dick. *Serving as a Board Member? Protecting Yourself from Legal Liability While Serving Charities*. Belleville, ON: Essence, 1998.

Lakey, Berit M. *Board Fundamentals: Understanding Roles in Nonprofit Governance*. Washington, DC: Boardsource, 2010.

Lencioni, Patrick. *The Five Dysfunctions of a Team*. San Francisco: Jossey-Bass, 2002.

Lewis, G. Douglass. "Governance: What is it?" *Theological Education* 44 (2009) 21–28.

Malphurs, Aubrey. *Leading Leaders: Empowering Church Boards for Ministry Excellence*. Grand Rapids: Baker, 2005.

McIntosh, Gary. *One Size Doesn't Fit All*. Grand Rapids: Fleming H. Revell, 1999.

Nanus, Burt. *Visionary Leadership*. San Francisco: Jossey-Bass, 1992.

Naufal, Michael. "The Chair-CEO Relationship: 10 Commitments for a Better Partnership," http://www.rayberndtson.ca/PDF/ChairCEO.pdf.

Olsen, Charles M. *Transforming Church Boards Into Communities of Spiritual Leaders*. Durham, NC: Alban Institute, 2001.

Orlikoff, James E., and Mary K. Totten. "New Approaches to Board Effectiveness." *Trustee* 63.1 (January 2010) 1–4.

Osborne, Larry. *Sticky Teams: Keeping Your Leadership Team and Staff on the Same Page*. Grand Rapids: Zondervan, 2010.

Pellowe, John. *Serving as a Board Member: Practical Guidance for Directors of Christian Ministries*. Elmira, ON: Canadian Council of Christian Charities, 2012.

Perkins, Larry. "The Delicate Dance of Congregational Government." http://www.churchboardchair.ca/the-delicate-dance-of-congregational-government/.

———. "Seven Habits of Effective Church Boards." http://www.churchboardchair.ca/175-seven-habits-of-effective-church-boards-habits-1-2/.

Plueddemann, James E. *Leading across Cultures: Effective Ministry and Mission in the Global Church*. Downers Grove, IL: InterVarsity, 2009.

Rendle, Gil, and Alice Mann. *Holy Conversations: Strategic Planning as a Spiritual Practice for Congregations*. Durham, NC: Alban Institute, 2003.

Robert, Henry M. *Robert's Rules of Order*. http://www.rulesonline.com/.

Roberts, Wess. *The Leadership Secrets of Attila the Hun*. New York: Grand Central, 1990.

Roxburgh, Alan J., and Fred Romanuk. *The Missional Leader: Equipping Your Church to Reach a Changing World*. San Francisco: Jossey-Bass, 2006.

Scott, Susan. *Fierce Conversations: Achieving Success at Work & in Life, One Conversation at a Time*. New York: Berkley, 2004.

Stahlke, Les. *Church Governance Matters. Relationship Model™ of Governance, Leadership & Management for Churches*. Edmonton, AB: Imperial Printing, 2010.

Stoesz, Edgar, and Chester Raber. *Doing Good Better: How to be an Effective Board Member of a Nonprofit Organization.* Rev. ed. Intercourse, PA: Good, 1997.

Taleb, Nassim Nicholas. *The Black Swan: The Impact of the Highly Improbable.* 2nd ed. New York: Random House, 2010.

———. "The Black Swan: The Impact of the Highly Improbable." *First Chapters* (blog), *New York Times*, April 27, 2007, https://www.nytimes.com/2007/04/22/books/chapters/0422-1st-tale.html.

Trower, Cathy A. *Govern More, Manage Less: Harnessing the Power of Your Nonprofit Board.* Washington, DC: Boardsource, 2010.

Walton, Elise. "Chairmanship: The Effective Chair-CEO Relationship: Insight from the Boardroom." The Millstein Center for Corporate Governance and Performance at the Yale School of Management, February 2011.

Wertheimer, Mindy R. *The Board Chair Handbook.* 2nd ed. Washington, DC: Boardsource, 2008.

What Makes an Exceptional Chairman? Required Qualities for Challenging Times. London: Alvarez & Marsal, 2012. https://www.alvarezandmarsal.com/sites/default/files/chairmans_research_report.pdf.